QUESTIONING SOVEREIGNTY

QUESTIONING SOVEREIGNTY

Law, State, and Nation
in the European Commonwealth

NEIL MacCORMICK

OXFORD
UNIVERSITY PRESS

OXFORD

UNIVERSITY PRESS

Great Clarendon Street, Oxford OX2 6DP

Oxford University Press is a department of the University of Oxford.
It furthers the University's objective of excellence in research, scholarship,
and education by publishing worldwide in

Oxford New York

Athens Auckland Bangkok Bogotá Buenos Aires Calcutta
Cape Town Chennai Dar es Salaam Delhi Florence Hong Kong Istanbul
Karachi Kuala Lumpur Madrid Melbourne Mexico City Mumbai
Nairobi Paris São Paulo Singapore Taipei Tokyo Toronto Warsaw

with associated companies in Berlin Ibadan

Oxford is a registered trade mark of Oxford University Press
in the UK and in certain other countries

Published in the United States
by Oxford University Press Inc., New York

© Neil MacCormick 1999

British Library Cataloguing in Publication Data

Data available

Library of Congress Cataloging in Publication Data

Data available

ISBN 0–19–826876–9

1 3 5 7 9 10 8 6 4 2

Typeset in Garamond by
Cambrian Typesetters, Frimley, Surrey
Printed in Great Britain
on acid-free paper by
Bookcraft Ltd., Midsomer Norton, Somerset

Preface

Law, state, and nation are concepts that seem distinct and yet overlapping. States have laws, and are sometimes said to be no more than personifications of legal order. Nations are sometimes said to have states, sometimes to be a part of the same thing, as in the common phrase 'nation state'. In Europe today, former understandings of state and nation seem out of date in the face of the development of the European Union. One of the pillars of the Union, the European Community, has its own body of law complete with the European Court of Justice as its most authoritative interpreter. The Court has held that Community law has direct effect in the member states and has supremacy over their domestic law. How far this claim extends, and subject to how much ultimate resistance from supreme courts in member states is a point on which there is no settled agreement. Yet this itself raises doubts about the 'sovereignty' of the states within this new legal order, and for some conjures up the spectre of a European 'super-state', a sovereign federal union exercising ultimate dominion over all its parts. In this context what becomes of nationalism, and how are we to account for the contemporary politics of identity? Is it a paradox, or a natural tendency, that in a world of globalized communications and commerce old identities like those of Catalonia or Flanders or Corsica or Scotland or Wales rise and seek to reclaim recognition among the nations of Europe and the World?

This book ranges over all these questions. The starting point is in the philosophy of law, within what Ota Weinberger and I have called an 'institutional theory of law'. I am grateful indeed for Weinberger's collaboration and encouragement over the years, and I give in the opening chapter of the book an introductory statement of my version of the institutional theory, before turning to the general theory of state and law. The institutional theory detaches 'law' conceptually from 'state'. It thereby opens the questions what is special about the law that is state law, and what is the possibility of ensuring that states as political entities can be effectively confined within law, attaining the status of a 'law-state', to use an unfamiliar English translation of the familiar German concept *Rechtsstaat*. Reflection on that idea in the British context reminds us how little the United Kingdom has had (or, perhaps, needed) in the way of a self-conscious theory of the state within domestic constitutional law. Hence when a problematic idea like that of the 'interest of the state' crops up in the context of the Official Secrets Act 1911, it shows a need for deep reflection on the character of the state.

There is a growing tendency among political commentators to reject the idea of the United Kingdom as a unitary state, archetype of a nation-state. Instead, it is portrayed as a 'union state', emerging from prior unions of distinct kingdoms. Chapter 4 pursues the question of how the 'Benthamite' or 'Diceyan' conception of the constitution developed in the circumstances of a union achieved by treaty in

1707. The following chapter discusses the tendencies both in the way of devolutionary movements and European involvements that seem to signal the end of that conception of the United Kingdom constitution. Then Chapter 6 engages in the debate whether the changes achieved through British accession to the European Communities must be counted as strictly 'revolutionary' in character. Our highest judicial tribunal can now treat Acts of Parliament as subject to being 'disapplied' in any case of conflict with Community law as authoritatively interpreted by the European Court of Justice. This seems to drive a wooden stake through the heart of the old constitution, the doctrine of parliamentary sovereignty.

It is not only in the United Kingdom, however, that concern has arisen about the extent of Community law and the competence of the European Court of Justice—far from it. In that light, Chapter 7 reviews the risks of state–union constitutional conflict, and considers suggestions about how to avoid this. Then Chapter 8 attempts a review of the idea of 'sovereignty' as we find it at the heart of all the difficulties covered in the preceding chapters. I believe that the forms of normative pluralism opened up by the institutional theory of law reveal the possibility that the countries and peoples of Europe can succeed in transcending sovereignty, going beyond the sovereign state, without at the same time simply transferring sovereignty from states to the union, as in the 'super-state'. This is a profoundly exciting possibility that can become an actuality only if people truly grasp its possibility intellectually and in their political imagination.

If that is correct, we face the issue of the kind of constitutional order that is proper to a 'commonwealth' such as the European Union. There are two problem ideas, democracy and subsidiarity. How can you make a reality of democracy in a polyglot union of many peoples and traditions? What kind of democracy makes sense in a post-sovereign commonwealth of this kind? And how can we state the principles concerning the need to retain maximal decision-making power as locally as possible, in accordance with the idea of subsidiarity?

In relation to all this, we confront again the worry about nations and nationalism, and the evidently powerful pull of ideas about local identity that operate alongside of the tendencies toward supra-nationalism the 'Europe' embodies. Chapters 10 and 11 contribute to the theory of 'liberal nationalism', aiming to state acceptable (because non-absolute) principles of national entitlement and national loyalty. Finally, I return to the question of union among the peoples and countries of the 'British Isles', suggesting that the old union has effectively run its course, and that new frameworks are presented both by the 'Council of the Isles' and the European Union. In this chapter alone does my own position as a political activist become directly involved in the argument. The general philosophical arguments of the previous chapters are not put in question by the more concrete advocacy in the concluding chapter, in this sense: one could not reasonably assent to the case made in that chapter unless one regarded most of the foregoing argument as sound. But it would be perfectly possible to accept all the premises of Chapters 1 to 11, and still disagree with the conclusion stated in Chapter 12. The preceding chapters are necessary but not sufficient for the conclusion. As with all points of political controversy, settling the principles is essential but insufficient. The right application of principles to concrete cases always calls for an appreciation of the actual situation of choice, and the possibilities present in it. These are matters of judgement, not of proof.

I have long believed that the academic community engaged in the study of legal philosophy has had an extraordinarily blinkered attitude to the questions about sovereignty, statehood, and the character of law posed by the development of the European Communities and now European Union. For some years I have been trying for my own part, and together with various colleagues, to make good this deficiency. Of course, there is a great risk here. The body of Community law and of learned and theoretically sophisticated commentary on it is now colossal. How can a mere amateur from another juristic specialism hope to cope with this? Will not the arrogance of mere ignorance shine from every page? Well, I think there is a risk here, yet one that is worth taking. The development of a new legal order of a special and unique kind is something no legal theorist can afford to ignore. The claim that there is such a thing here in Europe may be over-blown or even just plain false. But let us at least come to grips with the claim, both for the light it can cast on legal theory and for the light legal theory can cast on it.

Much of the present text results from re-writing and revision of work previously published, and I gratefully acknowledge permission to re-publish in this form from many sources, as listed below. Invitations to lecture and to present seminars in many universities and at learned conferences have provided many an occasion to start formulating my thoughts, and to profit from inestimably valuable criticism of the thoughts. The latter has made them at any rate better than they would otherwise have been, though I am all too conscious of remaining deficiencies.

I cannot begin to put in writing all the thanks that are due, but no list could fail to include the following: Zenon Bankowski and Andrew Scott, Joseph Weiler, Heike Jung, Richard Bellamy, Dario Castiglione, William Ewald, Aulis Aarnio, Nils Jareborg, Georg Ress, Vittorio Villa, Mario Jori, Anna Pintore, Ota Weinberger, Catherine Richmond, Marlene Wind, Hjalte Rasmussen, John Gardner, David Dyzenhaus, Tom Campbell, Jeremy Waldron, Roger Cotterrell, Pavlos Elevtheriades, Kenneth Munro, Beverley Brown, Bob Summers, Edward Mortimer, Gidon Gottlieb, Yel Tamir, Gordon Graham, John Haldane, Tom Nairn, Anthony Cohen, Brian Leiter, Ken Endo, Christine Boch, Caitriona Carter, Malcolm Anderson, the late Allan Macartney, Flora MacCormick, Sundram Soosay and many, many others. I have special debts to my students in seminars on these themes in the University of Edinburgh over several years and at the University of Texas in the Spring Semester of 1998. Zenon Bankowski and Andrew Scott received a grant from the Economic and Social Research council to run an interdisciplinary seminar in Edinburgh over the period, and I found participation in that extremely helpful.

Finally, I had the inestimable good fortune to be awarded a Personal Research Professorship by the Leverhulme Trustees for the years 1997–2003, for a project on

'Law, State and Practical Reason'. This is the first of several works to appear within that project. It would have been totally impossible without the enhanced opportunity for reading, writing, and reflection provided by the generosity of the late Viscount Leverhulme and the trustees of his foundation.

Neil MacCormick

Cairnbaan, Scotland
April 1999

Acknowledgements

Various of the chapters in this book are more or less substantially rewritten versions of work published (or presented for publication) earlier. I gratefully acknowledge prior publication, and consent to this publication of them, as follows:

Chapter 1
'Institutional Normative Order: A Conception of Law', *Cornell Law Review* 82 (1997) 1051–70; the original Otto Brusiin lecture, 'Law as Institutional Normative Order', was published under that title in *Rechtstheorie, Brusiin Sonderheft* 1997; 'New Approaches and Ways of Legal Thinking: the Otto Brusiin Lectures 1982–1997', edited by Aulis Aarnio and Werner Krawietz in cooperation with Panu Minkkinen (Berlin: Duncker & Humblot, 1998), 219– 34.

There is also considerable overlap with MacCormick 'My Philosophy of Law', in L. Wintgens (ed.), *The Law in Philosophical Perspective: My Philosophy of Law* (Dordrecht: Kluwer Academic Publishers, forthcoming, 1999) with kind persmission from Kluwer Academic Publishers.

Chapter 3
'The Interest of the State and the Rule of Law', in Peter Wallington and Robert M. Merkin (ed.), *Essays in Memory of Professor F. H. Lawson* (London: Butterworth, 1986), ch. 14, 169–87.

Chapter 4
The British Academy Lecture 1997; 'The English Constitution, the British State, and the Scottish Anomaly', *Scottish Affairs* (*Special Issue 'Understanding Constitutional Change'*), Edinburgh, 1998, 129–45; also to be published in *Proceedings of the British Academy*, 1998.

Chapter 5
'The Dialectic of Might and Right: Legal Positivisms and Constitutional Change', *Current Legal Problems,* 51 (1998), 37–63 (*Legal Theory at the End of the Millennium*, ed. M. D. A. Freeman, Oxford: Oxford University Press, 1998).

Chapter 6
'After Sovereignty: Understanding Constitutional Change', *King's College Law Review,* 9 (1998–9), 20–38.

Chapter 7
This chapter has considerable overlap, though not identity, with 'Constitutional

Pluralism in Europe: Are Collisions Avoidable?', in J. H. H. Weiler and Marlene Wind, *When High Courts Clash: National Resistance to European Supremacy* (Cambridge: Cambridge University Press, 1999, forthcoming), the proceedings of a CORE Conference held in Copenhagen in March 1998, which I am grateful to have attended. There is a genetic relationship also to: 'Risking Constitutional Collision in Europe?', *Oxford Journal of Legal Studies,* 18 (1998), 519–32.

Chapter 8
'Sovereignty: Myth and Reality' in *De Lege: Uppsala University Law Faculty Yearbook,* 1995, 'Towards Universal Law: Trends in National, European, and International Lawmaking' (ed. N. Jareborg, Uppsala: Iustus Förlag, 1995), 227–48 (also published, in a somewhat different version, in *Scottish Affairs,* 11 (1995), 1–13).

Chapter 9
'Democracy, Subsidiarity, and Citizenship in the "European Commonwealth"', in MacCormick (ed.), *Constructing Legal Systems: "European Union" in Legal Theory* Dordrecht: Kluwer Academic Publishers (1997), 1–26 (this was also published as *Law and Philosophy,* 16 (1997), 332–56), with kind permission from Kluwer Academic Publishers.

Chapter 10
'Is Nationalism Philosophically Credible?', in W. Twining (ed.), *Issues of Self-Determination* (Aberdeen: Aberdeen University Press, 1991), 8–19.

Chapter 11
This chapter overlaps with both of the following: 'What Place for Nationalism in the Modern World', in H. MacQueen (ed.), *In Search of New Constitutions* (Edinburgh: Edinburgh University Press, Hume Papers in Public Policy no. 2, 1994), 79–95 and 'Liberalism, Nationalism and the Post-sovereign State', 44, *Political Studies* (1996), 553–67.

Contents

1

The Legal Framework:
Institutional Normative Order

Introduction

The great jurist Hans Kelsen, who spent much of his life trying to clarify the concept 'norm', and the 'ought' that is the verbal sign of normative utterances, once remarked, almost despairingly, that the 'world of the ought' is a 'great mystery'. In Scandinavia, the disciples of Axel Hägerström doubted that any sense at all could be made of the ought. Said Karl Olivecrona of Lund: 'A mystery it is and a mystery it will remain forever.'[1] There continues to be controversy over the issue of properly accounting for normative elements in human thought and activity. It is a difficult thing to say just how (or if) a degree of order can be achieved in human lives, both individually and socially, by upholding and following normative requirements.

The basic idea of this book (and of companion volumes that will appear in the following years) is that norms belong within normative orders, of which some are, and some are not, institutional in character. A principal example of institutional normative order is law as this appears within contemporary states—municipal positive law. But this is by no means the only example, and it is illuminating for the purposes of reflection on the state to contemplate municipal positive law as a species of a genus, contrasting it with other species in the same genus. It is also of interest to compare and contrast morality as non-institutional order with law in its institutional character, and to contrast politics as institutional but not normative with law as both institutional and normative. These are fundamental contrasts for the present work, and this chapter works through them.

At any given time, any one of us has an idea of the world as it is now. But this is for the most part a broad and vague idea, with exactness and detail only in the contemporary foreground of perception and thought. Television, radio, newspapers, and other media keep us broadly informed about what is going on, though our attention is confined to particular subjects that interest us. Our awareness of history and geography let us locate ourselves somewhere terrestrially in the context of some narrative awareness of our present time in its continuity with past events, either directly recalled or spoken to in some memories or texts or reports available to us. Our own idiosyncratic understanding of the natural and social sciences gives us a

---

[1] See Olivecrona, *Law as Fact*, 1st edn. (London: Humphrey Milford, Oxford University Press, 1939), at p. 21. 'It is impossible to explain rationally how facts in the actual world can produce effects in the wholly different "world of the Ought". At one time Kelsen declared bluntly that this was in fact "the Great Mystery". That is to state the matter plainly. A mystery it is and a mystery it will remain forever.' The reference is to Kelsen, *Hauptprobleme der Staatsrechtslehre* (Tübingen: J. C. Mohr, 1911), 441.

broad idea of how things go along, and we have a common-sense grasp of how other people are likely to act and how our social situation is likely to change over time. We have some cosmological understanding of the earth in relation to the rest of the Universe, and either do or do not have an awareness of or faith in a divine being that underpins it all and in some sense guarantees it. With or without that, we have an actual perceptual consciousness of our immediate surroundings, and can to some extent give an account of what is going on here now, though by the time any such account is given, things have already moved on into some new state of being. Even the most learned and perceptive and well placed of us has only partial information in consciousness at any moment, always in a context of imperfect memory, possibly inaccurate scientific foundations, and rather inarticulate conjectures concerning probabilities.

Since David Hume's day, we have been used to contrasting the 'is' and the 'ought'.[2] It seems that this contrast has been mainly taken as highlighting the straightforward factuality of the 'is', in contradistinction with the somehow slippery character of the normative 'ought'. But is it not true, as just stated, that our grasp of the 'is' actually has a rather vague quality? If so, it is rash to jump into the assumption that the contrast drawn by 'Hume's guillotine' really favours the 'is'. Can we not usually be somewhat more certain about how things ought to be than about how they actually are? To hold or perhaps even to know that murder is wrong, or thus that people ought not to be killed wilfully and of malice aforethought, is to hold or know something that holds good everywhere and all the time. (If I am thinking in terms of municipal positive law, it holds good uniformly throughout the state in question.) Indeed, it is possible to be a good deal more confident that nobody ought to be murdered than that nobody is being, has been, or is about to be murdered, even in one's present quite near vicinity. I can be certain that murder is wrong, but not that it will not happen. And the same goes for jumping the red traffic light, or for acts of housebreaking, or for lying or breaking promises.

To think about the world, certainly to think of it beyond one's perceptual field, is to have some kind of picture or narrative account of it. This frames how I think it has been, has come to pass, now is, and will probably go on. The meaning of such thoughts is clear enough, for they either match the world or they do not, and if they do, that is how it really is. (The trouble is that we cannot check it all by direct immediate inspection—that is indeed the very trouble from which I started.) The 'ought' is of course different. The picture or narrative as I hold it ought to be is not one that is confirmed by how events are or turn out. It is an ideal picture or narrative, one to which I envisage the world being made to conform, as it does on all the occasions when no one murders a neighbour, breaks into another person's house or jumps a traffic light, tells a lie or breaks a promise.

If, however, I have some practical commitments concerning the way the world

<hr />

    [2] See Hume, *A Treatise of Human Nature* (Oxford: Clarendon Press, 1978, ed. L. A. Selby Bigge and P. H. Nidditch), Book III, Part 1, sect.1, last para.

ought to be, or the way it ought to go on, I can be fairly certain what these commitments add up to. In this way, I can have greater certainty about the 'ought' than about the 'is'. I can know better how the world ought to be (assuming my commitments are valid ones, and ignoring for the moment the question of what, if anything, validates such commitments) than I can know how it actually is. So far as concerns the positive law of the country I am thinking of, the rules in its statue book are nearly all cast in universal terms ('No one shall . . .', 'Whoever is in such and such a situation shall be liable/entitled to . . .', and so on). Their universality entails that, assuming I have a correct grasp of valid norms of the envisaged system of law, I can know with considerable certainty how things ought to be according to that system. This is so, even when I can never be so certain how things are or have been in the territory for which the law is valid.

Let us therefore acknowledge that the 'ought', however puzzling we may sometimes find it at the deepest ontological level, has at least the possibility of a degree of clarity and certainty that the 'is' often lacks. Nevertheless, all is not entirely simple. In a concrete situation I may wonder what some person (perhaps myself) ought to do or to have done, and may with some confidence conclude that the case is covered by a relevant norm. For example, 'thou shalt not kill' governs the case when I feel myself getting furiously angry towards Jim, and 'promises ought to be kept' governs the promise I made to Fred that is now due for performance. So I judge I ought here and now to calm down and avoid falling into some murderous impulse, or there and then to do the promised service. Or I may take a single simple norm like the no-killing one or the promise-keeping one, and reflect on it as in some way clearly valid for some context or jurisdiction. Yet it does seem to be the case that no such single normative judgement or proposition really makes sense on its own or in isolation. It is in its fitting together with a whole bundle of other norms that it makes sense. Especially in the context of the particular judgement—'what ought to be done or to have been done?'– or deliberation—'what to do now?'—there may be many normatively salient aspects of the situation, so that one's judgement or conclusion all things considered has taken account of more than one norm in its bearing on the situation. In this sense, normative judgements and deliberations do not relate to or presuppose or derive from single isolated norms. Rather, they depend on some larger conception of normative order, about the way things ought to be and ought to go on, taking the whole range of events things and possibilities as they appear to us at any particular time and place. This prompts an inquiry into the idea of 'normative order'.

Normative order

Normative order is a kind of ideal order. At any given time we may form a view of the world as we think it is, including the set of ongoing human actions and intentions for action. We may set against that a view of the world as it could be or could become, leaving out certain of the actions, leaving some actual intentions abandoned or unfulfilled, while other actions take place instead of those left out, and other intentions are fostered and brought to fulfilment. A view of the world as it could be or could become is an ideal view of it. An ideal view may be constructed in terms that rule out or imperatively exclude certain ways of acting on all occasions on which such action might otherwise be contemplated, and that insist on or imperatively include certain other ways of acting as always called for despite any contrary temptation.[3]

There is a notorious ambiguity in the term 'ideal' and most of its cognates in the various European languages. Sometimes we mean by it that which exists merely in idea, that is, within ideas held by some person or persons, whether for good or ill or in a neutral way. Sometimes, however, 'ideal' conveys the notion of a favoured or even highly favoured idea. Normative order, of course, is ideal in the sense of the favoured or preferred idea, not merely the neutral idea. Yet it falls short of any 'best of all possible worlds' perfectionism. Normative order is practical, both in the sense that it guides praxis, guides what we do, and also therefore practical in the sense of practicable. It is an order that is envisaged as a practically realizable state of the world given things as they are and persons as they are here and now; to the extent that it is realized, the world is a better, more satisfactory, world than if no such guideline were envisaged or followed.

'Norms' are propositions that we formulate with reference to, and as singled-out elements of, normative order. In primary form, they are either exclusionary provisions (negative duties, prohibitions) that rule out certain ways of acting on all occasions on which such action might otherwise be contemplated, or provisions of the converse type (positive duties, obligations) that call for or insist upon certain ways of acting as required of a person despite any contrary temptation, or countervailing reason for action.

This is not an attempt to explain norms or values in terms of value-free facts, of course. The notion of the 'better' or 'more satisfactory' built into the account of normative order as ideal order shows normative order to belong within, not independently of, values as fundamental elements in all human consciousness.

Also essential to making sense of these concepts is the way in which the practical concerns that which engages a person's will. Merely to envisage a possible world extrapolated from the actual one, even to think of it in some purely contemplative way as better than the actual is not to cross over into the realm of the normative. A steady commitment of the will to realization of some ideal order as a coherent and realizable state of the world is what is required for that transition. The will directed towards realizing a practicable, rationally coherent and humanly satisfactory ideal order constitutes it as normative order. Only by reference to such an order is it possible to establish the difference of right and wrong in action. Those actions are right

---

[3] Cf. G. H. von Wright, 'Is and Ought', in E. Bulygin *et al.* (eds.), *Man, Law and Modern Forms of Life* (Dordrecht: D. Reidel, 1985), 263 at 267–8, discussing norm-formulations and the use of the 'ought' therein.

that are not excluded from the conceived order, those that it excludes as actions and to which it denies fulfilment in intention are wrong. The dichotomy between wrong and not-wrong (or between wrong and right-in-the-sense-of-not-wrong) is the fundamental differentiation of actions or of intended or planned acts in a normative order. What a person engages upon when aiming to make normative order actual is the task of, or commitment to, avoiding wrongdoing.

The world as already-in-part-ideal order is that upon which we base our conceptions of normative order, the ideal order that would exist were practically removable imperfections purged from the way things go on now. Most promises that are made are in due course kept. Truthfulness and honesty are more frequent for most of us than lying and cheating. To formulate the principles that promises ought to be kept, that lies ought not to be told nor frauds perpetrated, is to set terms for an ideal order, but not one that stands absolutely apart from actuality, neither in terms of what is commonly done, nor in terms of what are commonly asserted as principles of acceptable conduct by others in our communities.

Thus normative order does not stand in absolute contrast with actuality. Quite a lot of what goes on is perfectly compatible with what is right from the point of view of any reasonable moral attitude. Moreover, this is the case, at least in part, because people share legal systems and moral attitudes or converge in the moral demands and conceptions of moral order they endorse. The world as it is does not unfold independently of human wills. On the contrary, the human world-as-it-is goes on as it goes on through human choices and decisions. However imperfectly, these choices and decisions reflect and conform to the conceptions of legal and moral rectitude held by the choosing and deciding agents. So normative order as ideal order does not by its envisaged contents or substance stand in any absolute contrast with the world as it is. Indeed, our normative commitments come out of our response to the world as it is, our satisfaction or dissatisfaction with it as it is and as it goes on, and our sense of the practicable alternatives to what does or might happen.

There are, it seems to me, three ways in which human beings come to an awareness and understanding of normative order. Through nurture, socialization, and education, we are exposed to and socialized into some common views of the right and the wrong, and gradually led to an ability to be at least partly self-regulating against the standing norms implicit, and partly explicit, in this common view. Then, in modern conditions, we fall into a series of rather institutionalized settings in which rules are made even more explicit than in the general familial and social milieu. For everyone nowadays this includes the experience of school, with compulsory attendance; for many, still, even in a secularizing society, participation to some extent in a church, mosque, synagogue, or other structured religious observance plays an important part. Nearly everybody participates in sports and games actively or as spectator or as both, and expertise about rules of play and rules of national and international competitions organized by officials and representative bodies is at least as widespread as knowledge and understanding of state-law. Thirdly, though, state agencies such as police and courts and in a more remote way other official organs up to and including parliaments and international agencies define one particularly authoritative, explicit, and highly regulated normative order for us.

At the very least, our picture of normative order emerges out of heteronomous orders, where others communicate norms to us and we learn to follow them, usually under some external incentive. The idea that any of us could invent a whole moral order for her- or himself is absurd; it is inevitable that we start from some learned or acquired framework of practical thought, and gradually develop our own critical awareness of it as something for which we take responsibility, and can adjust in the light of what seems to us reasonable. Our learning experience is one geared to developing an at least partial autonomy.[4] What we learn is to monitor and guide our own conduct against criteria of right and wrong that are conventional norms in some cases and formally enacted rules in others.

In a fundamental way, though, the possibility of developing fully autonomous judgement at the end of one's learning experience is that which makes intelligible the very concept of normative order. The telos of moral development is the fully responsible moral agent who takes responsibility for his or her judgements at all levels, and whose volitional commitment to some ideal of order is categorical, not conditional. Only a being that can act in a self-regulating way, judging between possible courses of action through voluntary commitment to some rationally willed order, and seeking to realize the willed order in action, can fully grasp the concept of 'wrong' action, or therefore the concept of right-as-not-wrong action. Only such a being can make full sense of auxiliary verbs such as 'ought' or 'should'. As Thomas Reid[5] observed in controversy with David Hume,[6] these are terms that every moral agent understands, but that are not definable in any terms simpler than themselves.

This account both presupposes and points towards reasons for believing the thesis that autonomy is fundamental to morality. Conceptually, I would suggest, the idea of autonomy that was sketched above is fundamental to any idea of normative order. For in the last result only an autonomous being can respond through acts of volition to the requirements of normative order. Normative order guides choices, but does not cause them. Choices are voluntary responses to an idea of order, not conditioned reflexes. On the other hand, the concept of a rationally coherent order in which universalizable principles find their place presupposes the agent's exposure to some conventional or institutional social ordering initially heteronomous in character from the agent's point of view. In the development of moral agency, heteronomy precedes autonomy.

Institutional normative order

Necessarily, normative order involves judgement. Being subject to a norm is being liable to judgement by oneself and by others in case one's conduct does not match

---

[4] See Jennifer Nedelsky, 'Reconceiving Autonomy: Sources, Thoughts and Possibilities', *Yale Journal of Law and Feminism*, 1 (1989), 7, 8-9, 21–2.

[5] T. Reid, *Essays on the Active Powers of Man* (Edinburgh: John Bell, 1788), essay V; see Reid's *Essays on the Powers of the Human Mind* (Edinburgh, 1819), vol. 3, 578.

[6] See Hume, *Treatise*, Book III, part 1, sect. 1, final paragraph.

up to what is required. Particular norms are to be envisaged as fragments drawn from a presupposed ideal order in the sense indicated, or as propositions formulated to capture the sense of that order in relation to a given type of situation. They are exclusionary or mandatory prescriptions that posit some course of conduct as wrong, or as obligatory. To engage with a norm as an acting subject is to judge what must be done in a given context; to reflect in normative terms upon one's own or another's conduct in a given setting is to judge, against some envisaged norm, whether what was done ought to have been done or ought not to have been done. The judgement that an act ought not to have been done normally entails a consequential judgement of the measure of penitence or restitution, or of censure, that is apt to the case. All in all, to think normatively is to think judgementally. This is a general and significant truth about all forms of normative order.

Judgement is sometimes purely personal and autonomous; sometimes it is conventional and heteronomous, without being institutionalized. It can also, however, be institutionalized, or, if you will, organized. The first step towards this can be seen wherever in a question involving two parties, a third is asked to help. Such a third party can be a relatively impartial judge between two persons on whom some norm impinges differentially. Reference to such an impartial third party can become a standing practice in a variety of situations. Thus over some range of topics, some persons may acquire a standing role as judges, to whom reference may be made. It can come about that the judgement of such persons acquires mandatory force within some normative order, in the sense that a person who wishes action taken in virtue of some normative judgement must either handle the matter in a purely voluntary way, or resort to compulsory action only under judgement of such a judge. Then appeals may or may not be allowed; but once judgement is institutionalized, there has to be some rule about the finality of judgement; a rule that it is obligatory to accept and carry out the judgement of the ultimate court, and that it is forbidden to take any further action beyond that ultimately authorized under the final judgement.[7]

Norms involve judgement, and judgement, as we noted, is either personal and autonomous or in some measure institutionalized. Institutionalization of judgement is a fundamental feature of the organization of normative orders. In one form or another, it occurs in a wide variety of settings, through churches, sporting organizations, commercial guilds, and leagues, international organizations, and agencies; and also, of course, paradigmatically in the state.

An inevitable effect of institutionalization of judgement, especially where there comes into being a group or a corps of judges acting in a coordinated way under a common structure of appeals, is that normative order must come to be conceived as systemic in character. The system in question then necessarily possesses, as Teubner and Luhmann point out, a self-referential quality.[8] For it has to be a question in any

[7] Cf. Neil MacCormick, *H. L. A. Hart* (London: Edward Arnold, 1981), ch. 9.
[8] See G. Teubner, *Law as an Autopoietic System*, trans. R. Adler and A. Bankowska, ed. Z. Bankowski (Oxford, Basil Blackwell 1993), 13–24; N. Luhmann, 'Law as a Social System', *Northwestern Univ. Law Rev.* (1989), 136 at 141–3.

dispute what the governing norm is and how it is to be interpreted. Finality of judgement entails final authority on the question what counts as a binding norm, and how it bears on the case. What makes the judgement final is a norm of the normative order that makes respect for judgements obligatory in every case. But the judgement that such a norm, or any other norm, belongs to the order, is itself one which can only be pronounced with final effect by an appropriate judge or court. And the same postulated normative order is that which makes a given judge or court appropriate, or (in the more technical term) 'competent' to judge on the question.

Whenever this is so, it follows that, relative to any institutional normative system, there is a way, conclusive within the system, for determining what counts as an authoritative norm of the system, or a definitely established right or duty of some person under the system. There is even a way of determining what counts as a person under the system, and what kinds of practical social and business arrangements can be set up with binding effect in the system.[9] The way is, of course, that of recourse to the judgement of those competent to judge. Otto Brusiin has remarked that, although questions about sales or marriages matter to us in quite diverse ways in the ordinary social milieu, what counts in law as a 'sale' or a 'marriage' is a question which the law-courts necessarily have ultimate authority to determine.[10] And they have associated authority to say what ulterior legal rights, duties, powers and the like follow consequentially upon the existence of a sale or a marriage according to law. But which law-courts? Could there be merchants' tribunals deciding about sales? Or sporting tribunals deciding about the valid transfer through 'sale' of a footballer's contract? Or Church Courts deciding about marriages?

As we know, each of these is possible. There can be tribunals of many kinds, and these can deal with similar questions affecting the same human individuals. But the characteristic of an institutional normative order is that competent judgement in it is conclusive within its own order, except to the extent that there is coordinated cross-recognition of different orders. Such cross-recognition obtained between Pope and Emperor in the Middle Ages,[11] and obtains between European Communities and member-state legal orders today. Where a plurality of judgements each conclusive within a particular order can be passed, the question is: 'Which ought to prevail?' As a question within a self-referential system, such a question is of course self-answering, for the system's agencies can never say other than that the system's norm ought to prevail. As a question for a person confronted by competing judgements of substantially the same question in practically different senses, the issue is which to respect, on grounds external to the self-referential answer provided by rival

---

[9]   See MacCormick, 'Institutions, Arrangements, and Practical Information', *Ratio Juris*, 1 (1988), 73 at 79–80

[10]   See Urpo Kangas, *Otto Brusiin: der Mensch und sein Recht* (Berlin: Duncker & Humblot, 1990), 182.

[11]   See Norman Davies, *Europe: A History* (London: Pimlico Press 1997), 336 ff. One can easily exaggerate the stability of church/empire jurisdictional relations in a period of considerable turmoil, but the independence of canon law from secular law remains a striking fact.

normative orders. Shall a state–court decree of divorce, or a church–court prohibition or nullification of the state's decree be taken as final? Shall the judgement of the state tribunal or the Trade Union tribunal be observed? And so on.

There are both prudential and moral elements in any reasonable answer to the question, 'Which to respect?' Which ought one to respect all things considered? Which is it least disadvantageous, all things considered, to ignore? In cases of conflict the answer to the latter question, the prudential answer, will be considerably affected both by the weight and balance of conventional opinions and by power-relations, and these will also be relevant, though with different scales of weighting, to the former, the moral question. But in so far as power-relations enter the question, the issue is, as I shall shortly try to show, one of politics. Whoever can make a judgement prevail in the last resort, in the sense of its being carried through by main force if necessary, and can reliably and predictably enforce such judgements in the general run, has political power. That political power backs and to a degree reinforces the authority and prestige of the tribunal whose judgement is enforced and that of the normative order to which the tribunal self-referentially belongs.

In the world as it has been, and still to a very large extent is, power of the relevant kind has been territorially concentrated, and each relevant territory has been that of a state. The coercively predominant normative orders have been those of states, though they have rarely if ever succeeded in absolutely eliminating rival orders of one kind or another. This is why there has been such a tendency to take for granted the equation of 'law' with 'state-law', though this has had serious distorting effects for legal theory.

Two obviously significant aspects of the interrelation of coercive power with normative order (thus also the interrelation of state with law) are of course that of executive power and that of legislative power. The executive possesses the direct or indirect command of the agencies of organized physical coercion that can back up the power of judgement—or, in cases of serious breakdown, disown and overthrow it. The legislature possesses, normally, the kind of democratic or quasi-democratic (or other ideological) legitimation that contributes significantly to the acceptability and durability over time of the coercive power that is organized under the executive. A delicate and shifting balance of power-relations normally obtains here. But always there is a question whether the due exercise of either legislative or executive power is a matter subjected to judicial judgement, and hence itself incorporated into the normative order which it so crucially supports. Where it is so incorporated, the state is a *Rechtsstaat*, a state-under-law, a 'law-state', as Åke Frändberg tells us to call it.[12]

In a law-state, the question what exercises of executive power are valid is a question of law; the political power of the executive is restrained under the authority of law. Likewise, it is for the courts to say what resolutions of the legislature constitute validly enacted norms of law, and how they are to be interpreted. The authority of

[12] The 'Law-State', as yet unpublished manuscript by Professor Frändberg of the University of Uppsala, Sweden; I am grateful for permission to borrow this term.

the legislature is not a matter of democratic or ideological or hereditary legitimacy extraneous to law, but is itself conferred by law, or at least confirmed by it on terms that effectively limit the power of law-making. Self-referentiality here shades over into 'autopoiesis',[13] in this sense: the law is 'self-making' since the acts that make it are law-defined and it is a question of law whether a purported act of law-making is valid or not. The court which answers that question itself exercises a power of judgement defined and conferred by law.

In such a state there can also be an independent profession of legal science, analysing the valid law, discussing the limits of its validity, offering interpretations that display some overall coherence and systematicity in the legal (normative) order conceived as an ideal unity. This scientific construction of order and system is itself an act of rational reconstruction[14] extrapolating from the given material. But in turn it is a reconstruction that reinforces the conception of law as a 'system', and which posits the systematic character of law as a guiding ideal for judges in particular, and also to a degree for legislators and officials of executive government.[15]

Law conceived as institutional normative order can thus come to be constitutive of a law-state. However, as Kelsen pointed out, there are two possible ways to conceive and represent the order as a working system. One way is a dynamic way.[16] Here, the process of change through time is central, including the way in which legal provisions themselves set the terms for valid change. This produces a representation of the order with a special focus on the processes of norm-creation, and on the processes of establishing institutional arrangements (contracts, trusts, and the like) within private and lower-level public law. When we represent a normative order in this dynamic way, we represent it in terms of the norms that regulate change, individuated as norms of competence, power-conferring rules, institutive rules of legal institutions.

The other way is what Kelsen called a 'static' representation.[17] Here, we represent the order by individuating rules or norms prescribing duties, or conferring rights either permissive or beneficial. Sometimes, in an even more microscopic way, we simply individuate particular duties and rights, depending on the current focus of attention. But this 'static' conception proves to be misnamed. For it concerns not stasis, but rather momentary normative judgement, whether the judgement envisaged is that of a court seeking to determine a litigated question, or that of a citizen engaged in practical judgement what to demand in a given setting, or indeed that of a scholar trying to produce a coherent representation of some branch of the law. The

[13] As the Greek etymology suggests, 'autopoiesis' is a characteristic ascribed to systems that are considered to be self-making and self-sustaining; for a full account, see Teubner, cited above n. 8.

[14] See MacCormick, 'The Ideal and the Actual of Law and Society', in J. Tasioulas (ed.), *Law, Values and Social Practices* (Aldershot: Dartmouth Publishing Co. 1997), 1–25.

[15] Cf. Joxerramon Bengoetxea, 'Legal System as a Regulative Ideal', *Archiv für Rechts- und Sozialphilosophie*, 53 (1994), 65 at 70–8.

[16] See Hans Kelsen, *The Pure Theory of Law*, trans. Max Knight (Berkeley and Los Angeles: Univ. of California Press, 1967), ch. 5.   [17] *Pure Theory*, ch. 4.

recognition of rights and duties in this practical–judgemental setting is in any event an intellectual procedure different from that of seeking guidance about the valid exercise of normative power within a normative order dynamically conceived; the two interact and overlap, but are not the same. Law as normative order has two aspects, the dynamic and the momentary. H. L. A. Hart sought to draw these together into a single structure of 'primary and secondary rules', but there is a notorious difficulty about the interconnection of his 'rule of recognition' with 'rules of change' and 'rules of adjudication'.[18] A proper representation of a legal system may reasonably take one or other of several forms, depending on one's practical concerns of the time. Material which is characterized in one way in a dynamic perspective takes a different shape when viewed in a momentary–judgemental perspective. There is no single uniquely correct reconstruction of the raw material of law into a single canonical form of 'legal system'.

Law and politics, law and morality

The final task of this introduction is to outline two distinctions, that between positive law and each of the two other realms of thought and action with which it is most intimately interrelated, politics and morality. For although interrelated and intertwined with these, positive law is nevertheless something clearly distinct conceptually. It is a genuine third term, not simply an amalgam of the other two. Politics is concerned with law—law making and law reform, appointments to key legal offices, maintenance of the forces of law and order, supporting the rulings of the courts. Yet politics is not law, nor law politics, despite occasional assertions to the contrary from the ramparts of Critical Legal Studies.[19] Morality is concerned with law, with the criticism of legal decisions and legal rules, with the issue of obligation to respect the law, with the question of law's claim to be genuinely normative, genuinely engaged with the world of the 'ought'. Yet morality is not law, nor is law morality, nor a sub-department of morality, for all that this has sometimes been claimed by thinkers in the tradition of 'natural law'. For making the distinctions that it seems vital to make, the key ideas are those of power, which seems to me especially focal for politics, and autonomy,[20] which seems to me definitive for morality. Let us see how these ideas help with the distinctions sought.

Politics is a matter of power, of the actual exercise of power within human societies or communities, and of elaborating principles for the proper exercise of power. Political power is the power to direct social agencies and individuals to certain

---

18   See Ch. 6 below

19   See D. Kennedy, *A Critique of Adjudication: Fin de Siecle* (Cambridge Mass.: Harvard University Press, 1997), 133–57; M. Davies, *Delimiting the Law: 'Postmodernism' and the Politics of Law* (London and Chicago: Pluto Press, 1996), 33–8.

20   This concept is more fully explained and developed in MacCormick, 'The Relative Heteronomy of Law', *European Journal of Philosophy*, 3 (1995), 69–85.

defined ends presumptively for the common good, to exercise control over available goods (economic and non-economic) and to determine or influence their distribution among persons and groups. This power is exercised over and among the members of a reasonably identifiable society of people. Essential to it is power to protect the society against serious interference from agencies external to it and from subversive sub-societies or groups within it. The power that we have in mind here is power-in-fact, not simply normative power; that is, power to make sure that somebody in fact acts in a certain way, rather than power to bring it about that somebody ought to act in a certain way. Political power is power-in-fact; but what is sometimes termed 'legal power' is power of the other sort, normative power, power confined to the realm of the 'ought'.

Law interacts with politics in many ways; sometimes as an object over and through which political power is exercised; sometimes as a control upon the use and abuse of power. But law is not itself constituted by the power-in-fact to effect social change. Law is a form of normative order, setting patterns of right and wrong conduct and conferring powers that are normative rather than coercive in their intrinsic character. Nobody doubts that the United States Constitution conferred and still confers the normative power to ban the manufacture, sale, and consumption of alcohol for beverage purposes. If exercised, this entails that according to law alcohol ought not to be manufactured, sold, or consumed for those purposes. The experiment of the 1920s, however, proved that this legal normative power was not conjoined with sufficient power-in-fact to change the drinking practices of Americans. This sufficiently exemplifies the distinction I have here in mind—politics about power, law about normative order.

Certainly, one might want to add that not every exercise of brute power is itself a matter of politics. We are often inclined to contrast political with military approaches to the solution of civil conflicts (e.g. in Northern Ireland or in Chechnya). The difference is in the element of persuasion, negotiation, discourse. Politics concerns the exercise of power through mainly peaceful discussion, persuasion, negotiation, within forms of government which at least purport to be directed towards a pursuit of the common good in a way that could in principle win general consent among the population governed. Still, however discursive politics may be, the discourse remains one that relates to the obtaining and the exercise of power in the sense defined. In its discursive aspect, politics has essential connections with morality. Morality in its most fundamental sense has to be grasped in terms akin to those of Kant's *Groundwork of the Metaphysic of Morals*, and with some regard to Jürgen Habermas's ideas on a 'procedural' account of the foundations of moral reasoning.[21] Morality concerns a normative order that is conceived to be valid independently of political or other power and yet to be universal in scope, addressing

---

[21] See H. J. Paton, *The Moral Law* (3rd edn., 3rd printing, London, 1961), which is a commentary on and translation of Kant's *Groundwork of the Metaphysic of Morals*; and J. Habermas, *Between Facts and Norms: Contributions to a Discourse Theory of Law and Democracy*, trans. William Rehg (Cambridge Mass.: MIT Press, 1996).

every moral agent as such. Since it is independent of power, it is necessarily autonomous in its force—for each agent, its binding force or normative validity lies in the commitment to it of that agent's own rational will. It is therefore discursive and controversial as well as autonomous. Moral principles are those we can argue out in conditions of free and uncoercive discourse, accepting that they must be universal in application and must take account of the interests and ideals of all persons capable of participating in the discourse or capable of being affected by its outcome. Each person is as fully entitled to enter into moral discourse as every other. The ultimate judgement of right and wrong in moral matters is for each agent a matter of the conclusions one draws after engagement in actual or imagined discourse with others, and of the commitments upon which one determines as a consequence. The drawing of conclusions characteristic of a rational will depends upon arguments from a sense of overall coherence of the positions that we commit ourselves to in essentially discursive, uncoercive, contexts.

Morality in a less fundamental sense is located in the common or conventional principles and rules held by persons in communities, often in connection with religious observances and traditions. To show why this sense is less fundamental, one need only ponder the question why these principles and rules have authority over a moral agent. One or other of only two answers is possible. Either their authority derives from the agent's own willing commitment to them, or it derives from the power, however crude or subtle, of community opinion and persuasion or disapproval that keeps the individual in line. In the former case, they are incorporated in the agent's morality through autonomous choice, hence conventional morality is subordinated to individual autonomy. In the latter case, individuals are subject, in however diffuse and ill-defined a way, to the exercise of power by others, and the rules of conventional morality are an element in the politics of community. If we are to understand morality as a distinct realm of thought and judgement, it can only be through giving conceptual primacy to the discursive–autonomous conception of morality.

Law has positivity. We look to law for answers to questions about what is obligatory or not, permissible or not, within some determinate and institutional sphere of decision-making. Inside that sphere of decision-making, the given rules and principles indicate what ought to be done, indeed what has to be done to satisfy the institutionalized system. The norms of a system of law lay down what is obligatory or permissible in the perspective of that system, not what from some ideal point of view ought to be obligatory or permissible. A properly taken decision that a certain rule shall be enacted into law does confer on that rule the character of being an actual rule of law. A properly taken decision about some disputed point of right between two persons settles conclusively the legal rights of each upon that point, just as a properly taken decision upon an accusation of crime settles conclusively the legal guilt or innocence of the accused person.

Law resembles morality in that it is normative. It resembles conventional morality in being a normative order commonly observed in some community or society, and backed by strong pressures of opinion, and by the regularly confirmed belief that others apply norms that are regarded as common standards for the group in question. States being territorial political communities organized under governments capable of wielding coercive power over individuals and groups and in response to external forces, the law of states is backed not only by opinion but also by the coercive force of political power. But it is important to remember these two things: first, the law of the state is not the only law that human beings have; secondly, the *Rechtsstaat* is, as was argued already, that particular form of state in which the law provides decisive and actually operative criteria for the rightful use of power. Such states have empirically a greater durability than police-states or party-states. In law-states, the exercise of governmental power is both limited and yet guaranteed by law. This can over time have a powerful effect in generating a popular sense of the legitimacy of government, as a 'government of laws not men'. Such a sense of legitimacy does not flow from the mere existence of an effectively functioning sovereign state. This further indicates that the legal and the political are not to be treated as identical however closely they interact in fortunate circumstances.

One manifestation of law's positivity lies in the way in which, on questions of law, there frequently seems to be a fact of the matter, checkable by reference to publicly accessible sources. If a person wants to find out whether there is a maximum speed limit on the roads of a country, or a maximum permitted level of blood alcohol for drivers, there are sources to which one can quite easily look for an answer. Explicit rules on such matters are to be found in pieces of legislation, frequently supplemented by pieces of subordinate legislation; and secondary sources such as legal textbooks or government publications about road traffic assist in identifying them.

On the moral question how fast it is right to drive, or how much if any alcohol it is morally acceptable to drink before driving, there is no interpersonally checkable source establishing a quantitative limit. Such questions are capable of being settled only through moral discourse, weighing relevant arguments, and establishing considerations relevant to the issue in hand. Their settlement from time to time depends on the conscientious judgement of a moral agent, whether or not in conformity with the conscientious judgement of other agents actually or potentially participating in the relevant discourse. Of course, it would be difficult to comprehend a claim that the norms of positive law in the state regulating alcohol consumption by drivers are irrelevant or weightless in a moral deliberation on the topic in question. But it would be even harder to comprehend, far less accept, a claim that morally the enacted rules could have the conclusive character they have within legal deliberation.

The settled, positive, character of law is jurisdiction-relative.[22] How fast one may drive is a question differently answered in different places governed by different legal systems under the jurisdiction of different organs or agencies. The fact of the legal

---

[22] For a fuller statement of this point, see MacCormick, 'Comment [on G. Postema's 'The Normativity of Law']' in Ruth Gavison (ed.), *Issues in Contemporary Legal Philosophy* (Oxford: Clarendon Press, 1987), 105–13.

matter is a fact about some discrete legal system, and, where the law in question is state-law, the answer normally holds good only in respect of the territory of the given state. Sixty miles per hour is the maximum permitted speed on roads in the United Kingdom other than designated 'motorways', on which the maximum is seventy miles per hour. That applies, of course, only to roads in the United Kingdom regulated by the Road Traffic Acts. If I visit another country, such as Canada, I expect the rules to be different, and even expressed in different units of measurement. There, I have to check on maxima in terms of kilometres per hour; and so on. In each jurisdiction, I look for some distinct piece of legislation (or other authoritative law-text) that settles the matter within that jurisdiction.

Moral judgements, however personal and controversial, are not in this way relativistic. If I hold that driving above a certain speed is inherently dangerous to life and limb, or wasteful of natural resources, and if I hold that humans ought not to endanger each others' bodily safety, or make excessive demands on non-renewable resources, then I must hold that speeding is wrong wherever it may cause danger or use too much fuel. These judgements apply universally. No doubt they are susceptible only to being supported with arguments in a moral discourse, without any interpersonally authoritative source to check against; but in their own character they are universalizable claims, not restricted by jurisdiction or territoriality. Certainly, circumstances alter cases morally; but they do so in a universalizable way. The truth of moral matters is not checkable by reference to established, public and institutional sources. But their truth is an unrestricted and universal truth to the extent we can establish it at all.

Here may rest the argument on the dual contrast of law with politics and with morality. Law is both a normative and an institutional order, and this connects it with the two poles of the contrast. As a normative order, it replicates certain features of morality, and connects necessarily to morality in certain ways. As an institutional order, it connects necessarily to politics and is in part constitutive of the political, while well-conducted politics is necessary to the maintenance of satisfactory systems of positive law, especially state-law.

Conclusion

I have tried to show in outline how to approach an understanding of law as institutional normative order conceptually distinct from morality and from politics. By focusing on an idea of institutional normative order, one negates the existence of any analytically necessary nexus between law and state. Law is institutional normative order, and state-law is simply one form of law. Conversely, the state is a form of territorial political order with some internal power-structure and power-relations, and the law-state is simply one form of state. This opens the question what are the possible, and the proper, relationships between state and law. Such will be the question pursued in the next chapter.

2

The State and the Law

Introduction

In the opening chapter, it was claimed that not all law is state-law, and not every state a law-state. This chapter will start to explain and vindicate in particular the second of those ideas, the argument continuing into the following chapter, with discussion of a test case. Essential to the argument is the differentiation that was drawn in the previous chapter between law and politics. Law is institutional normative order, politics is an order of power. The state is primarily a political entity, characterized by territoriality and stability in government. That is, a state has territory, and exercises effective government in that territory over the population, all or most of whom are citizens of the state. Typically, states are, or purport to be, 'nation-states', the process of nation-building having been one of seeking to develop among citizens a common consciousness of shared nationality. The less loaded term 'territorial state' will be used here.

Territorial states are not the only form of political entity, or polity, known to human history. The ancient world knew city-states and great empires. Many societies have lived in forms of tribal or clan-government. The political order of Europe in the Middle Ages was predicated on feudalism, with land-holding and socio-economic position dependent for everybody on having a place somewhere in the 'feudal chain', which was an extended set of bilateral relationships of service in return for protection and justice. Gradually, this was displaced in favour of the system of states we now see. Out of feudal kingdoms emerged centralizing monarchies with ever more absolutist pretensions. Out of reactions against royal absolutism emerged either constitutional monarchies or revolutionary republics, the former by somewhat slower and more evolutionary processes involving sometimes confrontation, sometimes negotiation, and sometimes mere chance, the latter in a more sudden and dramatic way, though often with many false starts.

It is a task for political history and political sociology to explain and account for the emergence, development, and character of the state. Gianfranco Poggi suggests that the state form of government is characterized by a cluster of attributes. This cluster includes organization of governing agencies, differentiation of their functions, effective use of coercive controls to implement acts of government, absence of any external power that can dictate policy to governing agencies ('sovereignty'), territorial sphere of the exercise of power, centralization of overall governance, and formal coordination of parts. Along with all that goes coexistence, by no means always peaceful, with other polities in a system of interacting states. As he remarks:[1]

---

[1] See Gianfranco Poggi, *The State: Its Nature, Development and Prospects* (Cambridge: Polity Press, 1990), 25.

[A]lthough one often speaks of 'the modern state' . . , strictly speaking the adjective 'modern' is pleonastic. For the set of features [characteristic of the state] is not found in any large-scale political entities other than those which began to develop in the early-modern phase of European history.

In previous large-scale political entities, political power was institutionalised in a different manner, and mostly to a lesser extent.

The prime question of this chapter is that of seeking to understand the relationship of law and state. William Ewald has commented illuminatingly that there are four possibilities in principle.[2] First, the state may be thought a creation of the law. Secondly, the state may be thought the unique producer of anything properly describable as 'law'. Thirdly, the state may be thought coexistent with law but not fully identical with it. And fourthly, the state and the law may be thought of as essentially identical, being but the same object viewed differently. He rightly points out that these need appreciation in the context of the history of ideas, as responses to various political controversies and ideological evolutions. But here, they will be taken in a somewhat schematic way with a view to a synthesis that I think apt to present political conjunctures.

Law and state: four possibilities

(i) The State as law-dependent

The first position depends on the theory of natural law. In such a theory, law is at its deepest level a set of rational norms of conduct built into the nature of things and of people, either by the arbitrary will of God the creator, or as a manifestation of God's intrinsic rationality and goodness. This natural law is also a moral law, and reflection on it enables us to see, given human weakness and wilfulness, that we must find our place in an ordered society of some kind. Whoever is found in the position of exercising governance in a human society has to make specific rules and ordinances for governing it and for securing that right conduct is upheld and wrongdoing adequately restrained and, when necessary, punished with appropriate severity.[3] Early versions of this theory were cast in a form appropriate to city states or to feudal kingdoms.

The upheavals of the reformation led to increasing difficulty in accounting for the legitimacy of one ruling house or party over another, indeed for the legitimacy of

---

[2] W. Ewald, 'Comment on MacCormick', *Cornell Law Review*, 82 (1997), 1071–9, at 1073–7; I must declare in full my indebtedness to the ideas advanced by Ewald in that comment on an earlier version of the present chapter 1. In what follows I adapt Ewald's ideas to my purpose, and superimpose an analytical view on a historicist conception. The resulting hybrid is mine, but the debt to Ewald incalculable.

[3] See, e.g., J. Finnis, *Aquinas* (New York: Oxford University Press, 1998), 255–74, and cf. Finnis, *Natural Law and Natural Rights* (Oxford: Clarendon Press, 1980), 245–52

governments at all. In response, there emerged 'social contract' theories in various forms. One line of thought associated particularly with the name of John Locke derived from the idea of a rational natural law the thesis that even in a 'state of nature', that is, outside any form of political organization, humans would have rights and would owe each other corresponding obligations. But these would be insecure, for their enforcement would rest entirely on private action, of a kind that would almost inevitably create a spiral of violence. Persons in the state of nature would therefore have compelling reasons to agree together on the establishment of a government. That government would be charged with upholding everybody's rights and legislating in clear terms common provisions identifying and delimiting otherwise dangerously vague rights. The agencies required for secure government to this end would include a legislature, an independent judiciary, and an executive branch concerned with external protection and internal law-enforcement.[4]

(ii) The law as state-dependent

The Lockean picture legitimates state institutions on condition that they uphold and give adequately concrete form to a law, and the rights derived from that law, which is perceived and presented as something anterior and superior to the state itself. But there have been many who have found such 'natural law' or 'natural rights' profoundly implausible. The counter thesis takes roughly this form: Human governments make laws and some of these laws confer rights. The only genuine rights humans can have are those that such laws confer, and only when there is power enough to enforce the laws and thereby secure the rights. This need not exclude the idea of a social contract. Thomas Hobbes had a vision of life in a state of nature even more disastrously insecure[5]—'solitary, poor, nasty, brutish, and short'—than that subsequently pictured by Locke.

Without law, humans are at war with each other, but know it is in their interest to seek peace. They can get peace only by agreeing with each other to subject themselves to a common ruler who exercises the whole power of the community. That ruler, or sovereign, whether a single person or an assembly of some kind, is the object of, not a party to, the original contract. Hence the ruler is not as such bound by the terms of the contract but acquires through it full power to enforce it as ruthlessly as necessary against any who go back on their word, and seek to disrupt the civil society their contract has set up. In this picture, there is no law anterior to the state, for law is the creature of the established human ruler, and is explicable simply in terms of the will and command of the ruler.[6]

The contract, however, is redundant in this account. Rulers or sovereigns can

---

[4] See John Locke, *The Second Treatise of Government*, 3rd edn., ed. J. Gough (Oxford: Basil Blackwell, 1966), ch. 2.

[5] See Thomas Hobbes, *Leviathan*, ch. 12, in Sir W. Molesworth (ed.), *The Collected English Works of Thomas Hobbes* (London: Routledge/Thoemmes, 1997), vol. 3.

[6] Hobbes, *Leviathan*, chs. 14–17.

come into being by conquest as well as by consent, and hold power so long as their rule is effective, giving enough people a strong enough sense of the advantages derived from settled government to make them effective collaborators in upholding the one in power. Thinkers like Jeremy Bentham[7] and John Austin[8] took Hobbes's theory without the 'fiction' of a social contract, saying that what mattered was the fact that people were in a 'habit of obedience' to a common superior, not a historical or mythical account of how this situation originally came about. Stable governments exist where there are stable habits of obedience, and the law is none other than the commands of those who are habitually obeyed. Sovereign rulers are those persons or assemblies who are habitually obeyed, but are not in the habit of obeying any human superior above themselves. An 'independent political society' is the group comprising a sovereign and all those living in the territory within which the habit of obedience obtains and the commands hold sway. A 'state' is either an alternative name for an 'independent political society' or is the collegiate governing entity that comprises the sovereign together with those subordinate power holders to whom have been delegated some portion of the sovereign's powers of command and enforcement.[9]

(iii) State and law as coexistent

Either of the former two approaches is exposed to the critique that they abstract from history, and take no account of the evolution of society, state, and law. Normative order (in the sense identified in Chapter 1) is a pervasive human phenomenon. It is perfectly possible for several orders to coexist, as when the law merchant (regulating international trading) coexisted with the canon law (regulating not only church organization but also family relations and aspects of succession law). Both in turn could coexist with the law administered in royal courts, or in local guild and other courts in cities, and so on. Centralization of governmental power was part of the evolution of the state as a form of polity. The Reformation and the wars of religion of the sixteenth and seventeenth centuries gave impetus to this. The claim by kings to exercise a monopoly over law was nowhere more dramatically exhibited than when in kingdoms such as England or Sweden royal supremacy over the church and its law was asserted and authenticated by acts of parliament, and enforced against dissenters with ruthless severity. But the tendency to establish monopoly over law should not blind us to the deeper underlying reality, of law rooted in the usages and practices of

---

[7] See J. Bentham, *A Fragment on Government*, in *A Comment on the Commentaries and A Fragment on Government*, ed. J. H. Burns and H. L. A. Hart (London: Athlone Press, 1977), at 441—it is Bentham who uses the term 'fiction' in this context.

[8] J. Austin, *The Province of Jurisprudence Determined* (ed. H. L. A. Hart, London: Weidenfeld & Nicolson, 1954), ch. 1.

[9] Austin, *Province*, 226–7; like Bentham, Austin preferred the concept 'independent political society' to that of 'state'; but 'state', he noted, could be used in the alternative, as indicated.

humans in social coexistence.[10] There remain in contemporary societies many forms of normative order, even institutional normative order, that are essentially independent of the state, even though the state may purport to regulate them in virtue of overall sovereign authority.[11]

To the extent that law can be seen as a form of customary normative order existing in popular consciousness and usage, there is a basis, not to deny the existence of state-law, but to deny its omnipresence and omnipotence. Those who seek to exercise political power in a society wish indeed to assert power of changing the rules by which people live, superseding older forms and imposing new ones, organizing sanctions to establish the force and authority of the state-order. But unless acknowledgement of the legitimacy of state-law becomes established as itself a part of popular custom, the government of the state is precarious, and the level of violence used to support its pretensions to rule will be high. Law promulgated by the state in these circumstances will be a very inferior species of the genus. Law and government should be seen as historically co-evolving systems, with state-law as simply one form of law,[12] most secure and genuinely law when supported by and partly grounded in custom rather then mere force.

(iv) Identity of state and law

States, on the other hand, are acting subjects. States do things. They mobilize armies and declare wars. They run health services and systems of agricultural subsidies and railway systems and goodness knows what else. The acts and movements in the physical world that are involved in all this are of course acts of human beings. Their acts are imputed to the state as the single organized reference point behind the myriad of human actings. What makes possible such imputation? The law, of course. The complexity of organization that characterizes the modern state is intelligible only in the light of a formidable body of public law authorizing people to act and investing their acts with the quality of being valid state-actions. But if you ask what is the real substance that lies behind the legal framework, the physical or metaphysical body of 'the state', the question seems unanswerable.

Hans Kelsen, in fact, argued that the question itself rests on a false dualism of law and state. The state simply is the territorial legal order personified. The state is simply the point of imputation to which public legal acts are imputed. More narrowly, it is

---

[10] See O. von Gierke, *Community in Historical Perspective*, ed. A. Black (Cambridge: Cambridge University Press, 1990), 84–95, 161–6; Gierke's influence on F. W. Maitland is well known—see F. W. Maitland (trans.), O. Gierke, *Political Theories of the Middle Age* (Cambridge: Cambridge University Press, 1900), intro., pp. xviii–xliii.

[11] Cf. also such 'institutionalist' thinkers as M. Hauriou; see *The French Institutionalists: Maurice Hauriou, Georges Renard, Joseph T. Delos*, trans. M. Welling, intro. by M. T. Rooney (Cambridge, Mass.: Harvard University Press, 1945), esp. at 93–124; cf. 'Institutionalism in Law' (by A. Pintore) in E. J. Craig (gen. ed.), *Routledge Encyclopaedia of Philosophy* (London: Routledge, 1998), vol. 4, 799–803.

[12] Cf. L. L. Fuller, *The Morality of Law*, rev. edn. (New Haven CT: Yale University Press, 1969), ch. 4, discussing non-state forms of law.

the corporate entity comprising the main organs of government organized through public law, and it is to this organization that we refer in speaking of the state or in imputing acts to it. Here, therefore, we find our fourth theoretical approach, that according to which there is effectively an identity of law and state. Neither does the state make the law nor does the law make the state, for in truth they are the same object viewed differently.

The theory may be gathered from either of the main English translations of Kelsen's work, viz, Max Knight's translation under the title *The Pure Theory of Law*[13] or Anders Wedberg's under the title *The General Theory of Law and the State*.[14] As well as being relevant to the current problem, Kelsen's theory has the considerable merit of being one of the most carefully articulated juristic theories of the state that we have. It has had very considerable influence on more general thought about the state, both in the United Kingdom, where H. L. A. Hart impliedly adopted it,[15] and in such countries as Italy or France, where such eminent scholars as Norberto Bobbio[16] and Michel Troper[17] have developed theories of the state, and national applications of these, out of originally Kelsenian materials.

Review: imperfect identity of state and law

We can in fact learn something from all of these lines of approach. Locke's and Kelsen's views, for example, have an important truth in common. They tell us that any state has to have a constitution that confers the general powers of government, and all the state's law then depends on being valid under the constitution, and is so only because of it. The constitutional legitimacy of law-making and law-applying follows from the fact that there is a constitution that ought to be respected, and that cannot be respected save by accepting laws validly enacted under it, and accepting the judicial application and police enforcement of the enacted laws. Indeed, that any person can be a head of state, or any gathering of persons a parliament or congress, or any group a bench of judges, requires there to be some constitution to which we can look as defining and conferring these offices. Imputation of acts to a state does require just such a constitutional organization.

Does it follow, though, that the constitution has to be envisaged in Locke's way as the terms of a social contract entered into by persons exercising contractual powers conferred by the law of nature? Surely not. The processes of constitution-making and

---

[13] Berkeley, Cal. (1967), 279–319.

[14] Cambridge, Mass. (1945), 180–95.

[15] See Hart, 'Definition and Theory in Jurisprudence', originally published in 1963; now in Hart, *Essays in Jurisprudence and Philosophy* (Oxford: Clarendon Press, 1983), 21–48 at 45–7; Hart, in his unpublished lectures on Kelsen in Oxford in the early 1960s, at least once (in my hearing) referred to Kelsen's theory of the state as 'a triumph'.

[16] See N. Bobbio, *Teoria dell' ordinamento giuridico* (Turin, 1970).

[17] See M. Troper, *Pour une Théorie juridique de l'État* (Paris, Presses Universitaires de France, 1994), 153–9.

constitution-giving, even, perhaps, constitution-evolving, have been many and various. Certainly, it is one democratic ideal that people cannot be bound by a constitution save by their own assent to it, and wherever there is a democratic form of government successfully maintained over time, one can portray the constitution as subject to a kind of ongoing agreement among citizens. But democracy is a desirable form of government for a state, not a condition of statehood, and democracy does not in itself guarantee the absence of disaffected minorities. As a regulative ideal, or an 'idea of reason',[18] one can picture a constitution as that which ought to have been open to consent and agreement by all. As a historical fact, real constitutions fall some way, in many cases a long way, short of the ideal. Social contracts are not real events.

What is true, as Kelsen points out, is that normativity attaches to laws made under a historically occurrent constitution only if some norm, some 'basic norm' or *Grundnorm*, is presupposed as conferring authority on the constitution and hence on those whom it authorizes to make and enforce law. Kelsen suggests that legal scientists must treat his as a pure hypothesis or even fiction—a norm that is presupposed, not posited, the content of an imaginary act of will.[19] Kelsen had a particularly austere view of the character and task of legal science, which he said had to be kept quite pure of ideology and of morality. Given this austerity of view, it may well be the case that a legal scientist committed to purity in Kelsen's sense just has to work with the unexamined presupposition of a 'basic norm'. Where one's concerns are, as in the present work, with the interface and overlap between law and politics such austerity is unproductive. Law is not only an object of study for legal science, but is in some form an element in the lives and actions of citizens and officials. It has a social dimension for which we must account—but how?

The historical approach holds the key to this. Normative order is a pervasive feature of human experience. Meaningful human actions always presuppose some normative framework. Even speaking or writing requires attention to (at least implicit) rules of grammar (syntactical and semantic, perhaps rhetorical and stylistic as well). Languages grow up and develop spontaneously, and only subsequently do some of them become official state languages, with national academies regulating their usage. Institutional normative order generally is a pervasive feature of our existence. Only at a certain point, or during a certain epoch in history, does human political order gradually assume the form of state-government. Then the state, that is, certain agencies, capture those elements of institutional normative order that are most essential to the maintenance of social peace, regulated economic activity, and external protection.

It remains true that there is always custom prior to any constitution, and there can be a widespread custom of respecting a constitution and demanding this respect as what is due. Such a customary norm of respect for the constitution is the securest normative underpinning of it. It is not a once-off social contract, but a shared

---

[18] See I. Kant, *The Metaphysical Elements of Justice*, trans. J. Ladd (Indianapolis: Bobbs Merrill/Library of Liberal Arts, 1965), 80–1.   [19] Kelsen, *Pure Theory*, 6–7.

custom extended in time that gives popular legitimacy to a constitution.[20] Moreover, it is only where states grow overweening in ambition that they seek to confine custom to the single function of working as constitutional foundation, or to negate it altogether as a source of law. At the same time, they are apt to seek to redefine all forms of institutional order as existing only by delegation from and permission of the state itself. But philosophical understanding of law and state should not give credence to overweening pretensions of states. States cannot turn their own contingent triumphs into necessary truths.

What of moral ideals? There is certainly no good reason to deny that there are sound moral ideals that we can set for constitutional government, and real moral values attendant on successful constitutional government. The conditions of respect for persons, and the possibility for the development of full and autonomous moral agency, depend on participation both in the institutions of civil society and in the self-governance of a state. At least a contemporary consensus concerning fundamental values for human existence can be expressed in some catalogue of fundamental rights that states have to respect, not throw aside.[21] 'Natural law' and cognate ideas have real resonance as critical ideals against which to judge actual performance. The more people are able to regard the actual functioning of a state as matching up to, or reasonably approximating toward, such ideals, the more ready will they be to sustain the custom and usage that underpin constitutional order.

Finally, the blunt realism of a Hobbes or an Austin is never to be wholly put out of mind. Many are the constitutions, many the Charters of Rights, that have been issued and proclaimed, perhaps endorsed by popular referendum, even with the approval of a suspiciously large majority of voters, and yet simply ignored in practice. Constitution-texts can be mere façade legitimation, mere window-dressing on actual state practice. The practice may be of one-party rule, of police torture, of corrupt and intimidated judges, of a military or militia barely if at all under civilian rule, of business practices distorted by the need for systematic bribery of officials, and so on. Yet even in such circumstances, order of a kind can be maintained. The 'habit of obedience' of the cowed masses may be never more real than under a bloodthirsty despotism carried on only with such deference to the published imperatives of the constitution as does not frustrate the stratagems and ambitions of the holders of power.

In extreme cases of this kind, the normal terminology of 'law' seems scarcely to fit the practical reality. Order there may to some extent be, institutions of a kind, but not normative order, not order essentially explicable in terms of reasonable efforts at reasonable conformity with some set of commonly acknowledged and pre-announced rules. In domains to which persons in government are largely indifferent, there may remain relatively efficacious bodies of private and commercial law, though

---

[20] See N. MacCormick and O. Weinberger, *An Institutional Theory of Law* (Dordrecht: D. Reidel, 1986), ch. 8 (MacCormick, 'Institutional Morality and the Constitution').

[21] Cf. Bobbio, *The Age of Rights*, trans. A. Cameron (Cambridge: Polity Press, 1996).

bribery of judges and court officials may amount to an unofficial tax on using the system. Human survival will require the discovery and devising of routines to manage the situation, and life will not necessarily be wholly unpredictable, but it will often be precarious.

Real life normally falls somewhere between the two limiting cases of what might be called Hobbes's nightmare and Locke's dream. No state can be imagined without some, at least purported, normative framework identifying office holders and the competence they can exercise. And to some greater or lesser degree, restraints and restrictions, checks and controls, separations of powers, may be observed and respected. The restrictions on governmental power may amount more or less to a reasonable scheme of individual liberty and fair collective security. Yet it remains the case that constitutions and laws enable or empower at least as much as they restrict. Moreover, as massively attested by the studies of Critical Legal Scholars and American Realists before them, a very considerable indeterminacy besets legal texts at all levels, constitutional, statutory, or precedential, quite as much in liberal states as elsewhere. This indeterminacy is exploited wherever powerful people are in contention over issues that depend, or can be made to depend, on some interpretation of the meaning and point of an apposite text. So the exact extent of governmental powers and of constitutional restrictions on them is always contestable, and there is rarely a shortage of competing interpretations at play when rival interests point in different directions.

The ends to which powers are used are not themselves set by the law or the constitution. They are determined by political programmes directed towards contested political ends, and driven in considerable measure by political leaders' and activists' personal ambitions for the trappings of power, for influence in great affairs, and for public recognition. Acquiring constitutional and legal authority is but one of the means to acquiring and using power over a society and its members. The state's activity comprises all that is done by way of exercising power in all its kinds by persons holding constitutionally defined offices or having control over those who hold formal office. In this sense, the state is a theatre of political power, not of pure legal authority. The state cannot live without some minimal law and minimal respect for it, and it cannot thrive without a considerable body of law and considerable respect for it. But straightforward identification of the state with the law is erroneous. This is true even though it is the case that we must look to a constitution to find out whose actions are the ones that can be imputed to the state as its acts for one or another purpose.

Our conclusion is that there is imperfect identity of law and state, overlap without complete identity. A state is a territorial organization of political power that requires constitutional definition and organization, but is not necessarily confined effectively by constitutional limits. Institutional normative order can exist apart from the state, and customary normative order is a condition for the grounding of the constitutional order that a state requires. States can, but do not have to, establish a monopoly on institutional normative order, purporting to make 'law properly so-called' fully and exclusively co-extensive with state-law. State power does not have to be exercised in accordance with the limits on constitutional authority, and is never perfectly so. It can decline into lawless gangsterism, but the character of institutional normative order, and thus of law, is not intrinsic to gangster-commands or the order of terror they may establish.

3

The Interest of the State and the Rule of Law

Introduction

Given the understanding established in the preceding chapter concerning the imperfect identity of state and law, it is an open question how far any particular state does live up to the rule of law, thereby achieving the character of a 'law-state'. This chapter will pursue that question in relation to the United Kingdom, focusing on one particular example, which raises a fascinating cluster of problems. I have in mind one particular incident in British public life from the mid-1980s. It was the case of a prosecution in London under the United Kingdom's Official Secrets Act of 1911.

A key section of that act makes it an offence if a person who possesses state secrets passes them on to anyone else, except if authorized to do so, or if under 'a duty in the interests of the state' to do so. In the prosecution in question, that of Mr Clive Ponting,[1] a civil servant in the Ministry of Defence, it was not disputed that Mr Ponting had passed secrets to a member of parliament. But the defence said he had acted out of a sense of his 'duty in the interests of the state' to do so. The judge was reported in the press as directing the jury about the meaning of that expression. He was reported to have told the jury that, as a matter of law, the interests of the state were determined by whatever were the policies of the government, that is, the executive branch, the Prime Minister and Cabinet. If a person was acting against the policy line taken by Ministers, he could not be acting in the interests of the state.

What was most striking to me at the time was the furious reaction this direction provoked among my academic colleagues. Sober and senior academics from disciplines other than law, some rather conservative in outlook, some moderately liberal, sought me out and demanded to know if this could possibly be the law. As citizens of a free country they expressed themselves outraged, and even sullied, by the claim that the state, their state as they thought of it, could have its interests treated as simply identical with governmental policy. If that was the law, they thought, it was high time for a change in it. In fact, the United Kingdom, like other countries in the common law tradition, lacks a body of doctrinal public law that articulates a well-developed theory of the state and its character. So there is not a lot in the way of legal doctrine on which to build an account of the meaning of section 2 of the Official Secrets Act where it uses the concept 'state'.

---

[1] An account of which, from the defendant's viewpoint, appears in C. Ponting *The Right to Know: The Inside Story of the Belgrano Affair* (London and Sydney: Sphere Books, 1985).

The state: a legal concept?

It may seem strange that, by and large, legal and constitutional parlance in the United Kingdom does not make much use of the term 'state' as a technical term. Where it does, as in the 'act of state' doctrine, this is really a borrowing from public international law, which necessarily uses the concept. Constitutional law in the UK does not offer much in the way of doctrines about the state and its competence. What elsewhere is treated as a unitary acting state is in the United Kingdom discussed through doctrines about 'the Crown' or occasionally the 'Executive', and about the prerogatives of the Crown, about Parliament—the legislature—and its privileges, and its omnipotence or indeed 'sovereignty'. Further, there are doctrines about the judiciary and about judicial independence. All this yields also a conception of the separation of powers, which is acknowledged to be only an imperfect separation of them.[2] The 'Rule of Law' has been held to depend on the fact that one single structure of courts is final arbiter of the legality of every action, governmental or non-governmental, and on the fact that it is primarily out of the traditional common law that the rights of the subject ('subject', note, not 'citizen') are defined.

The imperfectly separated powers of Crown, Parliament, and the Courts are all unquestionably powers (or functions) of state and government. But there is missing any tradition of articulated reflection upon the nature of states and the particular nature of the state whose powers the British Constitution (if indeed there is any one such thing) constitutes. By contrast, in the juridical traditions of the mainland of Europe there is a much greater inclination to treat the personified 'state' as the prime subject of constitutional law, that which constitutions constitute and whose powers they define, delimit, and distribute. Thus in these traditions 'the state' (*der Staat, L'État*, etc.) is a legal term of art, used in constructing and in construing the public law. One example of this is, indeed, the use within the Basic Law of the Federal Republic of Germany of the term *Rechsstaat—eine soziale Rechtsstaat*,[3] indeed—as defining one of the key qualities of the state constituted by that Basic Law.

The reason for the comparative silence of United Kingdom authorities in the matter of state-doctrine seems to be largely historical. It has to do with the evolutionary process of development of the modern United Kingdom out of an English feudal monarchy that moved sharply toward royal absolutism under the Tudor monarchs of the sixteenth century. It then saw the growth of royal power checked in the confrontation of monarch and parliament in the Civil Wars of the seventeenth century. Establishment of limited monarchy in what might best be called a 'polity of

---

[2] See Geoffrey Marshall *Constitutional Theory* (Oxford: Clarendon Press, 1971), ch. 2, 'The State, the Crown and the Executive'.

[3] See the *Grundgesetz* (Basic Law) of the Federal Republic of Germany, art 28, which requires the federated Länder to observe 'the fundamental principles of the republican, democratic and social *Rechtsstaat* in the sense of this basic law'. Consider also arts. 1–19.

estates', or *Ständestaat*,[4] came about through the pro-parliamentary *coup d'état* that was the 'Glorious Revolution' of 1688–9. That in turn was rendered secure through the Anglo-Scottish Union of 1707. The concomitant Hanoverian succession, under kings comparatively uninterested in the detailed governance of British affairs, had the effect of transferring real executive power into the hands of appointees who were indeed the 'King's ministers', but who had to have effective majority support in Parliament. By the end of the eighteenth century the real head of government was the 'First Lord of the Treasury' popularly called 'prime minister', in whose hands lay the gift of ministerial office and membership of the cabinet, and much else in the way of public patronage. The following century saw regularization and organization of the civil service, and the twentieth, extension of governmental functions to cover the full panoply of the 'welfare state'. New substance retained the covering of old forms, and the kingdom became a state without avowing its changed character through a formal constitution.

In these circumstances, it may not be surprising that when the concept 'state' does crop up in such a context as the Official Secrets Act, it subsists in something of a conceptual vacuum. This is not because the United Kingdom is not a state (it obviously is), but because it came to be one in an unusually picaresque way. In these circumstances, the challenge of achieving the actuality of a full-hearted *Rechtsstaat* or 'law-state' (assuming that to be desirable) is the more exacting. However, the home-grown tradition of the 'Rule of Law' may provide the necessary basis for doing so, since a law-state is effectively a state dedicated to upholding constitutionalism and securing the Rule of Law.

(*a*) The *Ponting* case: two theories

The outline facts of *R.* v. *Ponting* made headlines in 1985,[5] and deserve not to be forgotten. Clive Ponting was a senior civil servant in the Ministry of Defence. In March 1984, there was a period of public and Parliamentary controversy concerning the sinking of the Argentinian cruiser *Belgrano* early in the Falklands conflict of 1982. Mr Ponting was called upon to prepare for his Ministers (Mr Michael Heseltine, Secretary of State for Defence, and Mr John Stanley, Minister of State) a full study of the events surrounding the sinking of the *Belgrano*. In the light of his study it became clear that previous accounts given to Parliament had been incorrect, and that there were no good reasons of state security against giving the correct information. After a period of deliberation, however, the Ministers decided not to reveal the reveal the information in response to Parliamentary questions posed in particular by Mr Tam

---

[4] This term is translatable as 'polity of estates', see Gianfranco Poggi, *The State: Its Nature, Development and Prospects* (Cambridge: Polity Press, 1990), 40–2, and compare Poggi, *Development of the Modern State: A Sociological Introduction* (Stanford: Stanford University Press, 1978).

[5] See Ponting, *Right to Know; The Times*, 29 Jan.–12 Feb. 1985; *R.*v. *Ponting* [1985] Crim. R. 318.

Dalyell MP, and by the House of Commons Select Committee on Foreign Affairs. Three days after the delivery by Mr Stanley of a memorandum to the Select Committee on 13 July 1984, Mr Ponting sent two documents to Mr Dalyell. In relation to questions that had been raised by Dalyell, Ponting had drafted answers for use by his Ministers. The documents sent to Dalyell included these draft answers. They had not been used by the Ministers, who had instead chosen to 'stonewall' on the point. A further document was a text prepared by another civil servant (Mr Michael Legge) with a view to advising the Ministers how to avoid revealing to the Select Committee true information that would be at odds with accounts previously given by Ministers. Dalyell passed these on to the Chairman of the Committee, who in turn passed them to the Secretary of State. In due course Ponting was detected as the probable discloser of the documents and was, with the concurrence of the Attorney-General, Sir Michael Havers, prosecuted for a breach of the Official Secrets Act.

One defence mounted on Ponting's behalf at his trial was that that he had passed the papers to Dalyell in pursuance of a duty in the interest of the state. On this, the trial judge (McCowan J.) directed the jury that the defence depended on a wrong interpretation of the law. Therefore, on the facts as admitted, Ponting had done something which according to law he ought not to have done, and thus they as jurors ought to convict him of the offence against section 2 of the Official Secrets Act of which he stood indicted. The jury, having received this direction, retired to the privacy of deliberations in the jury room, and in due course returned and—to widespread astonishment—pronounced the verdict: 'Not Guilty.'

This could be thought a clear case of a 'perverse verdict'. The jury were told that the law was clear on a certain point; the facts were no less clear, being not, on essential points, subject to much dispute. But the jury's verdict did not fit those facts given that law thus understood. It must have decided to ignore what the judge had said. They respected what Ponting had done and disliked the spirit in which he had been prosecuted. So they acquitted him in defiance of the law as laid down.

Some people, most notably Lord Devlin,[6] have argued that the real function of the jury is that revealed through such perverse verdicts. In a democratic society, perverse verdicts should be issued from time to time. The real function of the jury is to be the plain person's censor of the law. If the law itself, or—even more importantly—the law as used by the executive or by the prosecuting authorities, becomes a moral affront to the ordinary decent person, then the jury is the ultimate protector of the harassed citizen. The jury can ignore, set aside, defy, such law—precisely by returning a verdict in the teeth of the law in an appropriate case.

When such a thing occurs, as most notoriously in the old death penalty cases, in which jurors refused to convict of thefts that were capital offences, it brings political pressure to bear on governments and parliamentarians. The political pressure is either to have the law changed or to bring to heel those members of the executive or

---

[6] Patrick, Lord Devlin, *Trial by Jury* (1956), 160–2. Cf. also W. R. Cornish, *The Jury* (1971), 127–33.

those prosecuting authorities who are using the law in an oppressive manner. (Candidates for such oppressiveness in the *Ponting* case were the Attorney-General, the Secretary of State for Defence, and the Prime Minister herself; though all hotly repelled the charge.)

The 'Perverse Verdict Theory' is, then, one possible account of what happened in *Ponting*'s case, a theory located at the heart of one conception of the special value of the jury system in criminal trials. If we try to fit it in with legal theory in a more general sense, we might find much in it to echo and confirm aspects of American Legal Realism. It fits well into those strains of thought which have been labelled 'rule scepticism' and 'fact scepticism'.[7] That juries can do such things reminds us not to take too seriously the theory of law as a pure normative order. Law is no simple set of established rules that are always applied in a perfectly deductive way by finding out the facts, subsuming the facts under appropriate rules, and reading off legal conclusions accordingly. The rules do not always matter as much as ideal theory suggests, and even if they did, what about the fact-finding process?

The facts may be as malleable as the rules, or more so, to borrow a thought from Jerome Frank.[8] The jury can say, just as it pleases, and in the face of any evidence at all, 'we do not find those facts proved'. Having shut its eyes to the facts as the judge thinks they are, the prosecutor thinks they are and indeed everybody else thinks they are, the jury can find the accused not guilty. They do so on the (pretended) ground of a lack of facts to which to apply a law whose effects would be only too clear were there but facts to fit it. The jurors' judgement of fact is, however, absolutely conclusive.

Whoever is master of the facts is in the last resort also master of the law (at least, of its application to particular concrete cases). So there is every reason for scepticism about the extent to which the law in action is—and perhaps about the extent to which the law ought to be—a scientific process of establishing facts without regard to any value-consequences of these findings of fact. The value-consequences depend partly on the logical consequences entailed by applying to these facts relevant legal rules according to some authoritative interpretation of them. As a theory of the case, the Perverse Verdict Theory has no shortage of support from some quarters in general jurisprudence.

But one can conjure up a rival theory of the case, for which no less powerful backing could be suggested. Using ideas drawn mainly from the thought of Ronald Dworkin,[9] one might advance the thesis that it was the trial judge's interpretation of the Official Secrets Act, not the jury's verdict, that deserved the epithet 'perverse' in this case. Let the rival theory of the case be called the 'Unsound Interpretation Theory'.

Here, one starts from the incontestable proposition that the *concept* 'interest of

---

[7] See, for this distinction, Jerome Frank, *Law and the Modern Mind* (English edn., 1949), pp. vii–x.

[8] Frank, op. cit., pp. xi–xiv.

[9] See Ronald Dworkin, *Taking Rights Seriously* (1979), esp. chs. 2–4 and 13; also *Law's Empire* (Cambridge Mass.: Harvard University Press, 1986).

the state' has a central significance in section 2 of the Official Secrets Act. In particular, it is crucial in certain cases as between being guilty or not guilty of an offence under section 2. But before the concept can be put into operation towards reaching a verdict in any case, the raw words 'interest of state' obviously have to be interpreted. We have to take the concept 'interest of state' and formulate some *conception* of that concept that could appropriately be applied in cases arising under *this* use of the concept. Always, of course, with abstract concepts like 'interests' or 'state', to say nothing of 'interest of the state', many rival conceptions may be open to be adopted as to the applicable meaning of the concept for the given context. Such concepts are contested concepts, the contests being between rival conceptions of them.

Nearly always, according to Dworkin, and at least sometimes, maybe even often, according to what I consider the better view, one or another conception is in the given legal context objectively better than any of its rivals.[10] And that gives us a criterion for detecting mistakes or misconceptions. Such mistakes can be made even by judges, whether or not for some purposes what they say or do is the last word (or deed) and final for practical purposes. This supposition opens the door to the possibility of perverse judicial interpretation of the law. Applied to *Ponting's* case, it generates the second theory of that case: the theory that the judge gave an unsound, indeed a wrong, interpretation of the phrase 'interests of the state'. What the judge did was to put before the jury a misconception of the concept, more or less directing them to convict on the faith of that misconception.

If that is so, then surely it was the jury that restored the sense to the law. The jury's conception of the interests of the state and of what is a person's duty in the interest of the state, it could be argued, was *even in law* a better conception of these concepts than that expounded by the judge in his direction to it. In this sense, one might wish to argue that the verdict in *R. v. Ponting* was the correct verdict. No doubt it was a hard case; but, as people like Dworkin argue, there can often be right answers even in hard cases. And maybe the jury got the legal answer right in this hard case. Maybe the judge got it wrong in this case but was faced with a stout-minded jury willing and able to get it right even in the face of his misdirection.

Each of the rival theories of *Ponting's* case: the Perverse Verdict Theory and the Unsound Interpretation Theory, has a recognizable background in a well-known general theory about law and legal processes. Of each of them, the question may well be asked: 'How does the Rule of Law fit in with this?' Given the Perverse Verdict Theory, we may wish to know whether it implies that the jury acted against or even in defiance of the Rule of Law. But would it then matter if the Rule of Law were flouted? If a law is a bad law, should not the rule of *that* law be flouted; and can not that be done without damaging the overall general fabric of the law, without subverting the Rule of Law in those matters in which it is of real value? Or is the Rule of

---

[10] Dworkin, op. cit.; and 'Taking the Rights Thesis Seriously', in MacCormick *Legal Right and Social Democracy* (1982), ch. 7; for Dworkin's reply to which see M. Cohen (ed,), *Ronald Dworkin and Contemporary Jurisprudence* (1984), 378–81. See also MacCormick 'Legal Reasoning and Practical Reason', in P. French *et al.* (eds.), *Midwest Studies in Philosophy VII* (1982), 271–86.

Law so important that we want juries and judges always to apply the law fully and faithfully regardless of their or our view of the merits or demerits, the justice or injustices of a particular law in particular cases? Whatever be our answer, the Perverse Verdict Theory certainly throws up some teasing questions about the Rule of Law.

No less so does the Unsound Interpretation Theory. This theory plainly has implications as to the Rule of Law. If it is true that the jury has and acts on the better conceptions of a key concept in the Official Secrets Act, then it is the jury after all which is upholding the Rule of Law, rescuing it from a misreading by the professional lawyer, the legally qualified judge. Furthermore, as I shall argue below, the very question of the interpretation of the 'interests of the state' may itself turn on the point of the relationship we suppose to exist between the state and the Rule of Law conceived as an ideal. If it is that intimate relationship characteristic of a *Rechtsstaat*, then this may favour one or other of our two theories—probably the second one.

(*b*) An argument for the Perverse Verdict Theory

The point in this section being to make out an argument for the Perverse Verdict Theory, it must start with a more exact statement of the exact way the concept of the interest of the state came into *Ponting*'s case. This requires recourse to the very words of section 2(1) of the Official Secrets Act:

If any person having in his possession or control any . . . information . . . which he has obtained owing to his position as a person who holds or has held office under His Majesty . . .

(*a*) communicates the . . . information to any person, other than a person to whom he is authorised to communicate it, or a person to whom it is *in the interest of the state his duty to communicate it* . . .
that person shall be guilty of a misdemeanour.

For the sake of emphasis, I have italicized the words that brought the concept of 'the interest of the state' into UK law as an operative concept of official secrets law. It is to be noticed, though, that this is encapsulated in the concept of a 'duty in the interest of the state'. To pass on information obtained in an official capacity is an offence unless the communication was to an authorized person or a person to whom one had a duty in the interest of state to give the information. There, for the *Ponting* case, was the rub. That Mr Ponting had obtained certain information in an official capacity, that he had passed it on to Mr Dalyell and that he did so without authority were not points in dispute. But the defence strenuously contended that he had done so in pursuance of what he regarded as his duty in the interest of the state, and that he was right so to regard it, for he was protecting the highest constitutional authority, Parliament, from being deliberately misled by persons who are subordinate to, and answerable to, Parliament in their role as ministers. Could this contention be upheld?

Certainly not, according to McCowan J. We need to look therefore at his conception of the interest of state. Unfortunately, for want of any better report, one is left with the newspapers as the only available source, in the news columns rather than the Law Reports. Here is how *The Times* recorded the key passage of his direction:[11]

As far as [concerned] the words *'in the interest of the state'* the judge said:

'I direct you that these words mean the policies of state as they were in July, 1984 . . . and not the policies of the state as Mr Ponting, Mr Dalyell, you or I might think they ought to have been.' He added: 'The policies of the state mean the policies laid down by those recognized *organs of government and authority*.'

. . . 'While it has [majority] support [in the House of Commons], the Government and its policies are for the time being the policies of the state.'

[Emphasis added.]

The words quoted are from a news report, without the care in checking and reformulation that can figure in a formal 'law report'. They may not be quite accurate as a record of what was said, though there is corroboration.[12] Or perhaps the words quoted are quoted out of context. At all events, it seems barely credible that one could assert an *identity* as between a state's 'policies' and its 'interests'. So even allowing that a state's policies are indeed exactly those determined by its lawful and recognized organs of government, it will not follow that its interests are whatever the government says they are. After all, if an individual made a policy of annually overspending his income, we would not necessarily conclude that this was in her interests; Mr Micawber's policy does not necessarily equate with Mr Micawber's interests, and so with the state.[13]

For the purpose of the Perverse Verdict Theory, however, we must read the judge's words so as to make the best possible sense of them. To this end, it has to be remarked that the question relates not to the state's interest *simpliciter*, but to what is an official's duty-in-the-interest-of-the-state. Taking that point, we may then acknowledge that although 'policies' and 'interests' are not the very same things, yet it is perfectly arguable that a public official has no duty in the interest of the state other than a duty faithfully to implement the policies of the state. It is, furthermore, arguable that the policies of the state are nothing other than the policies determined by the governing organs or authorities of a state. In the British case, on this view,

---

[11] *The Times*, 9 Feb. 1984. The *Criminal Law Review*, in its summary report, records the point in this way: 'As to the meaning of the words "in the interests of the state," the learned judge preferred the views expressed in the speeches of Lord Devlin and Lord Pearce in *Chandler v D.P.P.* [1964] A.C. 763, that the interests of the state meant what was in the interests of the State according to its recognised organs of government and the policies as expounded by the particular Government of the day. It was not, he held, for the jury to decide what the Government's policy should have been nor was it for them to enter into a political debate. In this case it was not in dispute that the policy of the Government was not to give the information which Mr. Ponting communicated.' [1985] Crim. L.R. 318 at 319.

[12] See Ponting, *Right to Know*, 190–4; on the other hand, the Crim. L.R. report quoted above seems clearer.

[13] On the possibility of a distinction between one's wishes or policies and one's interests, see Brian Barry, *Political Argument* (1965), 174–8, and cf. D. Parfit, *Reasons and Persons* (1964), 464–8.

state policy is determined by the government of the day, and so long as a government retains its majority it remains the government, and its policies are the policies of the state. Civil servants accordingly have a duty in the interest of the state that can be none other than to carry out those policies regardless of their personal opinion one way or the other. If the policies of the government include a policy of withholding certain information from Parliament or Members or Committees of it, the same goes for that as for any other policy. In general, whatever promotes the implementation of the government's policies is in the interest of the state, and whatever hinders their implementation is adverse to the interest of the state.

If this line of reasoning is sound, then the Perverse Verdict Theory can be upheld. That is, it can be accepted that the judge's statement of the law was in its essentials correct and the jury's verdict a perverse one given in despite of the law. Is the line of reasoning sound, then? Upon what sources might it rest? To answer these questions, it is helpful to notice that section 1 of the Official Secrets Act also employs the concept 'the interest of the state', albeit in a different context:

If any person for any purpose prejudicial to the *safety or interests of the state*
(a) . . . enters any prohibited place within the meaning of this Act; . . . he shall be guilty of a felony.

The leading authority for the interpretation of this section of the Act is the case of *Chandler* v. *DPP*.[14] This provision (as the sidenote to the section, 'Penalties for spying' indicates) was intended primarily to cover cases of spying, the Act having been rushed through Parliament during a somewhat factitious spy scare in 1911. Nevertheless, *Chandler's* case decided that its reach goes well beyond simple cases of spying on defence establishments. The primary instance of a breach of this section would be an entry upon a defence establishment for the purpose of spying—or, alternatively, for the purpose of sabotage. But the exact and precise gist of the offence is that one enters *for a purpose prejudicial to the safety or interests of the state.*

The issue in *Chandler's* case was whether the prohibition in the Act includes a prohibition upon breaking into a military airfield with a view to preventing the take-off or landing of planes armed with nuclear weapons and with the ulterior aim of drawing attention to the dangers attendant on the possession and possible use of such weapons. During one major phase of nuclear disarmament campaigning, certain members of the Committee of One Hundred planned such an entry with such an aim, this to form part of a protest at the Wethersfield Air Base, a 'prohibited place' under the Act. The persons concerned were frustrated in their purpose, but were nevertheless prosecuted for conspiring to commit a breach of section 1 of the 1911 Act. The conspiracy alleged was a conspiracy to enter a prohibited place 'for a purpose prejudicial to the safety or interests of the State'.

The case for the defence (apart from an unsuccessful point that the section was

---

[14]   [1964] AC 763, cited by McCowan J; see n. 11 above.

restricted in its application to spying only)[15] was obvious in the light of those words. So far were they from acting against the state's interests, it was argued, that indeed they were acting for the greater safety of the state. Nothing, in the defendants' view, could be more prejudicial both to the safety and to the interests of state and citizens alike than possession of nuclear weapons with their attendant risk of making the United Kingdom itself a target for nuclear attack. At least, they argued, it was their right to put this issue to the jury. Whether their purpose was a purpose prejudicial to the safety or interests of the state was a question of fact for the jury to decide.

In this, they were unsuccessful. The judge's ruling[16] was that the purposes emphasized by the defendants were matters of motive or ulterior purpose, while the immediate purpose of their planned entry was (or was to have been) the prevention of the movement of nuclear-armed planes on to or off the airfield. And, he ruled, if this immediate purpose or intent was a purpose to impede the operation of the armed forces of the Crown as directed by Ministers of the Crown, it was a matter of law a 'prejudicial' purpose under the Act. On appeal to the House of Lords, this ruling was upheld. It will be helpful to consider some of the reasoning of the Lords of Appeal; for example, the following words of Lord Pearce:[17]

Questions of defence policy are vast, complicated, confidential and wholly unsuited for ventilation before a jury. In such a context the interests of the State must in my judgment mean the interests of the State according to the policies laid down for it by its recognized *organs of government and authority*, the policies of the State as they are, not as they ought, in the opinion of the jury, to be. Anything which prejudices those policies is within the meaning of the Act prejudicial to the interests of the state.

I have italicized the phrase 'organs of government and authority' here as in McCowan J's charge to the *Ponting* jury, for here, I think, we must see the source of their later use in the latter case. To the extent that this was the authority for McCowan J's ruling in *Ponting*, it was no doubt a binding one in law, if applicable also in respect of section 2.

Lord Pearce's words may in turn be compared with the following by Lord Devlin,[18] the context being a contrast he was drawing between the concepts of 'the state' and of 'the country':

. . . [The more precise use of the word 'State', the use to be expected in a legal context, and the one which I am quite satisfied . . . was intended in this statute, is to denote *the organs of government* of a national community. In the United Kingdom, in relation at any rate to the armed forces and to the defence of the realm, that organ is the Crown. So long as the Crown maintains armed forces for the defence of the realm it cannot be in its interest that any part of them should be immobilised.

If it is true, as Lord Devlin here argues, that it is within the prerogative of the Crown to manage the armed forces and their conduct and disposition, then it must

---

[15] [1964] AC at 772, 789–90.   [16] [1964] AC at 773–4; and cf. Lord Reid at 789–90.
[17] [1964] AC at 813.   [18] [1964] AC at 807.

also be true that the interest of the state so far as concerns the armed forces is that nothing impede their conduct and disposition in accordance with directives issued on behalf of the Crown—that is, by duly appointed Ministers. But the one is indeed true, so the other has to be true. It is one of the most fundamental doctrines of the constitution, to be sure, that the armed forces are always subject to the command of the civil authorities. Nothing could be more in the interest of the state (setting aside the problem of unlawful orders) than that the armed forces be at the exclusive disposition of the lawfully constituted executive. Hence any impediment to the disposition of the armed forces as instructed by or under the civilian executive is, at first and perhaps also last sight, necessarily prejudicial to the state's interests.

At the very least, there is something to be said for this line of argument. As to the armed forces, the Crown's say goes; and so it should. The government of the day calls the shots (almost in a literal sense), and anyone who impedes the implementation of the call acts against this interest of the state. This follows from the sense properly to be ascribed to 'the state' in this context and for this purpose, viz. the context and purpose of the maintenance and disposition of the state's armed forces. So what looks like a rather blunt and unargued assertion of the meaning of 'state' and of 'the interests of the state' in Lord Pearce's speech as quoted above becomes in the light of Lord Devlin's speech a reasonable and (at least) highly arguable view. All the more so Lord Reid's speech, in which it is pointed out[19] that however controversial it may be whether to have armed forces and how to arm them, any constitutional state must have some means to resolve such controversies; and, in the UK, the constitutional resolution of the matter is that which ascribes the decision to the Crown and the executive, the executive in turn being subject to Parliamentary and hence democratic control through the doctrine of Ministerial responsibility to Parliament.

Supposing such an argument to be sound, the only question is whether the argument is transferable by analogy from its original application to the provisions of section 1 of the 1911 Act to an application to section 2 of the Act, the section under which Clive Ponting was charged. The difference between the cases is that in the former (in relation to the *Chandler* facts) one is concerned with the disposition of the armed forces. In the latter, one is concerned with the disposition of governmental information and (in relation to the *Ponting* facts) with the conduct of civil rather than military servants of the Crown. This difference, it can be argued, need not be taken as being crucial, especially in the light of the argument from democracy. It is a common view that it is all too easy for the permanent (unelected) civil service to frustrate the purposes, most especially the radical and reforming purposes, of elected Ministers; and a natural complaint that this is inimical to the democratic disposition of the affairs of the state. But nothing is more vital to statecraft than the control of governmental information, and nothing more essential to democracy than that officials subordinate their will to that of the elected Government and its Ministers.

Accordingly the policies of Ministers as to the disposition of available informa-

---

[19]   [1964] AC at 790–1.

tion and their explicit instructions to civil servants about its concealment or disclosure may well be held to be governed by exactly the same principles as govern the decisions about armament and disposition of the armed forces. The interest of a democratic state is that ministers who are members of an elected government and answerable to an elected parliament should be accorded meticulous obedience by their civil servants.

It appears, therefore, that there is both authority for McCowan J's view in *Ponting* and also reason in favour both of the precedent and of its analogical application to the problem situation in the instant case. So perhaps the Perverse Verdict Theory is true. And perhaps even the perverseness of the perverse verdict amounts not only to technical legal perversity but also even to moral, constitutional, and political perversity—*trahison des jurés*, treason against democratic values as well as the rule of law.

(c) The case for the Unsound Interpretation Theory

There still is a case to be made for the rival theory. There is a strong argument for the Perverse Verdict Theory, but could there be a yet stronger one for the Unsound Interpretation Theory? Let us see.

The gravamen of the counter-case would have to be that the above-mentioned analogy is too weak a link to bear the load suspended from it. What would have to be stressed was the crucial qualifying phrase in Lord Devlin's speech: 'in relation at any rate to the armed forces and to the defence of the realm.' It is only in relation to those matters that Lord Devlin is holding the Crown to be the relevant organ of state, that whose decisions and interests are *for this purpose* the state's decisions and interests.

Here, too, one might note dicta of Lord Reid's in the *Chandler* case, dicta which Clive Ponting tells us to have been crucial to defence submissions in his case:[20]

On the crucial question of 'interests of the state' Jonathan [Caplan] quotes two Law Lords in the crucial case [of *Chandler*]. Lord Reid said: 'State is not an easy word. It does not mean the Government or the Executive . . . the interests of the majority are not the same as the interests of the state.' Reid talks about 'the realm' and the 'organised community' and on the issue of the public interest says: 'Governments or Ministers do not as a general rule have the last word about that.'

McCowan remarks facetiously: 'He's your high spot, isn't he? . . .

High spot or not, Lord Reid himself did not uphold the defence's proposition in *Chandler*, explicitly on the ground that the control and disposition of the armed forces has always been within the Crown's prerogative in Britain. He held that the state's interest is that the Crown's decisions be put into full effect in relation to the armed forces, even though 'Crown' and 'State' are not identical conceptually. Yet,

---

[20] Ponting, *Right to Know*, 163; the quotation from Lord Reid being from [1964] AC at 790.

even more clearly than in Lord Devlin's speech, this makes clear that the identity *in connection with the defence of the realm* between the state's interest and the implementation of ministerial policies is an identity for that purpose only.

What this brings into focus is the possibility that what really matters is the proper interrelationship of the organs of the state. Here, one starts from the question how the armed forces are to relate to other state functionaries. The answer, an answer of fundamental constitutional importance in this case, is—they must be subordinate to the civil authorities. Hence, in any dispute about who says where the armed forces shall go, bearing what arms, it is vital to our constitution that the Crown's solution to the dispute is final. This will hold good even if the dispute is between the Government of the day and a group of citizens as passionately sincere as the Committee of One Hundred at Wethersfield was.

This, however, will not be conclusive for all other issues. Other interrelationships between other organs of state also command our attention. Other organs of state may, after all, have constitutional powers as against the executive or the Crown. And here lies the key point of the Ponting defence. The doctrines of the constitutional supremacy of Parliament and of Ministerial responsibility make Ministers of the Crown answerable to and before Parliament—subordinate, indeed, to the will of Parliament. So whatever actions or activities make the Crown, or, rather, its Ministers, effectively answerable to Parliament are actions that uphold the proper relations between Parliament and the executive and, in so doing, uphold the constitutional order of the state. As actions that uphold the constitutional order of the state, they must, by the very same argument as underpins the expressed reasoning in *Chandler*, be actions in the interest of the state.

Thus the key point in favour of this theory would be one which stresses that even if the *Chandler* argument is a sound one, it is a qualified one. The qualification excludes the *Ponting* case, for here we are not talking about the armed forces, but about the relationship between Parliament and the Ministers of the Crown and about securing the full answerability of the latter to the former.

This seems to presuppose that a primary interest of any state is an interest in the integrity of its constitution. For states exist in virtue of constitutions, and a state can have no higher interest than that its constitution be sustained and upheld. This interest is fundamental beyond any interest in securing the implementation of the policies of a Government, however democratically elected. That any state has a real and serious interest in the implementation and the non-obstruction of its Government's policies is surely true. But it is true, surely, because of the role the constitution gives the Government, not vice versa—the upholding of the constitution is not to be deemed an interest of the state only so far as upholding it is the policy of the current Government.

On this view, the interest of state in the implementation of Government policy about information (or about anything else) would be an interest in its implementation on all points on which the constitution makes Government policy conclusive, but not on anything else. And that could well set limits on a civil servant's duty to act as directed by Ministers. If it came to upholding the constitution even against a Minister's expressed command, to defy the command would surely be the civil servant's duty in the interest of the state.

That says enough, it appears, to show a persuasive argument for the second theory, according to which there was no perverse jury verdict but only an unsound judicial interpretation of the law. The argument can proceed no further without returning to the questions about the theory of the state that were left hanging open at the beginning of the chapter.

The theory of the state: Kelsen and the *Rechtsstaat*

One theory according to which it is a necessary truth that a state's highest interest is in the upholding of its law and constitution is that of Hans Kelsen, summarized above. Kelsen's theory has rather strong relevance to the present concern, given the identity that it asserts for some purposes between 'the state' and the legally identified organs of government and authority. Kelsen's writings are the likeliest source, though probably an indirect source, for the various judicial pronouncements that have been considered so far.

The first point of the theory is that the existence of a legal order is necessary but not sufficient to the existence of a state. As was said already, there cannot be a state at all unless there is a legal order. A legal order is a legal system in operation in a by and large efficacious way, whereby the conduct of people in some kind of a social whole is ordered in accordance with a set of genetically interrelated norms whose authority or validity is derivable from a single constitution. That is itself in turn validated by a non-positive basic norm. For a legal order to constitute a state, it has to have other properties: it has to be an order of coercive norms, stipulating the application of sanctions upon certain events. It has to be relatively centralized. It has to have a distinct territorially defined sphere of validity, and has to be actually effective within that territory or a large part of it. Given all that, legal order is, in Kelsen's account of it, sufficient as well as necessary for the existence of the state.

But what then *is* the state that is so constituted? Kelsen's answer, at first sight both puzzling and unhelpful, is that it is a 'personification' of the 'unity' of the legal order. To resolve the puzzle of such a way of putting it and to render the theory helpful: it is a 'personification' exactly in the sense that we envisage states as acting beings. States do things, engage in activities, pursue policies, have interests and so forth. Our concept of the state is that of an acting subject, a subject which acts in (at least) the spheres of politics, international relations, international law, and domestic public law.

How then can such an abstract entity be said to act? The answer is—as J. C. Gray observed before Kelsen[21]—in the same way as other abstract entities, namely by

---

21 J. C. Gray, *The Nature and Sources of the Law* (2nd edn., ed. R. Gray, New York: Macmillan, 1921), ch. 3. MacCormick, 'A Political Frontier of Jurisprudence: John Chipman Gray's Theory of the State', *Cornell Law Review* 66 (1981) 973–88.

virtue of the actions of people whose acts are attributed to the abstract entity. The Vice-Chancellor's act of proclaiming the conferment of a degree on a person may be said to *be* the act whereby 'the University' confers that degree, or the company secretary's affixing of the seal in the presence of witnesses may *be* the execution of a conveyance of property by the company. In these cases we impute the action of a human being to a corporate entity as its act for purposes of law. It need be no different in the case of the state. But who are then the persons whose acts may be imputed to the state? The answer, ostensibly circular, is of course that the persons who are organs of the state are the persons whose acts in certain circumstances may be imputed to the state, as when an official signifies the monarch's assent to the enactment of an Act of Parliament in the UK, all prior parliamentary stages of legislation having duly passed.

This answer is ostensibly circular because it defines 'the state' in terms of organs of 'the state'. But the circle can be broken by redefining the relevant organs as organs holding certain superior positions within the normative hierarchy of the legal order and thus as being superior organs of the legal order. This explanation is necessarily connected to the notion of 'centralization' that was introduced earlier as one of the conditions of statehood. The point is that functions such as legislation, adjudication, and the enforcement of law and imposition of legal sanctions may within a hierarchically arranged legal order be assigned to sets of persons hierarchically arranged so as to secure common policies of law making, adjudication, and law enforcement. The persons deputed to performing these and other like functions are organs of the legal order. On the Kelsenian theory, it is their acts that are imputable to the state, as the personification of the unity of this hierarchically organized, that is, 'centralized' legal order. In his own words:[22]

The state is, so to speak, a common point into which various human actions are projected, a common point of imputation for different human actions. The individuals whose actions are considered to be acts of State are designated as 'organs' of the State.

Or again:

To impute a human action to the State, as to an invisible person, is to relate a human action as the action of a state organ to the unity of the order which stipulates this action. The state as a person is nothing but the personification of this unity. An 'organ of the State' is tantamount to an 'organ of the law'.

Both McCowan J in *Ponting* and Lords Pearce and Devlin in *Chandler* clearly based their reasoning on a theory that identifies the state's actions and interests with those of its 'organs of government and authority' and their policies. That is, they assumed a theory whose concepts are those elucidated by Kelsen.

So far as concerns the present discussion, it does certainly seem that to support and promote the implementation of the very policies that are determined by the duly

---

[22] Kelsen, *General Theory*, 191–2.

constituted organs of a state would be to uphold and promote an interest of the state. But, all the more, to uphold the order which constitutes the organs, and to uphold the constituted relationships of super- and subordination, of supremacy and answerability, between different organs must be also to uphold an interest of the state. And, at least on the face of it, the latter interest must be one that overrides the former in any case of conflict. Since the state is, in a sense, the personification of a given legal order, whatever upholds that law upholds that state; and the interests of the state must include an interest in the integrity of the legal and constitutional order as a superior interest of state.

It appears that McCowan J's direction to the jury did not leave room to acknowledge this interest as a superior interest, and did not leave to the jury the question whether Ponting's actions in the given case could properly be said to be actions fulfilling a duty to uphold this interest. It is at least arguable, therefore, that he was misinterpreting the law as it is illuminated by the juristic theory that he was implicitly relying on.

The argument is not, however, a conclusive one. Analytical theories do not yield substantive results in concrete cases. They may indicate questions of substance that ought to be asked, but they do not themselves answer those questions. Beyond doubt, we can show that in *Ponting* the judge ought to have asked the questions stated above about the interest of the state in the upholding of the lawful and constitutional order of things. But we cannot from this theory derive final guidance about the proper answering of that question. After all, the very issue was whether the law either required or even permitted civil servants to go over their Minister's head (or behind his back) and disclose to Members or Committees of Parliament information that the Minister had refused to disclose. To say that a civil servant has a duty to do so if by doing so he or she would be upholding the law may well be true; but it is empty. For everything then depends on what the law is.

Kelsenian legal theory therefore fails to settle the issue between Perverse Verdict and Unsound Interpretation. On Kelsen's own account of interpretation, there is nothing for it in a case like this than but that a decision be made by an authorized person. The trial judge is the authorized person to state the general interpretation, the jury the authorized organ to apply it in the given case. The decision of each is valid in its own sphere, and that is all that is to be said about it.

This leaves us no better off than with the thought that what counts as upholding the Rule of Law depends wholly on what the law's rules are and who has the final authority to interpret and to apply them. Nor does it really help to appeal to the doctrine of Parliamentary supremacy. On the one hand, it may be argued that Parliamentary supremacy requires the answerability of Ministers to Parliament, and hence requires those things to be done that will best secure that answerability. Yet on the other, it can be argued that this very doctrine requires the full-hearted implementation of every Act of Parliament including the 1911 Act, and accordingly cannot be called in aid to justify one particular interpretation of that Act. Since Parliament could, if it chose, secure the dismissal of a Minister who refused to answer questions on any ground whatsoever, there is all the less reason for being impressed here with the argument from parliamentary supremacy. (Doubtless what keeps Ministers safe from dismissal is not a neglect of the law, but the arithmetic of party representation in Parliament.)

The equivocal quality of Kelsen's theory as between the two views of the *Ponting* case is mirrored in one of the corollaries he derives from his theory of the state. This is the thesis that every state is a *Rechtsstaat*. For if every state is a personification of the unity of the legal order, and if law as such can have any content depending on the decisions of authorized lawmakers, then there is no way to discriminate between states that are and states that are not ordered in accordance with law. All states are, and it is only a question of 'what law?' Some states, that is, some legal systems, may vest very wide, or even virtually unlimited, discretion in some superior organ of executive government. Then the law requires whatever is required by the rulings, however arbitrary they may be, of that organ of state. The state remains a *Rechtsstaat* defined by this body of law having this highly discretionary character. In a Kelsenian sense, the 'Rule of Law' prevails here too. Certainly, the laws may be broad and vague in the discretionary power they confer, but that only means it will be easy for those in authority to be sure they are acting lawfully.

On the other hand, Kelsen does also acknowledge that there is an ideological use of the concept, under which positive value does attach to the *Rechtsstaat*. Where there is a constitutional separation of powers, with checks and controls on arbitrary discretion, and a requirement that government be conducted under clear and pre-announced laws, and above all when these laws include a justiciable catalogue of fundamental rights that limit governmental power, the *Rechtsstaat* in a substantive, not merely a formal sense, exists.

Just as it is an error to try and derive substantive conclusions from formal analyses so is it an error to regard descriptive analytical theories as yielding substantive concepts like *Rechtsstaat* in its ideological, or substantive sense, and Kelsen does not commit this error. In effect, he warns legal theory against assuming that it can derive the substantive doctrine from a mere analysis of law and state. He is correct. The concepts of *Rechtsstaat* and of Rule of Law both express certain closely related values that have been advanced in respect of legal order. Some of the proponents of these values in the past and the present may have thought it possible to derive them from pure analyses of the concept of law and have thus been, as Kelsen rightly observes, in error. But from the fact of their error it does not follow that the values in question are empty or absurd. The truth of the matter is that the relevant values are perfectly intelligible and deeply hostile to arbitrary power even when it takes the form of wide and uncontrolled discretion conferred by legal rules. By '*Rechtsstaat*' we should not understand 'a state under any kind of law whatsoever', nor by 'Rule of Law', rule under any kind of law whatsoever. Both require forms of law in which at least certain kinds of process-values are securely observed.

So, useful or indeed essential as Kelsen's theory of the state is to elucidating a concept such as 'duty in the interest of the state' and to evaluating the two present theories of *Ponting's* case, it is in the end indeterminate as between the two theories. It shows that both are possible, but does not adjudicate between them. It does not connect up satisfactorily with the substantive concept of *Rechtsstaat*, for which the term will henceforward be reserved in this book. Although it is necessarily in the interest of any state that its constitutional order be upheld, that tells us nothing as to the kind of constitutional order any particular state has or is. Properly understood, only a certain kind of constitutional order will suffice to constitute a *Rechtsstaat*. What is needed is an order that fulfils (at least) the process values essential to constituting the Rule of Law as an ideal quality which legal systems should be committed to realizing. (But realization of them is not in fact necessary to a system's qualifying as a *legal* system.) If the United Kingdom were not merely a state but also a *Rechtsstaat*, not only a legal order but also a legal order under the Rule of Law, this would clearly add some substance to any reflection on what is in the interest of the United Kingdom as a state. Only by proceeding beyond the Kelsenian analysis while retaining the sound insights in it would it be possible to resolve the competition of the two theories. We must therefore so proceed.

The Rule of Law and the interest of a *Rechtsstaat*

The classical British exposition of the Rule of Law is Dicey's, with his stress upon the universal applicability of a single legal order within the United Kingdom and the answerability of all, officials and citizens alike, before a common set of courts.[23] From this he derived the conception of the Rule of Law as essentially hostile to arbitrary power (because excluding the exemption of officials and state organs from answerability before the same courts as the ordinary citizen, and because entitling the ordinary citizen to vindicate his or her rights even against state organs in those courts). But since Sir Ivor Jenning's famous refutation[24] of Dicey's version of the doctrine, it has been clear that it is inadequate to bear the weight Dicey put on it. As Jennings remarked, Dicey attended too much to the question of rights and ignored problems concerning the powers vested in officials.

This should challenge public lawyers not to abandoning the Rule of Law as an empty concept but to re-stating it. A somewhat more Lockean interpretation might be suggested, and in this vein a good starting point is Lon L. Fuller's view of the 'inner morality of law'.[25] Whether or not we agree with Fuller in taking this to be of the essence of the very concept of law, we certainly do well to adopt it as disclosing the kind of ideals for well-ordered law that characterize part at least of what we called 'Locke's dream'. Here is a brief account of the view he suggests.

---

[23] A. V. Dicey, *An Introduction to the Study of the Law of the Constitution* (10th edn, London: Macmillan, 1964), ed E. C. S. Wade; T. R. S. Allan, 'Legislative Supremacy and the Rule of Law' [1985] *Cambridge Law Journal* 111.

[24] W. I. Jennings, *The Law and the Constitution* (1933), 45 f.

[25] See L. L. Fuller, *The Morality of Law* (rev. edn., 1969).

Laws should be *prospective* in operation, should be *published,* and should comprise *general rules,* not individualized directives; but they should also avoid the trap of over-generality and thus extreme vagueness. For laws have to be acceptably *clear* in their terms, in order to serve the function of being guides for the right conduct of rational beings; and this in turn requires reasonable *constancy* through time (not an ever-changing set of rules, so that no one can tell moment by moment what to do) and reasonable *consistency* among laws (for contradictory laws afford no real guidance), and must not require people to do the impossible (for these, like sets of inconsistent laws, would really be licences to officials to indulge in arbitrary punishment). Finally, and most crucially, the conduct of legal officials has to be *congruent* with the law as laid down; officials owe the same respect to the same laws as do ordinary citizens, and laws exhibiting the other seven characteristics would necessarily limit the scope for official arbitrariness.[26]

The insistence that there be publicly acknowledged rules and that official conduct be congruent with them echoes or mirrors the historic German programme for insisting upon a statutory footing for all official actions and a self-limitation by the state to governing itself and its citizens on an explicitly statutory footing. The nineteenth-century conception of the *Rechtsstaat* can practically be summed up in those terms.[27] Dicey's insistence on the unitary character of private and public law—no special law and tribunals for administrators—has the same fundamental point; as also, perhaps, his misunderstanding of the French *droit administratif.* The same ideas must, presumably, have the effect of erecting a doctrine of separation of powers into one of the pillars of constitutionalism. Demands that there be congruence of conduct with law become empty if those whose pursuit of policy comes under question are *either* identical with those who make the law *or* identical with those who adjudicate upon issues of congruence or not.[28]

This in turn must draw attention to the processes of acquisition of information. Where the question is whether or not conduct actually has been conformable to law, this question of fact has to be resolved under constraints of due process and natural justice. No one should be judge in his or her own cause, the various sides to a dispute must be heard, and conclusions of fact must be grounded in objectively statable evidence up to some reasonable standard and discharging some reasonable burden of proof upon the asserter of the fact. And other aspects of fair investigation of allegations ought to be required as a matter of law and observed as a matter of fact. To put it at its most general there has to be a regard for reasonableness and a due sense of proportionality (*Verhältnismässigkeit*) in the actions of public officials. Such ideas can be found more fully developed by writers such as John Finnis and Joseph Raz, who have carried the discussion of the Rule of Law beyond the point at which Fuller left

---

[26] Op. cit., ch. 2.   [27] See, e.g. O. Bähr, *Der Rechtsstaat* (1864).
[28] Cf. Marshall, *Constitutional Theory,* ch. 5; Allan, 'Legislative Supremacy' at 125–9; R. Zippelius, *Allgemeine Staatslehre* (9th edn, 1985), s. 31.

it in his enumeration of his eight principles.[29] They are also familiar in German discussions of the concept of the *Rechtsstaat*.

It is open to question whether such purely formal virtues and process-based values are sufficient to a proper conception either of the Rule of Law or of the *Rechtsstaat*. It can be argued that requirements of substance, such as observance of basic civil and political rights or even of various economic and social guarantees are also essential. Undoubtedly the specific concept of 'a social *Rechtsstaat* in the sense of the Basic Law [of the Federal German Republic]' clearly incorporates such matters of substance in its meaning.[30] But not all good things need to be thought of or named as the same good, and there is a specific value in the formal and processual ideals that were more traditionally ascribed to the Rule of Law and *Rechtsstaat*. This perhaps justifies one in sticking to the relatively formal elucidation of these concepts advanced above.[31] Even those who doubt that they are sufficient to either concept are not disposed to deny their necessity to both.

The question next to consider is *why* these formal virtues and process values really are of value. Of what good are they? Are they not simply obstacles to the expeditious and efficient pursuit of policies of state, and hence barriers to democracy in those states where governments have a democratic mandate? The standard, and correct, answer to this question is that while they do indeed involve some sacrifice in efficient policy-implementation on the part of governments and official agencies, they are essential to respect for persons—and thus to respect for the moral personality of the citizens of a state. Whatever be the content of a given law, if it fulfils such Fullerian criteria as those of generality, publication, prospectivity, clarity, and the like, it makes possible a rational and autonomous choice by citizens for or against obedience. Granted observance of the 'due process' and related corollaries of Fuller's 'congruence' requirement, people's actual fates are determined by its being provable that they have acted of their free will against true law and are then treated reasonably in proportion to the seriousness of an infraction. Taking the rules seriously and taking the facts seriously are essentials of respect for persons.[32]

A further point to which Fuller himself gave particular stress was that of *communication* between persons. A community of mutually respectful and self-respecting citizens would be one within which freedom of communication between and among persons would be both maximized and most of all at a premium; this whether or not some citizens hold official positions and others not. Freedom of communication is the antithesis of manipulation—so here again, the case for the Rule of Law comes

---

[29] J. Finnis, *Natural Law and Natural Rights* (Oxford; Clarendon Press, 1980), ch. 10, s. 4; J. Raz, *The Authority of Law* (Oxford: Clarendon Press, 1979) ch. 11.

[30] See e.g. O'Hagan, op. cit., above, n. 3; also E. W. Böckenforde, 'Entstehung und Wandel des Rechtsstaatsbegriffs', in *Festschift für A. Arndt* (1969), 53 f; A. Herzog, art. 20, VII Rdn. 25 in Maunz-Dürig-Herzog-Scholz, *Kommentar zum Grundgesetz* (1980); R. Zippelius, op. cit., above, n. 33, ss. 30–4.

[31] MacCormick, op. cit., above, n. 3; and cf. A. Baratta, 'Zur Entwicklung des modernen Rechtsstaatsbegriffs', in *Festschrift für Bernard C. H. Aubin zum 65. Geburstag* (1979), 1–14. In broader view; that would strengthen, not weaken, the present case.

[32] Cf. Raz, *Authority of Law*, 221–2.

down to and rests upon the value of respect for persons and its particular corollary of the desirability of maximal unimpeded intercommunication among persons.[33]

These views, if sound, give us some view as to what would best serve the interests of a state that aspired to being a *Rechtsstaat*. Whatever tends to promote the particular qualities of law essential to the Rule of Law serves the interests of the state as *Rechtsstaat*; likewise, whatever tends to promote the values underlying the value of *Rechtsstaat* and Rule of Law. This is obviously not going to be identical with whatever tends to promote the expeditious and efficient implementation of the policies set by the government of the day—the executive branch of government—even when the government has a democratic mandate. But that should not surprise us. For in its origins *der Rechtsstaat* is the concept set up in opposition to that of the *Polizeistaat* or *État de Police*—the state governed ultimately by considerations of policy rather than of legality, that is, in the non-vulgar sense, the 'Police State'.[34] These reflections, it seems to me, indicate why those judicial reasonings that have, or appear to have, equated the interests of the state with whatever tends to promote governmental policy gave such particular offence to reflective and loyal citizens. It remains true of any state and thus also of the United Kingdom that the state has an interest in the successful pursuit of government policies *within the range of discretions constitutionally allocated to the executive branch* under a given constitution. But this is not an exclusive or overriding interest. It remains subject to the interest in the upholding of the whole framework and balance of the constitution.

Constitutions themselves require interpretation in the light of fundamental principles, the scope for interpretation being doubtless the broader the greater the extent to which a constitution depends (as the United Kingdom's does to a considerable extent) on common law interspersed with statute law. So then the question is what principles are to guide the interpretation of a constitution. Unless one actively wishes the United Kingdom to tend more towards the condition of a 'Police State' in its classical sense, one must wish that the principles defining the Rule of Law or the *Rechtsstaat* in at least the formal sense have predominance. This must surely be a stance that favours the interest in the maximal communication of information and favours the effectual answerability of the executive branch of government in its pursuit of policy. Of course, in this, many values are at stake and may come into competition with each other. It cannot be supposed that the state's interest is always best served by publication of everything, and it must be the case that the interests of security and defence can override the interest in disclosure. But it will always be a legitimate question whether it can be an official's duty in the interest of the state-as-constitutional-state to disclose to Parliament information that Ministers of the Crown wish to hold back from Parliament. The question which was withheld from

---

[33] Fuller, *Morality of Law*, 186–7.

[34] See Gianfranco Poggi, *The State: Its Nature, Development and Prospects* (Cambridge: Polity Press, 1990), 50–1 and cf. Zippelius, op. cit., above, n. 33, s. 29.1.1.; also O. von Gierke, *Community in Historical Perspective* (ed. A. Black, Cambridge: Cambridge University Press, 1990), 84–95, 161–6; 110–15, 257–8.

the jury by McCowan J is, on this argument, a question that ought to have been put to them, with careful guidance as to the constitutional principles to be reviewed and balanced in considering the proper answer to it in the given case.

Moreover, the extreme breadth and vagueness of the Official Secrets Act (particularly section 2) and the ways in which it effectively reverses the balance of proof on important points make it on the whole an Act which is in several ways hostile to the above discussed conception of the Rule of Law. If nothing else, it leaves a vast range of Ministerial discretion as to who shall and who shall not be prosecuted, and for what. This in itself would justify giving a restricted interpretation to the prohibitions in section 2 and a generous and liberal interpretation to the exceptions.

No doubt this argument all depends upon a particular conception of the concepts Rule of Law and *Rechtsstaat* and on the view that the principles defining that conception do belong to, and ought to be given priority in the interpretation of, the constitution of the United Kingdom. No doubt both these points are contestable. They are, however, the fundamental points for this chapter, and points that the argument has tried to justify. Their implications are clear in respect of the two theories of *Ponting*'s case set out at the beginning. It cannot be said that the jury, in acting against the judge's directions in *Ponting*'s case, acted against a reasonable interpretation of the particular law in issue or of the Rule of Law. Their view of 'the interest of the state' appears to have been at least as well conformable to a reasonable conception of the interest of the state as constitutional state—the state-under-the-Rule-of-Law—as that put to them by the judge. In this light, it is sad to note that when the Official Secrets Act was amended in 1989, making it more restrictive in a number of ways, the government of the day steadfastly refused to accept any amendment that would have created a 'public interest' defence in an open and plain way.

However that may be, the argument shows why Kelsen's formal analysis of the state, illuminating and sound as it is up to a point, needs supplementation with other elements belonging to what he would deem ideology rather than scientific analysis. Moreover, in the perspective of power politics, the state has a manifest capacity to act through lawfully established organs in a way that goes outside its own legal framework, and fails to live up to the ideals of Rule of Law or *Rechtsstaat*, even when these are taken in a relatively formal sense. This indicates why we should insist on the view proposed in Chapter 2: the state is a political form that is in its nature only imperfectly or incompletely identified with the law. That makes clear that a demand for conformity to the ideals of rule of Law and Law-State is no trivial striving after a tautology.

4

The United Kingdom: What State? What Constitution?

Introduction

The previous chapters discussed the possibility of construing the United Kingdom as a law-state, on the assumption that this is a desirable thing for a state to be. It might, however, be argued that the propositions put forward are unconvincing, since they make assumptions about states and constitutions that are unwarranted in the case of the United Kingdom of Great Britain and Northern Ireland. Brief allusion has already been made to the historically unusual character of the United Kingdom, and the curiously evolutionary character of its constitutional arrangements. That evolutionary character has the outcome that the United Kingdom has a body of highly flexible constitutional law, by way of customary elements, conventional elements, common law elements found in judicial precedents, statutory elements, and possibly elements derived from the treaties constituting the European Union in more recent years. An evolved state is bound to differ from a deliberately constituted one based on a historic constitution. The evolved state may well exhibit the virtues of the rule of law, may even do so with a special excellence along the lines argued by F. A. Hayek.[1] But it will just be a confusion even to ask whether it could be a *Rechtsstaat*. The very term is one that has no currency in English, and 'law-state' is a barbarous neologism devised to spatchcock into British constitutional theory a concept which has no native home there.

To deal with this potential objection, I should like to give some thought to the foundation of the British state, and the way in which its constitutional law came to be perceived as it now is. The perspective in which I approach this issue remains that of constitutional theory and the philosophy of law. The aim is to conduct an analytical and critical, but also partially a historical, inquiry into the constituting of the United Kingdom, and thus the character of the state it has established.

Uniting the kingdoms

In most parts of the world, though no longer in the domestic media and official discourse, the United Kingdom is commonly referred to as 'England', 'Angleterre', 'Inghilterra', and the like, and we may in due course reflect why this should be so. But this 'England' is properly the British State, at present the United Kingdom of

---

[1] See F. A. Hayek, *Law, Legislation, and Liberty* (London: Routledge & Kegan Paul, 3 vols, 1973, 1976, and 1979), vol. 1, *Rules and Order*.

Great Britain and Northern Ireland. And if we look for origins, we do not look very far into the past. Here are sonorous words culled from almost[2] the last Act of the Parliament of Scotland enacted in January 1707:

Article 1: That the two kingdoms of Scotland and England shall upon the 1st day of May next ensuing the date hereof, and forever after, be united into one kingdom by the name of Great Britain. . . .

Article 2: That the succession to the monarchy of the united Kingdom of Great Britain, and of the dominions thereunto belonging, after Her Most Sacred Majesty, and in default of the issue of her Majesty, be, remain, and continue to the Most Excellent Princess Sophia Electress and Duchess Dowager of Hanover, and the heirs of her body, being Protestants . . .

Article 3: That the United Kingdom of Great Britain be represented by one and the same Parliament, to be styled the Parliament of Great Britain

These opening clauses of the first three Articles of Union encapsulate the theme of this section of the present chapter. Why is there a British state? When did it come into existence? How was it first constituted? Reciting the Articles takes you to the answer. But the Articles themselves are, as is obvious, only necessary, not sufficient in themselves to the explanation. They were agreed between Commissioners for Scotland and for England appointed by Queen Anne in 1706 pursuant to appropriate resolutions respectively of her Scottish and her English Parliaments. Mere agreement by the Commissioners on the Articles as terms of a possible Union did not put them into effect. For England to accept the Articles as terms of a Union, the English Parliament had to pass legislation giving effect to them as law; likewise, for Scotland, the Scottish Parliament had to enact them into law.

As is well known, the Scottish Parliament debated and legislated first. The debate was passionate, the sense of betrayal of a long independent history appears to have been palpable, the leader of the anti-Union coalition, the Duke of Hamilton, conducted himself in such a way as to dissipate the strength of the opposition.[3] Otherwise, the opposition might well have defeated these Articles of Union as decisively as had previous similar proposals slipped into oblivion in the past. Certainly, opposition speakers, especially Fletcher of Saltoun, delivered the more telling speeches. The Government deployed as little eloquence as necessary and as little drama as possible. As later administrations have done when faced with the task of securing parliamentary validation of unpopular treaties, it kept its head down and its patronage personnel at work, and ground systematically through the Articles, one at

---

[2]   Yet later was the Act of 5 February 1707, determining the mode of election of Scottish members to the two houses of the Parliament of Great Britain.

[3]   See, for example, A. V. Dicey and R. S Rait, *Thoughts on the Union between England and Scotland* (London: Macmillan, 1920), 206–29; W. Ferguson, *Scotland 1689 to the Present* (Edinburgh: Oliver & Boyd, 1968), 47–57; C. H. Dand, *The Mighty Affair* (Edinburgh: Oliver & Boyd, 1972), 144–69; P. H. Scott 1707, *The Union of Scotland and England* (Edinburgh: Chambers, 1979), 55–65; Paul H. Scott, *Andrew Fletcher and the Treaty of Union* (Edinburgh: John Donald, 1992; G. Lockhart of Carnwath, *Scotland's Ruine: Lockhart of Carnwath's Memoirs of the Union*, ed. D. Szechi, foreword P. Scott (Aberdeen: Association of Scottish Literature Studies, Annual), vol. no. 25.

a time, winning the vote on each by a sufficient majority, and by use of all the forms of pressure and inducement available to it. Eventually, in January 1707, the ratification of the Articles was enacted into law, with an appended 'Act for Securing the Protestant Religion and Presbyterian Church Government'. The question then passed to the English Parliament. There was some unease and dissent over the issue of preserving 'in all time coming' a Presbyterian establishment in Scotland at odds with the Anglican establishment in England. But the opposition did not add up to much, and the English Ministers had an easier time of it than their Scottish counterparts had had. So the Act of Union with Scotland was enacted into law in good time to secure consummation of Union on 1 May 1707, with in due course the resultant summoning of the first Parliament of Great Britain.

Membership of that Parliament comprised the English Lords of Parliament and the Commons Representatives who had sat in the last Parliament of England, no new general election having been considered necessary. In accordance with Article 22, they were joined in the upper house by sixteen representative Peers elected from the peerage of Scotland, and in the lower by the forty-five MPs elected from the designated Scottish constituencies. By the method of calculating representation in Parliament that then prevailed, namely according to value for land-tax, Scotland was over-represented with forty-five members in the Commons. But this was done by reference to an argument that has continuing resonance. Since a whole country was being incorporated into a larger, there was special reason to secure that its interests could not be ignored or belittled. There was also concern about unfair discrimination against the interests of a minority with a long prior history of conflict with the new majority. On both accounts, but particularly the former, it was agreed that Scottish representation should by a reasonable amount exceed that which would be properly proportional given the prevailing rationale of representation, forty-five rather than the thirty-eight originally proposed by the English Commissioners.[4]

The subsequent transition to a democratic principle of representation was a drawn-out affair, universal and equal adult franchise coming only after the Second World War. Under the Representation of the People Acts, Scottish (and indeed Welsh) representation has been subject to a required minimum number of seats, and this has produced a level of representation that is higher than strict proportionality by reference to the democratic principle of representation that now prevails. It is a common saying that this scale of Scottish representation is arbitrary and unprecedented.[5] The common saying is ill informed. There is a precedent from 1707, and it

---

[4] Cf. Dand, *Mighty Affair*, 124–5, Scott, *Andrew Fletcher*, 156–7, citing Bishop Burnet; cf. Lockhart, *Ruine*, 132, suggesting the Scots could have got even more if they had really tried. Whether there really was an attempt to make an in-principle fair provision for a national minority, or just a stitch-up among leading Commissioners is a point on which one should not be overconfident.

[5] But note that Iain McLean has shown that the introduction of the modern disproportionality through the number fixed for Scotland seems to have had no explicit rationale such as might have been derived from the 1707 compromise, and was to that extent arbitrary, albeit not unprecedented after all. See I. McLean, 'Are Scotland and Wales over-represented in the House of Commons?', *Political Quarterly*, 66 (1995), 250–68.

establishes a principle that justifies departure from strict proportionality judged solely by the main prevailing rationale for representation. There is a subsidiary principle of reasonable assurance for minority countries. Perhaps this will be cancelled in the circumstances of devolution, but the point should be argued, not merely assumed.

The Articles of Union can be summarized around three themes: what was to be common to the whole of Great Britain? what was to remain distinct in the formerly separate parts? and what were to be the transitional arrangements? Common were to be, of course, the Crown (and thus the Executive) and the single bicameral Parliament. So were to be the flag and other public insignia, and currency and coinage. Taxation, and customs and excise and other impositions and drawbacks on trade and commerce were to be equalized, so as to realize the conditions of free trade throughout the new Kingdom and with 'the dominions thereunto belonging'. This was to be a customs union with a common market and single currency, administered by a single executive branch under a single legislature. It was incomparably the largest such customs union in the world at that time, when, even within a powerful and centralized monarchy such as France, inter-regional customs barriers were extensively in existence.

The continuing separate identities that were to survive Union lie in civic institutions, in courts and common law, in churches. For the system of local government, specifically the Royal Burghs, was to remain unaltered. (It has been altered, but Scottish local government retains a distinctive pattern and its own legislative framework.) The Scottish Courts, and also all heritable jurisdictions were to remain in being, with no appeal from the former to 'any . . . court in Westminster Hall'. (The heritable jurisdictions have gone, and their going was integral to the trauma of the Highland clearances; but the Court of Session and the High Court remain undiminished.) The whole of the public and private law were to continue except for whatever was inconsistent with the union. In future, the Parliament of Great Britain was to have power to amend the law in Scotland. But this was subject to an important limitation:

with this difference betwixt the laws concerning public right, policy, and civil government, and those which concern private right, that the laws which concern public right, policy, and civil government may be made the same throughout the United Kingdom, but that no alteration can be made in laws which concern private right, except for evident utility of the subjects within Scotland. [This arrangement has been pretty well respected.]

Finally, there was the already noted provision for securing the Presbyterian church establishment in Scotland, and along with that protection of the system of education both at university and at school level. None of these remains exactly as originally foreseen, but distinctiveness, and even a measure of distinction, survive.

The transitional provisions related to phasing in new systems of taxation and to compensation for Scotland's incurring a share of the English national debt. They also made provision to compensate for losses to investors in the Company of Scotland whose disastrous failure in attempting to establish a colony on the Darien Isthmus was held substantially imputable to the hostility of the late King William and his English ministers. When Bur.is said that the 'Parcel o' Rogues in a Nation' had been 'bought and sold for English Gold', this was what he had in mind. Fletcher had earlier remarked in even more pointed terms that the Scots of 1707 were not being bought with English money, but with their own.

Given all that, it was natural to conclude the Articles by insisting on their over-riding status as the basis of the new union. This was done in Article 25:

[A]ll laws and statutes in either kingdom, so far as they are contrary to or inconsistent with the terms of these articles, or any one of them, shall, from and after the Union, cease and become void, and shall be so declared to be by the respective parliaments of the said king-doms.

This is a provision so obvious in its sense and context as almost to go without saying. The terms of a new union must prevail if the union is to come effectively into being. These new provisions must be fundamental, and prior laws different in tenor cannot stand up against them.

The opponents of Union argued that those terms in the Union that aimed to protect their distinctive Scottish institutions were mere paper guarantees, for in the necessary logic of things the new Parliament could by majority vote change them at any time. In due course, indeed, the greatest of English constitutional lawyers, A. V. Dicey was to argue that in point of law the most solemn and expressly unalterable provisions of the union had no greater constitutional sanctity than the Dentists'Act.[6] In like vein, F. W. Maitland, prince among legal historians, was to insist that 'we have no irrepealable laws'.[7] But this was not the only way to look at it. Daniel Defoe, as pamphleteer (and spy) for the pro-Union side in 1707 argued that the Articles of Union being the foundation of union would have to be accepted as fundamental law in it.

[N]othing is more plain than that the articles of the Treaty . . . cannot be touched by the Parliament of Britain; and that the moment they attempt it, they dissolve their own Constitution; so it is a Union upon no other terms, and is expressly stipulated what shall, and what shall not, be alterable by the subsequent Parliaments. And, as the Parliaments of Great Britain are founded, not upon the original right of the people, as the separate Parliaments of England and Scotland were before, but upon the Treaty which is prior to the said Parliament, and consequently superior; so, for that reason, it cannot have power to alter its own foundation,

---

[6] See A. V. Dicey, *Introduction to the Study of the Law of the Constitution* (10th edn., London: Macmillan, 1964), 145: 'There are indeed important statutes, such as the Act embodying the Treaty of Union with Scotland, with which it would be political madness to tamper gratuitously; there are utterly unimportant statutes, such, for example, as the Dentists Act, 1878, which may be repealed or modified at the pleasure or caprice of Parliament; but neither the Act of Union with Scotland nor the Dentists Act 1878, has more claim than the other to be considered a supreme law.'

[7] See F. W. Maitland, *The Constitutional History of England* (Cambridge: Cambridge University Press 1908), 332.

or act against the power which formed it, since all constituted power is subordinate, and inferior to the power constituting.[8]

This is an argument which has been repeated by many persons on many occasions since 1707. The high water mark, so far as concerns judicial pronouncements, came in 1953 with Lord President Cooper's opinion in the case of *MacCormick* v. *Lord Advocate*[9] where he held that the Union of 1707 did constitute fundamental law. The petitioners in the case had argued that the Queen's Ministers, in advising her to assume the title of Elizabeth 'the Second', had violated the basic provision of the Treaty of Union whereby a new kingdom had been constituted. Since monarchs of the prior separate kingdoms had been monarchs of distinct states, her Majesty was the first Elizabeth of the United Kingdom, and to entitle her otherwise was unwarrantable. The First Division held that the choice of royal style and title was a matter of prerogative power, not controllable by the courts. Further, even if the Treaty constituted fundamental law, it was unenforceable in face of an Act of Parliament, though if it ever came to legislation trenching upon the existence or powers of the Court of Session itself, the position would have to be reconsidered. Hence the petitioners' case was rejected, though without award of expenses to the Crown. But the *dicta* of the Court made clear that the provisions of the Articles of Union could not legitimately be assimilated to ordinary Acts of Parliament, and should be interpreted with special regard to the provisions expressed to be permanent in all time coming.

The Scottish Courts have been on the whole cool towards arguments challenging contemporary governmental policies by reference to the Articles, especially when recent legislation is in issue.[10] Last century, in the litigation on the powers and liberties of the Kirk that led to the Disruption of 1843, Lord President Hope took indeed a high Austinian view on the indivisibility of sovereignty and the illimitable legal authority of a sovereign parliament.[11] So it must be said that Defoe's argument, however sincerely stated in its time, has not been borne out by the main course of history. According to Dicey, its critical weakness lay in this fact: the Parliaments that delegated power to the new Parliament wholly abolished themselves in the very act of constituting that new Parliament. Had they remained in being for the one purpose of authorizing changes to the terms of union, they would have retained sovereignty. As it was, they had necessarily passed it in its totality to the successor.

Analytically, I think the problem can be stated in terms of a pair of possible distinct interpretations of Article 25. Either the Union effectively overrode all prior constitutional law in both countries, and constituted a completely fresh start incorporating

---

[8] See Paul Scott, *1707: the Union of Scotland and England* (Edinburgh: Chambers, 1979), 62 quoting D. Defoe, *The History of the Union Between England and Scotland* (London: 1786), 246. In this and at many other points of the argument I am very particularly indebted to Paul Scott for his deep scholarship in matters concerning the union, its origins, and continuing utility. See also his splendid *Andrew Fletcher and the Treaty of Union*.   [9] 1953 S.C. 396.

[10] See Colin R. Munro, 'The Union of 1707 and the British Constitution', in *Scotland and the Union*, ed. Patrick Hodge, *Hume Papers on Public Policy*, 2 (Edinburgh: Edinburgh University Press, 1994), 87–109.

[11] See the *Auchterarder* case (1838) 16 S. 661 and Robertson's Report (2 vols.).

only such elements from the past as would fill out its own rather skeletal framework—call this the 'Defoe View'; or the Union was simply an adaptation and modification of a pre-existing constitution that continued subject to the express amendments and implied repeals to be spelt out from the text of the Articles—call this the 'Dicey view'. This latter view implies that, even if a new state called 'Great Britain' was set up in 1707 by treaty, the constitution of that state was effectively the English constitution, amended so far as necessary to incorporate the provisions of the (English) Act of Union. The Scottish Act had constitutional force only so far as adopted by the English Act. Otherwise, it was implemented fully in the very act of incorporating Scotland into Great Britain, a consummation achieved by the summoning of the new Parliament with the solemn admission of Scottish peers and MPs thereto. Then it passed into legal history as the basis on which union was achieved peacefully and by agreement rather than by force of arms. As a law, its force was spent, and its author disbanded.

The English constitution

Very well, then. How much of the pre-existing laws of Scotland and England prior to 1707 must be deemed abolished as inconsistent with the Articles of Union? Obviously, all particular laws concerning special provisions for one or other country, and laws concerning the descent of the Crown, and such like. But the key question concerns constitutional laws themselves. Notoriously, the old English constitution was an unwritten one, deriving from custom, convention, and common law, and from the royal prerogative within the spheres of its existence as acknowledged by common law. The authority of Parliament, that is, of the monarch in Parliament, was an authority absolute and sovereign in kind. For it derived from the powers held by conquering monarchs who gradually over several centuries were forced to, or agreed to, exercise their powers only by and with the consent of parliament, while delegating others to their judges. And that was a matter of English common law, pretty clearly established by at least 1688.

The old Scottish constitution, as Scots authorities like George Buchanan were very insistent, was never a constitution based on conquest. Hence the *Ius Regni*, the law of the kingdom, could never be interpreted as constituting an absolute monarchy whether in or out of Parliament, but only as authorizing a limited one dependent on popular assent. From this, and from such other iconic texts as the Declaration of Arbroath, has derived the thesis that in Scottish constitutional tradition, sovereignty belonged to the people, to the community of the realm, rather than to Parliament, or, strictly, King or Queen in Parliament.[12]

One view of the meaning of the 1707 Union is that it must have been fundamental and hence overrode the customary constitution of England as well as that of

---

[12] Cf. O. D. Edwards (ed.), *A Claim of Right for Scotland* (Edinburgh: Polygon, 1989), 13–15.

Scotland, setting the whole on a new footing. That view, the Defoe view, if it prevailed, would of course entail that the UK did start with a written constitution, admittedly a somewhat sketchy one. I have suggested elsewhere[13] that this is both the fairer and a possible reading of the case. But I am under no illusion that this is the prevailing view. The other view, the Dicey view, is the one that lays stress on the very concept of an 'incorporating Union'.

The phrase 'incorporating union' is a telling one. In the early 1700s, and in the parliamentary debates of 1703–5, most Scots appear to have wanted a better Union with England, or none at all. As of that date, the union was only a union of the crowns, not of the countries or their parliaments. Kings and Queens were still in a real way heads of government as well as heads of state, and ministers were 'their' ministers in much more than a merely formal or ceremonial sense. Hence the smaller of the pair within this regnal union was particularly exposed to the risk of government through a ministry hostile or indifferent to the opinion and popular will of the country at large. In effect, the King's or Queen's English Ministers had the key part to play in determining policies of state; then the King's Scottish Ministers had the task of reconciling their own Parliament to the policy in question. This was unsatisfactory to say the least.

One idea for remedying the situation proposed 'union' in a sense different from the one that in the end prevailed. The idea is largely attributable to Fletcher of Saltoun. A continuing Union of the Crowns was possible only given agreement on a treaty that would do several things. It would distinguish the sphere of required common action to be accomplished through a common head of state-and-government from the spheres of action of separate Scottish and English concern. In respect of these latter spheres, Parliaments would hold sway, and the responsibility of Ministers would be rather to the respective Parliaments than to the monarch. The treaty would also aim to secure peace by protecting each country against the risk of attack from or through the other, and should provide for freedom of trade and commerce.[14] Such a Union Fletcher and his associates dubbed a 'federal union', in a sense of the term derived from the concept 'treaty' hidden in the Latin root. It was their preferred option, but if it were unattainable, the option of a continuing Union of Crowns would have few attractions. The card that was played to try and draw England into such an agreement was refusal to confirm for Scotland the Hanoverian Succession already determined for England by the Act of Settlement of 1701. Playing that card led to tension and drama in the years 1703–5.[15]

The English riposte as it unfolded in the period prior to, and the period of, the Union negotiations, was that if the Scots wanted Union, they could have it. But they could have it only in the form of an entire or incorporating union. Federal union was

---

[13] See N. MacCormick, 'Does the United Kingdom have a Constitution? Reflections on *MacCormick v Lord Advocate*', *Northern Ireland Legal Quarterly*, 29 (1978), 1–20.

[14] See A. Fletcher of Saltoun, *State of the Controversy betwixt united and Separate Parliaments*, ed. P. H. Scott (Edinburgh: Blackwood, for the Saltire Society, 1982), 14–17, and cf. Scott *1707*, 22–4.

[15] See ibid., *passim*; Dicey and Rait, *Thoughts*, ch. 4.

not an option. And moving back to a fully separate Scottish crown with succession different from that for the English crown would entail that Scots in England would revert to alien status, and that any threat to English security in the North would be met with overwhelming and pre-emptive force. It seems fair to say that the Scots had not a lot of room for manœuvre, and that even leaders more skilful, public-spirited, and resolute than those they had would have had difficulty getting out of the corner into which history had painted them. As it was, all the leaders were anxious to ensure that if Union were inevitable, they and their families would do well out of it. The Duke of Hamilton's is here an instructive case. If he could have kept Scotland out and his skin and assets entire, there seems no doubt he would genuinely have preferred to. But the risk of ruin in an unsuccessful rearguard action stared him in the face. The result was his crippling attack of psychosomatic toothache the day he missed attending Parliament and the last die was cast.[16]

However that may be, the record as between federal and incorporating union is clear. The Scots Commissioners were mandated to put the proposal for federal union, and they made it their opening gambit, but knowing the reply it would receive. The English Commissioners rejected it with unconcealed contempt,[17] and indicated their own terms for an incorporating union. After the briefest of recesses, the Scots agreed to discuss these terms, and the rest of the time was spent working out the details of the deal, with the Scots squeezing any advantages they could along the way.

How are we to analyse the notion of incorporating union? In form, the Union constituted a new state with a new name. But in substance, the underlying assumption was that the larger partner was a continuing entity. Institutionally and in terms of personnel and procedure, the new Parliament of Great Britain was continuous with the predecessor English Parliament, save for the addition of a few Scottish peers elected from the whole peerage of Scotland, and two score and a quarter Scottish MPs. The Crown, the armed forces, the executive became one, and the preserved Scottish institutions got on with their work over the horizon of visibility in the North, with occasional legislative interventions that strayed in some cases well beyond the spirit, let alone the letter, of the agreed limitations. In this context, it is easy to interpret the constitution as a continuing evolution of the old English customary constitution as a patchwork of convention, common law, and statute. The Act of Union is a not insignificant statutory element in this patchwork constitution, in so far as it extended the authority of parliament geographically and enhanced its membership in a matching way. But there was no disturbance of the prevalent balance of parliamentary forces, and no new constitutional doctrine, no development of popular or other powers attributable to it. Really, it was a completion and consolidation of the Revolution of 1688, not a new step in a new direction.

---

[16] Cf. Scott, *1707*, 65–6.

[17] See Lockhart, *Ruine*, 130 'the English commissioners telling them in a saucy manner that they did not incline so much as once to take it into consideration (their very words) [the Scots were content to] resile pittifully and meanly from it without one word to enforce it'.

This view is strongly attested by the great majority of authors who have treated of British constitutional law and constitutional history from within the paradigm of English common law; and that means a very large majority indeed. This is as true of Scottish as of English writers within the dominant tradition. Sir David Lindsay Keir was a distinguished Master of Balliol College, author of a highly regarded work in constitutional history. His *Constitutional History of Britain: 1485–1937*,[18] takes the long view of the development of parliamentary democracy in Britain from its beginnings in the growth of parliamentary rule in England. The Act of Union merits a couple of two-line throwaway comments relating to the balance of power among Queen Anne's Ministers. Yet Keir was a Scotsman, a son of the manse and proud of it, so his taking the common law perspective on the constitution was by no means genetically or ethnically predetermined. Maitland a generation previously had a good deal more to say in his Lectures on *Constitutional History* about the creation, first of Great Britain and then, in 1801, of the United Kingdom of Great Britain and Ireland. He did see these as constitutionally momentous events. But his structural perspective on the driving forces of the constitution suggests that the extensions of the sway of the British State, however important geopolitically, were byways from the point of view of the evolution of an essentially unitary constitution.

A moment ago, and quite pointedly, I used the term 'the Act of Union'. From the standpoint of incorporating union in the common law interpretation, that is, in the Dicey view, this is the common and probably the correct usage. There was one essential Act of Union that extended the sway of Parliament over Scotland on agreed terms. Agreement of the terms may indeed have necessitated legislation in Scotland also. But the continuing constitution, the continuing chapter by chapter chronological series of Acts of Parliament requires only the English Act as the bridge between the Parliament of England at the beginning of 1707 and the Parliament of Great Britain at the mid-year and thereafter. This was the self-same Parliament enlarged and renamed.

Close observers of present-day constitutional debates are well aware of the ideological resonance attaching to key phrases: 'the Act of Union', 'the Acts of Union', 'the Articles of Union', 'the Treaty of Union'. Only the casual users of the singular 'Act of Union' are unaware of their singularity, for holders of a majority ideology are usually indignant to discover that they have an ideology at all.[19] When it is drawn to their attention, their astonishment matches that of M Jourdain when he discovered that prose was what he had been speaking all along.

The story has been a long one to this point. But our exploration of the British state has led us to understanding the strange survival of the English constitution. Even if there is a British state, and even if we can date its commencement exactly to

---

[18]   3rd edn. (London: A & C Black, 1946).

[19]   Even Linda Colley, in her admirable and sensitive *Britons: Forging the Nation: 1707–1837* (New Haven and London: Yale University Press, 1992) uses throughout her book the singular 'Act of Union', whereas though there was but one union it required two acts, except if we presuppose the Dicey view without further discussion.

1 May 1707, its constitution can be and commonly is deemed to be the old English constitution continuing. The very provision that preserved a distinct body of Scottish common law necessarily preserved and continued the English common law as well. Hence issues of constitutional law arising before the English courts have assumed the very continuities that are implicit in the ideology of incorporating union. All in all, it need not surprise us that the workaday name of the British State in most of the world is now and always has been 'England' and its cognates. Here, an honourable exception must be made for that two generations of well-spirited people in public agencies of all kinds who have striven to use only the terms 'Britain', 'British', and 'the United Kingdom', not 'England' in its over-inclusive sense. In so doing, they have apparently given themselves a new headache. They are now not sure what is English as distinct from British where their predecessors had a weak grasp of what is British as distinct from English.[20]

Despite first appearances, therefore, there is from one point of view an indisputable logic of coexistence between the British State (first 'Great Britain', later 'The United Kingdom'). This logic depends on a particular reading and interpretation of our constitution and constitutional history. This reading is neither uncontestable nor uncontested, as witness the doughty efforts of the late Professor Sir Thomas B. Smith, aided and abetted (or, perhaps, led on) by the petitioners John MacCormick and Ian Hamilton in the *Queen's title* case mentioned above.[21] Contested though it is, however, the incorporationist view is the majority view and the dominant one. It was clearly asserted in the incoming Labour Government's 1997 White Paper *Scotland's Parliament.* There, the Government proposed in bold terms the establishment of a devolved Scottish Parliament. But in the same breath it insisted on the continuing and absolute sovereignty of the United Kingdom Parliament in respect of the whole United Kingdom, Scotland necessarily included (see paragraph 4.2). That power is merely delegated to the Scottish Parliament established under the Scotland Act 1998 and makes it in constitutional principle no different from any Parish Council in England, as the future Prime Minister Tony Blair said during the run-up to the election campaign which his party won so convincingly on 1 May 1997.

The very Government which produced the White Paper contained many signatories of the 'Claim of Right for Scotland' of 1989, the foundation document of the Scottish Constitutional Convention.[22] The Convention, in turn, was the body that worked out the proposals for a devolved Scottish Parliament that were adopted by the Labour and Liberal Parties in the elections of 1992 and 1997, and that formed the basis of the White Paper scheme put to the Scottish electorate in the Referendum of 11 September 1997, and approved by an overwhelming majority. That 'Claim of Right' seems no less categorical than the White Paper on the issue of sovereignty, but in an apparently opposite sense. 'We, gathered as the Scottish Constitutional

---

[20] See J. Paxman, *The English* (Harmondsworth: Michael Joseph, 1998), ch. 1 and *passim*.

[21] Cf. MacCormick, 'Does the United Kingdom have a Constitution? Reflections on *MacCormick v Lord Advocate*', *Northern Ireland Legal Quarterly*, 29 (1978), 1–20.

[22] See Edwards, *Claim*.

Convention, do hereby acknowledge the sovereign right of the Scottish people to determine the form of Government suited to their needs . . .'.

The Secretary of State for Scotland, the Chancellor of the Exchequer, the Foreign Secretary, and many other senior members of the 1997–8 Government were signatories of this Claim of Right. If not a contradiction, there is at least something of an apparent antinomy here. Exactly here also lies what may be called the 'Scottish anomaly' at the heart of the British state. The Union encompasses both an English constitution and a special dispensation for Scots law, Scots Courts, Scottish education, and Scottish local government. It also provides for a separate church establishment, and this has been matched by separate hierarchies in Catholic and Episcopal churches.

All this has meant the continuing existence within union of a strong civic identity alongside a continuing if often 'kailyard-like' popular culture. It has made possible a strong Scottish identity among many internal diversities, of highland and lowland, Gaelic and Scots, country and town, East and West, North and South. And a strong Scottish sense of identity has indeed survived three centuries of Union, growing more, not less, evident, as the three-hundredth anniversary year of 2007 approaches. This concatenation of circumstances made possible just such appeals to a continuing background constitutional tradition of popular sovereignty rather than Parliamentary sovereignty as that which the Scottish Convention recited in its 'Claim of Right'. This is then the anomaly: Scotland was incorporated, but Scotland stayed different.

The Scottish anomaly

Scotland has been the anomaly that has made an ostensibly unitary state, an archetype of 'nation state' in certain political-theoretical terms, function internally in a markedly federal way. This has been hitherto a federalism of political management and judicial separation rather than a federalism of constitutional form. Indeed, according to the Dicey view of the (incorporating) constitution, as we have noted, nothing that protects the Scottish institutions has the least force as a legal guarantee or entrenchment. The 'Autonomy of Modern Scotland', as Lindsay Paterson has observed,[23] is quite a remarkable phenomenon judged by the fate of most submerged small nations in Europe. It is an autonomy that has made possible the continuing assertion of a submerged constitutional tradition of a distinct Scottish stamp. The continuing claim to a historically attested sovereignty of the people is part and parcel of that. It includes the implication that assent to the union involves a continuing *plébiscite de tous les jours*. So long as the will of the majority sustains it, it will continue. If it ceases to do so, it will cease.

---

[23] See L. Paterson, *The Autonomy of Modern Scotland* (Edinburgh: Edinburgh University Press, 1994).

For whatever reason, though, managed federalism, or quasi-federalism, had by 1997 ceased to be acceptable. Not a single candidate representing the unreformed union was returned for a Scottish constituency in the 1997 General Election, and the September referendum was even more decisive. The democratic deficit had become too glaring for contemporary sensibilities. Linda Colley in her remarkable book *Britons* suggests that the union succeeded in the eighteenth century because it gave insular Protestants a sense of unity against the threat from continental Catholicism, represented in particular by France, and because it created a shared pride in the massive common enterprise that was the British Empire, largely won during the conflict with France. The empire was, perhaps, the 'British thing' *par excellence*. Now it has gone, and now Europe is, as once before for Scots, far more a theatre of opportunity than a threat to identity. These deep-running secular changes must also have a part to play in the explanation of change in electoral preferences. In this, the rise and solid continuance of support for the Scottish National Party in the period between 1945 and 1997 cannot be ignored. It must be ranked as one among the causes of change; yet it cannot be denied that it was also in important measure one of its consequences.

However that may be, a time of great change was at hand at the close of the millennium. The Scotland Act that established the Scottish Parliament elected in 1999 substituted a new anomaly for an old one. Subject to reservation of powers deemed essentially UK-wide to Westminster, there was set up a Parliament empowered to make laws for the peace, order, and good government of Scotland. Yet Scotland continued to be represented in the Westminster Parliament by a full complement of MPs, with some reduction intended in due course. In place of managed quasi-federalism, there had emerged democratic quasi-federalism. England's only Parliament remained and remains also the United Kingdom Parliament. The government of England continued to be determined by whatever is at any given time the largest party UK-wide in that Parliament, while for Scotland there had come into being both a domestic Parliament and government and also the opportunity to participate in UK institutions. Scottish MPs necessarily and properly share in performing Parliament's UK functions, but parliamentary arithmetic will sometimes make it necessary for them also to play a decisive role in purely English matters, if a government is in power without a majority among the representatives of English constituencies.

The old anomaly was an invisible one. The point was that, under the managers of the day, Scotland went its own way, block-funded according to the Goschen proportion or the Barnett formula (used to determine a proportional share of UK public expenditure to be set aside for those expenditures in Scotland that were delegated to the Scottish Office, or will be devolved to the Parliament). Nobody in other parts of the UK gave this much serious attention. The new anomaly could not but be much more openly visible, and on that account it looks (in the spring of 1999) unlikely to endure long as originally designed. The incorporating union has finally run out of steam. The question now, as in 1706, is whether federal union in either the older or the newer sense is available in the alternative.

The nearest equivalent to what Fletcher envisaged in the way of federal union involves the European Union. The kind of relationship between the countries of these islands that would exist if they were all fellow members of a European union, especially one with a common currency, would broadly satisfy the criteria that he expounded or assumed. This prospect finds favour with some, myself included. Others suggest that a form of federal constitution internal to the United Kingdom may be devised. If all parts have Parliaments or assemblies, and the UK Parliament would deal only with common questions at the federal level, the new anomaly would disappear, since Scotland would not have the only sub-Parliament, Wales not the only executive assembly.

Further questions that arise about resolution of this situation must be postponed to the concluding chapter of this book. We have, however, brought the story to a point where we can deal with the issue raised at the beginning of the chapter. How could it be that a curiously evolved 'union state' such as the United Kingdom could actually exhibit the characteristics that we have ascribed to a 'law-state'. The answer is that it could do so only imperfectly, given that the originally constituent Articles were never seriously acknowledged as a constitution, nor, therefore, ever reviewed or amended in a deliberate way so as to develop an articulate and encapsulated constitution that might have been adopted or endorsed by all the people in the union. The new process of devolution, with other related elements of constitutional change or reform that will be discussed in the next chapter, could well lead in the direction of some kind of constitutional moment at which the whole will be pulled together in an orderly way.

Meantime, however, it can be quite legitimately claimed, as will also appear in the next chapter, that there is a deep-seated conception of the 'rule of law' built into United Kingdom legal and constitutional usages. This depends on judicial and political practice, not on any entrenched guarantees. As in the case of the Official Secrets Act, discussed in the preceding chapter, the practice sometimes falls short of the ideal. When it does, there is no remedy, at any rate not within domestic law and institutions. This ideal of the rule of law belongs within the ideas developed by A. V. Dicey, who drew largely on the inspiration afforded by Jeremy Bentham, and it will be discussed in the next chapter under the name of the 'Benthamite constitution'. To the extent that the rule of law is a principle, part positive, part aspirational, in the constitutional law and practice of the British state, we can properly say that *Rechtsstaatlichkeit*, the quality of being a law-state, is an aspirational ideal of the British state, and one that it has to a considerable extent realized in its practice despite the absence of an explicitly framed and adopted constitution, and the kinds of entrenched guarantees that such instruments may afford.

5

The Benthamite Constitution—Decline and Fall?

Introduction: the roots of anti-naturalism

Whoever poses the issue of 'Might against Right' effectively issues a rhetorical invitation for all to line up on the side of Right. Who does not prefer that those who exercise power exercise it only by guidance of plain justice, so that power serves right and fair dealing among humans? Who is openly willing for power to be exercised arbitrarily and unrighteously? It is all too easy to see why there is a yearning in us all after some form of 'higher law'. Whether given by God or implicit in the nature of things or the nature of humankind (or all three), a higher law comprising clear prescriptions and prohibitions would set a pattern of right against which to measure human arrangements and human dispositions of power. Then the plea for Right to rule Might would not collapse for want of an objective test to tell us what is right.

Alas, there has been a plethora of competing claims to revelation or derivation of the single true higher law. Many such claims have been associated with one or another religion or sect, some with none at all. This cacophony of competing interpretations or versions of 'higher law' or 'natural law' has led to disappointment of the hope for this ideal security against misrule. There is not after all a clear test for what counts as misrule (for example, was the *fatwa* pronounced against Salman Rushdie for his *Satanic Verses* a deliverance of higher law or an affront to it?) Even if there is a higher law, the bitter disputes its proper interpretation has generated have deprived it of practical applicability in any cross-cultural or liberal-secular context, though surrogates have to some extent been found in entrenched or internationally agreed charters of human rights, not that the interpretation of these has been unproblematic either. Anyway, such charters are higher law positivized, not higher law in 'natural' form.

The problem of multiplicity of claimed revelations, whether by the direct word of God or through the collaboration of human with divine reason is not a new one. A solution that emerged in the eighteenth century related to adopting the lowest common denominator of many variants on 'natural law'. Most variants of natural law theorizing, at any rate of the post-reformation rationalist variety, included the claim that, while there are several foundational principles of the law, there is one residual principle that backs them all up and gives guidance where they are silent. This is the principle that human happiness ought to be promoted and misery prevented as far as possible. Through its application, human love to a degree replicates divine love. Hence, within many branches of natural law thinking, the usefulness, or 'utility' of human laws for upholding rights derivable from higher law and, beyond that, for fostering human happiness in general, has been one ground for commending such laws, or for recommending improvements in them.[1]

Thinkers like David Hume and Jeremy Bentham, who found themselves unimpressed by the assertions concerning self-evident or revealed principles of higher law, were more impressed with the argument concerning utility. But why, they asked, is utility only a residual principle? If in the last resort it all comes down to utility, why not in the first resort, too?[2] They further argued that our attachment to the principle of utility can be accounted for in terms of human psychology, or in terms of our unmediated approval of that which tends to our own happiness and that of our fellows. So a mixture of introspection and study of our fellows gives us evidence in favour of the principle that human institutions ought to promote human happiness and minimize human misery. This, they thought, is a principle to which all are inclined to assent once they attend clearly to it. Its thoroughgoing application as a guide to the adoption or retention of happiness-serving human laws makes redundant appeals to assertedly self-evident principles and rights, capricious and contested as such appeals usually are.

Just as the principle of utility was wrested out of natural law thought, by stripping away claims about a plurality of other equally fundamental principles of 'natural law', so was the command theory of law salvaged from natural law thought. What had to be trashed here were claims about social contracts that set up the agreed human commander(s), or about natural rights that restricted the commander's rights of governance, and other claims about the derivation of existing human legal institutions from the principles of natural or divine law. So far as concerned the existing laws, the hallmark of the new thinking was voluntarism: law as the will of the powerful.[3] How to ensure that those in power were actually motivated by what they ought to be motivated by, namely, a concern for the happiness of all within their power, was

---

[1] See, e.g., Stair, *Institutions of the Law of Scotland*, 2nd edn., ed. D. M. Walker (Edinburgh: Edinburgh University Press, 1981), 1.1.18, 'There are three prime principles of the positive law, whose aim and interest is the profit and utility of man.' A parallel remark in the Blackstone's *Commentaries*, I.1 provoked the special scorn of Bentham, *Comment on the Commentaries*, ed. J. H. Burns and H. L. A. Hart (London: Athlone Press, 1977), 17–18; Locke, Erskine, and others all have similar points to make—see J. Locke, *Second Treatise of Civil Government* (many eds)., J. Erskine, *An Institute of the Law of Scotland*, new edn., ed. J. B. Nicolson (Edinburgh: Bell & Bradfute 1871), I.1. In its first edition, Erskine's work is closely contemporary with Blackstone's; Stair dates from 1681, with a second edition in 1693.

[2] See D. Hume, *An Enquiry Concerning the Principles of Morals* (many eds.), section III, part 2; note Bentham, 'A Fragment on Government', in *A Comment on the Commentaries and A Fragment on Government*, ed. J. H. Burns and H. L. A. Hart (London: Athlone Press, 1977), 439–40, praising Hume's *Treatise of Human Nature*, Book 3, for having shown the redundancy of contractarian and other like arguments on the ground of the direct and more reliable derivation of similar conclusions from purely utilitarian premises. For Bentham's own view of the principle of utility, see *An Introduction to the Principles of Morals and Legislation*, ed. J. H. Burns and H. L. A. Hart (London: Athlone Press, 1977), ch. 1.

[3] This, of course, is more Bentham's than Hume's view, for Hume was more inclined, rightly in my view, to stress custom than command. Bentham's position was stated early in the 'Fragment', with refinement but no great alteration in *Of Laws in General*, ed. H. L. A. Hart (London: Athlone Press, 1970), see ch. 1. But note the many antecedents for the view of law as command; Erskine's *Principles* opens with the sentence 'Law is the command of a sovereign containing a common rule of life for his subjects.' (See J. Erskine, *Principles of the Law of Scotland*, 19th edn., ed J. Rankine (Edinburgh, Bell & Bradfute, 1895.) Blackstone likewise mingles command theory with natural law, and remarks in *Commentaries*, I.1 that 'municipal law is a rule of civil conduct, prescribed by the supreme power in the state'.

a practical problem of constitutional design, a problem which might more likely be exacerbated than alleviated by facile appeals to so-called fundamental rights.[4]

The argument had a pleasing simplicity at its heart. Then as now, there was not much dispute but that human governments in fact exist and exercise more or less effective authority over human communities and societies, and that they are in the way of issuing general directives that are recognized as law, and put into effect by judges appointed by the same governing authorities. Therefore, it was said, we need no mysterious account of 'higher law' to establish what law among us actually is. We already know it to be (as most natural lawyers also said) the command or mandate issued by those in authority. And they are those who, for whatever reason and by whatever means, have come to be habitually obeyed, not being mere intermediaries who themselves obey another. It was indeed no new revelation to say that sovereigns' commands are laws. To say that there are no other laws was to trigger what we now call a paradigm-shift.

Out of this revolution in thought, coupled with persistent unease about the category of command, emerges the broader generalization that law depends entirely on social interactions among humans. Out of unease over the claims to empirical provability and calculable applicability of hedonistic utilitarianism emerges the thesis that law is necessarily open to criticism against some rational or reasonable standard of evaluation, hence cannot be assumed to be already a morally justifiable code by its very existence as law. Thus does the descriptive theory of the nature of law called 'Legal Positivism' emerge as one main descendant of the Benthamite project. We should stress, though, that for Bentham descriptive theory was always the handmaiden of practical reform. Law as the expression of might could and did often fall far short of the rational standard of right, the greatest happiness principle. The task was to devise constitutional reforms and projects for sound codification that would stifle the forces of sinister interest and weave the fabric of felicity through law.

In Bentham, there is not even a hint of moral non-cognitivism. By contrast, non-cognitivism of the style of Hans Kelsen[5] leaves positive law to stand as humans' only objective standard of right. In such a posture, the epistemological, descriptive, aspect of positivism necessarily holds sway, any particular critical or reformist notions being characterized as ideology not science. Others have rejected non-cognitivism without embracing Benthamite utilitarianism, and have continued the descriptive programme under the guidance of the twin theses of the conceptual separation of law from morality and the derivation of all law from some social practice or practices, not necessarily, however, the simply voluntarist picture of the sovereign's mandate or command.

---

[4] Bentham's voluminous constitutional writings are now to a substantial extent available in readable form: *Constitutional Code, Vol. I*, ed F. Rosen and J. H. Burns (Oxford: Clarendon Press, 1983); *Principles Preparatory to Constitutional Code*, ed. P. Schofield (Oxford: Clarendon Press, 1989); *Securities Against Misrule etc*, ed. P. Schofield (Oxford: Clarendon Press 1990), *Official Aptitude Maximized: Expense Minimized*, ed. P. Schofield (Oxford: Clarendon Press, 1993).

[5] See H. Kelsen, *The Pure Theory of Law*, trans. M. Knight (Berkeley: University of California Press, 1978), 62–7.

Rather than calling Bentham himself a 'legal positivist', I think we do better simply to characterize him as an anti-naturalist, building a practical philosophy for law reform and remodelling one element in the traditional descriptive account as an element in his overall project. Legal positivism, or, perhaps, legal positivisms, so many and internally various are the variants,[6] are in intellectual descent from this or from the strands of Germanic neo-Kantian thought that flow into English-language theorizing through scholars like Kelsen and more recently Weinberger.[7] Here, I shall test such thinking particularly in the context of present discussions about constitutional reform in the United Kingdom.

The Benthamite constitution

In the previous chapter, an account was given of the constitution of the United Kingdom that discussed the way in which, notwithstanding the composite and originally treaty-based character of the British state, there came to prevail what was called the 'Dicey view' of the constitution. It is important to acknowledge that this was no merely arbitrary choice, but belonged to, or became consolidated through, the very great influence of Benthamite thought in nineteenth-century public life in Britain. To read Dicey's *Law and Opinion in England* is to be struck again and again how deeply wedded Dicey was to a form of individualistic utilitarianism that he took to be rooted in the teachings of Bentham read faithfully to the master's genius.[8]

Dicey's contribution to the critique of collectivism in law and state in early twentieth-century Britain came four-square out of his reading of Bentham and the Bentham tradition. It was, of course, this same Dicey who in the same period authored the greatest and most influential statement of the law of the British Constitution as that stood in the United Kingdom's period of transition from a traditional and oligarchic to a substantially though imperfectly democratic polity at home.[9] Abroad, the sweep of British imperial dominion was at its widest, and the might of which I speak was still thought capable of growing mightier yet. I think it is not unreasonable to label the constitution of that epoch, or at any rate the then-prevailing interpretation of constitutional order, the 'Benthamite constitution'.

The central idea is one that identifies law with power. As was remarked in the Introduction above, the power in question is grounded in the habits and usages of people rather than in any formal agreement or social contract. It is not necessarily

---

[6] See R. George, *The Autonomy of Law: Essays on Legal Positivism* (Oxford: Clarendon Press, 1996), chs. 1 & 2; but cf. W. J. Waluchow, *Inclusive Legal Positivism* (Oxford: Clarendon Press, 1994).

[7] See O. Weinberger, *Law, Institution and Legal Politics: Fundamental Problems of Legal and Social Philosophy* (Dordrecht,: Kluwer Academic Publishing Co., 1991).

[8] See A. V. Dicey, *Lectures on the Relationship Between Law and Public Opinion in England* (London: Macmillan, 1920), 20: 'Individualism as regards legislation is popularly, and not without reason, connected with the name and principles of Bentham.' These lectures dated from Dicey's visit to Harvard in 1898.

[9] *An Introduction to the Study of the Law of the Constitution*, 10th edn., ed. E. C. S. Wade (London: Macmillan, 1960).

mediated through any formally established constitution; constitutions presuppose power more than they constitute it. Order comes from the habits of obedience of people to some one or several others. Such habits might or might not be based on some prior agreement or constitutional understanding, but this is quite contingent. Provided the habit of obedience exists, order exists, political society exists, and law is possible, in the form of the mandates of the person or persons habitually obeyed.

Unlike Austin, Bentham considered it possible for the ultimate power of commanding to be divided, so long as people could be discriminating in their postures of obedience to different authorities, say Emperor and Pope. And he did think that restrictions could be put on the use of sovereign power by the device of 'laws *in principem*'. These might be in effect promissory in relation to self-imposed limits on sovereign exercises of power, or might alternatively be conventional in the sense of being encapsulated in treaties. Of this latter, in one of his youthful writings, he discerned an example in the Treaty of Union between England and Scotland.[10] Such limits operated, he thought, by setting a line beyond which the obedience of the subjects could not be guaranteed, or a line indicating a sphere of policy the sovereign could not safely trench upon.[11]

In this light, Bentham might not have had excessive difficulty accommodating into his theory an account of the Treaty of Accession by the UK to the European Communities (as they then were) and the European Communities Act 1972 that gave domestic effect to the treaty.[12] However that may be, he was convinced that any attempt to establish unalterable laws was hostile to the public interest, and usually a cloak for sinister interest. In fact, the issue for him was not that of restricting the law-making power, but that of ensuring it was in the right hands. Rendering the legislative power answerable to those whose interest the legislation affected came to seem the ultimate security against misrule. So far from being a danger to social stability, democracy would more likely be an effective way to guard against the enactment of partial laws, and a way of furnishing people with the rights it was genuinely expedient for them to have. Oren Ben Dor has shown how far Bentham's own constitutional proposals went towards thinking out democratically effective ways to eliminate the effect of sinister influence in legislative and governmental processes.[13]

When Austin in due course identified the true sovereign of the United Kingdom as the electorate working in consort with monarch and hereditary peerage, he captured part of this underlying idea. He, however, particularly in his later writings, set his face against moves toward a fully democratic franchise, on the ground that a weakening of an unreflective habit of obedience to a Parliament representing the

---

[10] See Bentham, 'Fragment', 490–1.   [11] See Bentham, *Laws in General*, 64–71.

[12] Bentham has the notion that a convention (in the sense of a treaty) can be one basis of a 'law *in principem*' setting a limit to the habit of obedience by marking a point beyond which a sovereign commits itself not to legislate. One could argue that each of the member states' sovereigns has done this very thing, through the various European Treaties up to and including the Maastricht Treaty on European Union, ceding to European organs a certain domain of legislative power, revocable only by agreement of all.

[13] See Oren Ben Dor, Ph.D. Thesis (University of London, 1997); another source of great assistance which I gladly acknowledge is G. Postema, *Bentham and the Common Law* (Oxford: Clarendon Press, 1986).

superior class of persons would tend to subvert social order and peace.[14] In this he departed from Bentham. But formally, he clarified and simplified the kernel of voluntaristic positivism in the well-known formulae that are almost too trite to mention here. The sovereign is the habitually obeyed one who or which habitually obeys no other. An independent political society is the association formed by a sovereign and that sovereign's subjects. 'The state' is either a synonym for the independent political society, or a collective term for the sovereign together with those public servants who exercise governmental powers as delegates of the sovereign.[15] Law is thus a creature of the state, and cannot as such govern the state, though it can and should control the activity of the individuals who hold offices of state, including membership of the supreme legislative body. What was logically impossible was for the sovereign itself in its corporate and law-making capacity to be bound by anything that could strictly be called a 'law'.

Dicey in turn rejected the identification of electorate with sovereign in the legal sense. The habit or custom that enshrined the position of sovereign was a habit encapsulated in the common law and the common usage of courts, politicians, and people. By that common law, Parliament was sovereign, and this was an unchallengeable legal sovereignty containing only the logically necessary disability of Parliament at any point in time to pass legislation that could set legal bounds to the power of successor Parliaments to legislate as they chose.[16]

Sovereignty in a purely political sense would be a different thing, and would rest with whoever could exercise effective long-run influence on Parliament and thus control the general direction of legislative and administrative policy. So the sovereignty that the electorate did enjoy was political rather than legal.[17] This was a political sovereignty that could be exercised only though the mediation of enforceable laws enacted by the legal sovereign, the Parliament.[18] In turn, the laws enacted by the Parliament took effect in society only as mediated through the decisions of the judges. These judges sat in courts with undifferentiated powers of adjudication in issues of public as well as of private law, and administered the same body of common law and statutory rights and obligations over all persons, whether public officials or private persons. Having a duty to recognize and implement every piece of legislation emanating from the sovereign power of Parliament, the Courts were nevertheless expected and entitled to exercise their powers of interpretation of laws to secure that any intrusion upon prior rights operated in an even-handed way and was kept to an appropriate minimum.[19]

---

[14] See J. Austin, *A Plea for the Constitution* (London, 1859).

[15] See id., *The Province of Jurisprudence Determined* (ed. H. L. A. Hart, London, Weidenfeld & Nicolson, 1954), 226–7; like Bentham, Austin preferred the concept 'independent political society' to that of 'state'; but 'state', he noted, could inter alia signify either the governors of an independent political society, or its totality, governors and governed together.

[16] See *Law of the Constitution*, 3–4, 27.

[17] Ibid. 27 whereas as a 'merely legal conception', sovereignty is 'the power of law-making unrestricted by any legal limit', by contrast 'that body is "politically" sovereign or supreme in a state the will of which is ultimately obeyed by the citizens of the state' (also p. 27).

[18] Ibid. 289.   [19] Ibid. 107–22, 268–73.

It is at first sight implausible to claim, as Dicey claimed, that the Rule of Law and the Sovereignty of Parliament are mutually reinforcing rather than mutually opposing constitutional principles. But, on closer inspection, one can see that the claim is based on a particular vision of the dynamic balance within the constitution that did to a considerable extent obtain in Dicey's day.

The picture remains, however, one of an ultimate identity of state and law. Even when one introduces the common law as that which underpins the habit of obedience, there is a direct two-way mutual interdependence of law and state. In this, the Benthamite conception of a constitution is mirrored in later forms of positivism that challenge some of the premises of the Benthamite enterprise. Hans Kelsen, though dismissive of a detected confusion between mere commands and binding commands in Austin's version of the theory,[20] came (as we saw in Chapter 2) by a different route to the conclusion that the state and the law are effectively a single identical object viewed in different lights. The state is the law personified and conceived as an acting subject.[21] H. L. A. Hart, who never directly addressed this issue in his published work, effectively agreed with it in a sidelong glance in his 1962 Inaugural Lecture 'Definition and Theory in Jurisprudence',[22] and endorsed it in his (never published) 1960s lectures at Oxford University on Kelsen.

Kelsen's conclusion, as we have seen, deliberately weakens the ideological resonance of the German constitutional theorists' conception of the '*Rechtsstaat*', the state-under-law, or law-state. For if there is an identity of law and state it follows that every state is formally a law-state, and the critical cutting edge of the demand that states be subjected to law is blunted.[23] The same uneasiness lingers over the Benthamite constitutional project, even with Dicey's gloss on the rule of law. For it turns out that the law that must rule is ultimately a law that depends fundamentally on a sheer power of coercion grounded in the habits of obedience we have. Can law set bounds on politics if law is simply the output of politics? How do we fit together might and right, how can we back right with enough might to be effective, how do we then secure that might cannot always override right? The highest apogee of a decisionist positivism, found in Carl Schmitt's work puts it bluntly to us that this is a delusory hope.[24] Must we rest content with that disturbing conclusion?

---

[20]   See Kelsen, *General Theory of Law and the State*, trans A. Wedberg (Cambridge. Mass.: Harvard University Press, 1945), part I, ch. 5, section C.

[21]   Kelsen, *Pure Theory*, 286–311.

[22]   Hart, 'Definition and Theory in Jurisprudence', originally published in 1963; now in id., *Essays in Jurisprudence and Philosophy* (Oxford: Clarendon Press, 1983), 21–48; see also id., *Essays on Bentham: Studies in Jurisprudence and Political Theory* (Oxford: Clarendon Press, 1982).

[23]   Cf. Ch. 2 above, and see Kelsen, *Pure Theory*, 312–13. As is clearly stated in Professor Bill Ewald's 'Comment' discussed in Ch. 2, while Kelsen is committed to the proposition that each state is formally speaking a *Rechtsstaat*, there is a narrower use of the term to denote a politico-constitutionalist ideology favouring separation of powers, entrenched rights, and the like (see Ewald, 'Comment on MacCormick', *Cornell Law Rev.* 82 (1997), 1071–79 at 1072–3). The latter, says Kelsen, cannot be derived simply from the concepts of law and state.

[24]   See D. Dyzenhaus, *Legality and Legitimacy: Carl Schmitt, Hans Kelsen and Hermann Heller in Weimar* (Oxford: Clarendon Press, 1997), chs. 1 and 2, esp. at p. 54; cf. P. Caldwell, *Popular Sovereignty and the Crisis of German Constitutional Law: The Theory and Practice of Weimar Constitutionalism* (Durham N.C. & London: Duke University Press, 1997).

Might and right : two tendencies

To challenge the Schmittian conclusion, the discussion will now turn to a review of the programme of constitutional reform that was undertaken by the 'New Labour' Government that took office in the United Kingdom in May 1997. Its approach to that task was an ambitious one, involving devolution to Scotland, Wales, and Northern Ireland, re-establishment of all-London local government with a directly elected mayor, administrative regionalization in England, reform of the upper house of Parliament, and domestication of the European Convention for the Protection of Human Rights and Fundamental Freedoms (hereinater, the 'Human Rights Convention'). Within that programme, it will be argued, there are in fact two conflicting or at any rate competing strands or tendencies. I shall call these respectively the 'diffusionist' and the 'sovereigntist' tendency. A few brief and programmatic words will serve to give an initial summary of each.

(i) The Diffusionist Tendency

This term refers to the strand in policy that looks with favour at a distribution of power among functioning power-centres, both 'upwards' to the organs of the European Union and Community, and 'downwards' to the component countries of the United Kingdom, and perhaps to regions as well. Three points stand out:

(*a*) The general election of May 1997 seemed to give solid confirmation of the United Kingdom's membership of the European Union and European Community. Sir James Goldsmith's Referendum Party put the issue of Europe fully before the electorate, and the outgoing Government, though divided on the issue, was markedly more 'Euro-sceptic' in stance than the Labour Party, which won the election by so substantial a margin. The incoming Government has interpreted its mandate as justifying a full-hearted though not uncritical commitment to the rights and responsibilities of membership in all pillars of the European Union

(*b*) The Government has secured enactment of legislation to make the European Convention on Human Rights effectively justiciable before British Courts.

(*c*) Under legislation enacted for Scotland and for Wales, there is substantial devolution of legislative and domestic governmental power to a Scottish Parliament and Executive, and at the same time a weaker form of representative domestic government was implemented for Wales through a directly elected administrative Assembly. These forms of devolution were endorsed by referendum in the two countries, though the massive 'Yes' majority in Scotland was far from repeated in Wales, where 'Yes' had but a tiny majority. A restoration of internal self-government with power-sharing between unionist and nationalist communities, and with new cross-border institutions involving Northern Ireland and the Republic of Ireland, was agreed in the Good Friday Agreement of 1998. This also envisaged a 'British–Irish Council', popularly known in the alternative as the 'Council of the

Isles', to create a forum for discussion of common issues among the governments of Ireland and the UK, the three devolved administrations and the Isle of Man and the Channel Isles. The reform of London Government has involved creating the office of a directly elected Mayor together with some form of elected regional assembly for London. Whether or in what way the process of devolution and decentralization may be developed in relation to other English regions remains to be seen, but the question is at least open for discussion.

(ii) The Sovereigntist Tendency

This term refers to the counter-tendency in governmental opinion, contending that final power remains centralized where it has been ever since emergence of the modern English-and-then-British Constitution, namely in Parliament, with the monarch-in-Parliament. This is still the kingpin of a democracy secured by ensuring the electorate's political sovereignty through Parliament's legal sovereignty (and this democracy will be further buttressed by abolishing the hereditary element in the House of Lords). The sovereigntist tendency can be expressed as counterpoints to the three points of diffusionism:

(*a*) It is a misinterpretation of the situation to say that EC membership upsets the traditional doctrine of parliamentary sovereignty in its fundamentals. It merely calls for a reinterpretation of it in the light of contemporary conceptions of democratic government.[25]

(*b*) In relation to the European Convention, the Government is careful to reserve parliamentary sovereignty. For the Courts are merely to be required to interpret UK legislation with a view to avoiding so far as possible any conflict with the Convention, but to refer to Parliament, through a 'declaration of incompatibility', any provision of statutory law that appears to conflict with the Convention despite best efforts of benign interpretation. It is intended then that Parliament will make its own choice whether and how to cure the conflict.[26]

(*c*) The White Paper *Scotland's Parliament* was careful to insist that the Scottish Parliament's powers would be merely devolved, and that sovereignty would remain with the Parliament at Westminster, and the Scotland Act makes provision substantially to that effect.[27]

---

[25] See T. R. S. Allan, 'Parliamentary Sovereignty: Law, Politics, and Revolution', *Law Quarterly Review*, 113 (1997), 443–52, arguing against Sir William Wade that the emergence of judicial review of Acts of Parliament for conformity to European Community law is an evolution within constitutional law, justifiable by an appropriate interpretation of the relationship between democracy and sovereignty. But see also Sir W. Wade, 'Sovereignty—Revolution or Evolution?' *Law Quarterly Review*, 112 (1996), 568–75; Wade is surely correct that Dicey's conception of sovereignty has been wholly subverted by recent developments, though that is not necessarily decisive as to the issue of contemporary constitutional interpretation.   [26] Human Rights Bill 1998, clauses 3, 4, and 5.

[27] See *Scotland's Parliament* (1997 Cm. 3658, para. 4, 2: 'The UK Parliament is and will remain sovereign in all matters; but as part of Parliament's resolve to modernise the British constitution Westminster will be choosing to exercise that sovereignty by devolving legislative responsibilities to a Scottish Parliament without in any way diminishing its own powers.' And see Scotland Act 1998 section 28(7), providing that the UK Parliament's power to legislate for Scotland is unimpaired by the Act.

In these two partly competing, perhaps even conflicting, tendencies of policy, it is easy to see Benthamite constitutionalism as the mainspring of the sovereigntist tendency, or certainly one of its most powerful buttresses. The insistence is that while power may be delegated in various directions, it remains and ought to be secured as essentially unitary and central. Economic and other benefits may be gained from delegating powers to the organs of the Economic Community. This may indeed be an agency whose own court of justice claims 'supremacy' for its laws. In a British constitutional perspective, however, this would be properly interpreted as explaining the implications of Parliament's recognition within UK law of 'enforceable Community rights' through sections 2 and 4 of the European Communities Act 1972. Such rights are recognized as highest-level legal norms in the UK so long as the Act remains unrepealed. But this highest-level legal validity is conferred under the constitution, by the Parliament that passed the European Communities Act and which retains under the same constitution the power to repeal it. This does not derogate from the constitutional position of Parliament, even if in the meantime the upshot is the possibility of 'disapplication' of Acts subsequent to the 1972 Act when these conflict with enforceable community rights as in the last resort interpreted by the European Court.[28]

Similar considerations of economic and political benefit may in due course be held to justify commitment to Economic and Monetary Union, and adoption of the common currency, the Euro, in preference to the pound sterling, with an inevitable delegation of monetary policy to European organs. This would no doubt increase the practical difficulty of a future withdrawal, in particular a unilateral withdrawal, from the European Community and Union. But nothing in British constitutional law and custom would countenance the thesis that the legal-cum-constitutional power to secede had been or could have been surrendered in the processes of adaptation to European institutions. From the standpoint of the United Kingdom constitution, all that has happened has been a delegation of powers to common European organs *pari passu* with a like delegation by other European states, whose constitutional tribunals have been at least as ready as ours to insist on the surviving and unimpaired integrity of the national constitution even after delegation of certain 'sovereign rights' to European institutions.[29]

Likewise, the domestication of the European Convention on the terms proposed, so far from undermining the sovereignty of the Parliament, underlines it. For Parliament will have the ultimate decision whether to uphold or elide a difference of view about the true demand of human rights in contentious domains of public policy. Faced with a 'declaration of incompatibility', it is up to Parliament to decide

---

[28]   See Wade and Allan, above n. 25, compare A. W. Bradley, 'The Sovereignty of Parliament—In Perpetuity?', in J. Jowell and D. Oliver (eds.), *The Changing Constitution*, 3rd edn. (Oxford: Clarendon Press, 1994), 79–108.

[29]   Cf. D. Rossa Phelan, *Revolt or Revolution: the Constitutional Boundaries of the European Community* (Dublin: Round Hall/Sweet and Maxwell 1997), discussed in Ch. 7 below, reviewed, MacCormick, 'Risking Constitutional Collision in Europe?', *Oxford Journal of Legal Studies*, 18 (1998), 517–32, and cf. id., 'The Maastricht-Urteil', below n. 32.

whether or not to choose compatibility or to continue with the incompatibility according to its own sovereign preference. Finally, it may be true that many members of the Government did put their hands to the Scottish Constitutional Convention's 'Claim of Right' asserting the 'sovereign right' of the Scottish people to determine their own constitutional framework.[30] But this has now to be seen as no more than a rhetorical flourish or a special version of the claim about political sovereignty. Unitary state, unitary law, and unitary ultimate power remain undisturbed by a series of delegations which make government both more effective and more sensitive, an improved version of the Benthamite constitution, not a subversion of it.

Some will, however, hear in all this something of the desperation of the denizens of riverine flood-plains who seek to dam leaking levees with paltry sandbags. The grounds for scepticism over claims about sovereignty grow more solid the clearer it becomes how very problematic in practice would be any act of one-sided secession from Europe. And surely in any event sovereignty in Dicey's classical conception collapses with the discovery that the 1972 Parliament could bind its successors, even if not in an absolutely irrevocable way. The European Communities Act is certainly the first to which the maxim of *lex posterior*, that the later Act derogates from the earlier, does not apply. The 1972 Act derogated from the Merchant Shipping Act 1988, not *vice versa*.[31] Likewise, a deliberate choice by Parliament to defy the European Convention would carry heavy costs in terms of relationships within Europe and beyond. This may be power more in theory than in practice, and after time one will wonder why to treat as sacrosanct a theory that bears so little upon practice. Perhaps what we see is not the death of sovereignty but its rebirth in new splendour. But if this thesis is to prove finally convincing, its proponents have some work to do. The implications of this new sovereignty need to be spelled out and justified. Later in this book I will advance a rival thesis, that the United Kingdom and its European partners are 'post-sovereign states' as members of a European Community that is also not a sovereign federal union nor fatally predestined to become one. Nothing here can be taken for granted, and it is worth trying to figure out what does come next on the assumption that the game is up for sovereignty and sovereigntists.

---

[30] See O. D. Edwards, *A Claim of Right for Scotland* (Edinburgh: Polygon, 1989); I have discussed this in two forthcoming papers, 'Sovereignty or Subsidiarity: Some Comments on Scottish Devolution', in A. Tomkins (ed.), *Towards Devolution* (London, 1998); and 'The English Constitution, the British State, and the Scottish Anomaly', *Scottish Affairs, Special Issue 'Understanding Constitutional Change'* (1998), 129–45.

[31] The reference here is, of course, to the *Factortame* case (*R v Secretary of State for transport ex. P. Factortame* [1989] 1 All E. R. 692 and (No 2) [1991] 1 All E. R. 70, Case C 213/89) as discussed in Wade and Allan, above n. 25. See also MacCormick, 'Beyond the Sovereign State', *Modern Law Rev.* 56 (1993), 1–18, and cf. MacCormick, 'Sovereignty, Democracy and Subsidiarity' in (1994–5) *Juridisk Tidskrift*, 2, 290–7, id., 'Sovereignty: Myth and Reality,' in *De Lege* (Uppsala University Law Faculty Yearbook, 1995), *Towards Universal Law: Trends in National, European, and International Lawmaking*, 227–48. (Also published, in a different, earlier, and more home-oriented version, in *Scottish Affairs*, 11 (1995), 1–13), MacCormick 'The Maastricht-Urteil: Sovereignty now', *European Law Journal*, 1 (1995), 259–66, id., 'Liberalism, Nationalism and the Post-sovereign State', 44 *Political Studies*, 553–67 (1996), and 'Democracy, Subsidiarity, and Citizenship in the "European Commonwealth" ', *Law and Philosophy*, 16 (1997), 332–56) (also in MacCormick (ed.), *Constructing Legal Systems: 'European Union' in Legal Theory* (Dordrecht: D. Reidel, 1997), and substantially contained in Ch. 9 below).

At least there is room for doubt about the nature of sovereignty and its local manifestation. In these circumstances it must also be remarked that the United Kingdom Parliament acquiesced rather than took the initiative in setting up a Parliament for Scotland, not through the wise judgement of decentralizing metropolitan intelligence, but in response to a very long-standing and strongly articulated demand from a region considered a nation by its inhabitants. The unitary sovereignty of the incorporating union agreed in 1707 seems to be at best in its twilight.

Thus, although for each of the points in the diffusionist tendency there is a sovereigntist counterpoint, the matter does not end there. The diffusionist tendency can be read more boldly as pointing towards something altogether less monolithic than the Benthamite conception either of law or of constitution. It points towards acknowledging a plurality of interlocking sets of standards of right and wrong, operated by different authorities in different spheres of responsibility. These spheres of responsibility engage in some cases larger, in some cases smaller, participant populations to take part in one or another scheme of collective self-government. Perhaps it is not, or will over time prove not to be, necessary to have or to assert a single all-purpose supreme authority. Certainly, if there were none, the situation emerging would require careful management at all levels to avoid deadlock or damaging conflict among rival authorities. Each level would need to respect the sphere of competence of every other, and there would have to be ongoing dialogue to secure common understanding of the scope and limits of various authorities. A diffusion of legal authority would entail a parallel diffusion of political power. Those who hold power at particular levels or for particular purposes would be likely to find themselves subject to checks and controls on their action that emanate from different authorities and are not amenable to change by processes in the power of those controlled by them. To cope intellectually with such developments would require a legal theory that is pluralistic rather than a monistic in its approach to legal and political order.

Let it for now be acknowledged, however, that sovereigntists today as in the days of Hobbes can properly warn us what is at stake. The scenario envisaged may point not so much towards exciting new openings for legal and political theory, but simply towards chaos. Here may lie but the mere anarchy that is let loose when the centre cannot hold and things fall apart, when the question, 'Who is in charge here?' admits of no clear answer.

Were chaos to ensue, the next move in a Hobbesian dialectic would then be an inevitable movement to a reimposition of new certainty on a situation in which there has been a momentary lack of clarity about the true location of power, the true dispositions of people to obey or disobey. This has been much in the mind of the present Lord Chancellor.[32] Whether the sovereignty that will emerge is the one he

---

[32] See Lord Irvine of Lairg, 'Judges as Decision-Makers: the Theory and Practice of *Wednesbury* Review' [1996] *Public Law* 59-78, at pp. 76–8, responding to Sir J. Laws, 'Law and Democracy' [1995] *Public Law* 72–93; note Laws's view that it is the constitution that is sovereign, not any organ operating under it. This is an interesting notion, but one that makes short work of the classical United Kingdom constitutional interpretation, and most of the legal theory of sovereignty.

advocates is not perhaps as clear as he would have us believe. But if sovereignty there must be, it will emerge at one or another level in the pile, whether by transfer to the centre, as Eurosceptics fear, or by retention and reassertion at the level of present EU member states, as they desire, or at that lower level, of Scotland or Wales or Catalunya or England or Bavaria or Flanders to which the inexorable logic of the decentralizing tendency may in truth point. Sovereignty is a zero-sum game, for as between two or more contenders for it, only one can win.

Let us not reach any hasty conclusion on these questions. It has been conceded that there is a powerful and challenging account of legal and constitutional theory that makes sense of the sovereigntist claims. What is not clear is whether any adequate theoretical structure could be built up that would make the diffusionist view seem at least intellectually coherent, whether or not in the end it is accepted as guiding us to a radically new conception of law-and-politics. I shall suggest that there is such a theoretical structure available, one built out of different materials presented to us by other strands within the positivist tradition than those with which I have been working until now. This is what I call the theory of 'institutional normative order'.

Institutional normative order and legal pluralism

For the purpose in hand, there is also a theory at hand, that which was adumbrated in the introductory chapter of this book. The theory of law as institutional normative order has built into it an inherently pluralistic conception of legal system. Distinct systems can co-exist without any one having to deny either the independence or the normative character of another. Hans Kelsen believed that any objective cognition of normative order would be driven by its own rationality to see the totality of that which is normative in monistic terms,[33] so that every objective normative order must be part of a dynamically integrated whole. But the present theory can fully endorse the normative quality of law while allowing for a radical pluralism such that objectively valid normative orders may give conflicting answers to the same point. That being so, there will not necessarily be any specifically legal method for eliminating the conflict—it is perfectly possible that conflicts will simply go unresolved, or that the resolution may be a matter for political rather than legal processes. To reject the claims of Kelsenian monism on this point is to call in aid some of the insights of Hartian jurisprudence.[34] This is not surprising, since the characterization of normative order rests substantially on pressing further than he did with Hart's insights concerning the 'internal aspect' of conduct that is governed by norms. It has to be said though, that however open Hart was conceptually to a more

---

[33] See Kelsen, *Pure Theory*, 332–44.
[34] Cf. S. L. Paulson and B. L. Paulson (eds.), *Normativity and Norms: Critical Perspectives on Kelsenian Themes* (Oxford: Clarendon Press, 1998), 553–82.

pluralistic approach,[35] most of his legal writing sticks rather firmly within a common law approach, usually in its Anglocentric form. There is a line of thought here awaiting development.

Secondly, we have already seen how this approach permits drawing a clear conceptual divide between law and state. This depends on differentiating the normative form of power, 'authority' as it is sometimes called, from non-normative social power, human power in its factual sense, political power. It has been a characteristic of political power at least in the modern world that it is exercised territorially, normally with a claim of exclusive legitimacy in respect of a more-or-less definite territory. For Bentham and Benthamites it both accounts for and depends on the 'habit of obedience'.

A political conception of the state takes it in the wide sense to be the whole societal entity comprising governors and governed within the claimed territory. In the narrow sense, it takes the state as acting entity to comprise the people and agencies whose decisions determine the exercise of political power in the state in its wide sense. Such a conception (in wide or narrow senses) neither needs to, nor is wise to, deny the significance of legal order in the fabric of the state. For the state's pretensions to legitimacy, which are a large part of the success the governors have in exercising power, usually depend on a self-representation as embodying and institutionalizing a satisfactory normative order, either in secular or in sacred terms, or in some mixture.

There is a converse truth, that no institutionalized normative order is likely to be durable or credible without some element of power to uphold its decisions and dispositions. Hence, in a world of states, one significant manifestation of law will be the legal orders of the territorial states. A possible, but not necessary, feature of the state will be that it accept a thoroughly legal definition of state agencies and powers through a customary or statutory or mixed body of constitutional law. Within that framework, there can be a more or less effective realization of the 'rule of law', under which decisions of public authorities, in particular those affecting individuals and organized groups, are genuinely controlled by legal norms that are effectively policed and administered by impartial and relatively independent courts.

This makes possible a kind of demand fully within the spirit of Benthamite legal politics, a demand of the kind expressed most recently by Tom Campbell in *Ethical Positivism*.[36] This is the demand for a rigorous view of the separation of powers, with reservation of the task of articulating general rules to the legislature, while limiting to an inevitable, but not always particularly welcome, minimum the law-making activities of courts. Just how far this should be pressed is itself a debated question, but alongside of Campbell on this general point we may range thinkers such as Joseph Raz and Frederick Schauer, the latter of whom has given particularly careful

---

[35] See Hart, 'Kelsen's Doctrine of the Unity of Law', in *Essays in Jurisprudence and Philosophy*, 309–42

[36] T. D. Campbell, *The Legal Theory of Ethical Positivism* (Aldershot: Dartmouth, 1996), 69–90.

thought to the extent to which and the grounds on which it is right to insist on a relatively rule-bound approach in adjudication within institutional normative order.[37] Nor is this line of thinking necessarily confined to those who would characterize their own thought as positivistic—suffice it in this context simply to mention the name of Lon Fuller, who was himself most insistent on a pluralistic vision of legal order in human society.[38]

The pluralistic potentialities of the present approach enable one to recover some of the decided virtues of older 'institutionalist' approaches[39] to legal thought, such as those represented by Gierke[40] and Hauriou,[41] though without the element of social vitalism advocated by the latter. Among the points such thinkers wanted to stress was a denial of the undue pretensions of the state to total mastery of a territory and all that went on within it. Partly, this was a matter of asserting ecclesiastical independence, in Hauriou's case with particular concern for the rights of the Catholic Church in secular, republican, France. Partly, there was a more general concern for the independence and vitality of the manifold communities, guilds, associations, and corporations to be found in civil society. The idea that recognition of corporate status was something wholly and arbitrarily in the gift of the state was to them anathema in terms of political morality and misleading in terms of social history and contemporary social reality. Surely it is true both that the State is not the only significant human association that we know, and that the State's arrangements for taking account of the corporate existence and intrinsic normative order of other social entities should not be supposed to disclose the ontologically necessary conditions for the actual existence of such associations, such orders. One part of the objection that legal positivism has aroused has been an objection to the implicit, or sometimes explicit, statism inherent in the monistic or monolithic strand of positivism. Statism is certainly a creed worthy to be rejected, positivism a stance that should be embraced only to the extent that it can be carefully distinguished from statism.

Finally, we are in a position to reassess the balance of might and right. Normative order is not sustainable without some disposition of power and in the end brute force. This is not, however, because of a conceptual dependence of norm and coercion, like the conceptual dependence Austin saw between 'command', 'sanction', and 'duty'. As Eerik Lagerspetz has shown with conspicuous lucidity in his recent *The Opposite Mirrors*,[42] the possibility of normative order as a source of solutions to human co-ordination problems can be explained in terms of structures of mutual

---

[37] See Raz, *Practical Reason and Norms* (London: Hutchinson, 1975), 193–9; F. Schauer, *Playing by the Rules*, 158–66.

[38] See L. L. Fuller, *The Morality of Law*, rev. edn. (New Haven, Conn., 1969), 33–94 on the rule of law; 122–37 on the plurality of law's manifestations.

[39] See 'Institutionalism in Law' (by A. Pintore) in E. J. Craig (gen. ed.), *Routledge Encyclopaedia of Philosophy* (London: Routledge, 1998), vol. 4, 799–803.

[40] See O. von Gierke, *Associations and Law: The Classical and Early Christian Stages*, trans. and ed. G. Heiman (Toronto: University of Toronto Press 1977), Heiman's introduction at pp. 37–9 being of particular help on this point.

[41] See *The French Institutionalists: Maurice Hauriou, Georges Renard, Joseph T. Delos*, trans M. Welling, intro. by M. T. Rooney (Cambridge, Mass.: Harvard University Press, 1945), esp. at 93–124.

[42] See E. Lagerspetz, *The Opposite Mirrors* (Dordrecht: Kluwer, 1995), 30–50.

belief among different agents who are disposed to interact with each other. But, especially in large-scale, relatively impersonal contexts, people risk being exploited where they act in the faith that the order will be observed by others, who in fact then take advantage of them. There needs to be some security against this to sustain a system of norms grounded in or connected to mutual beliefs. This can be provided by the organized exercise of power, disposing of effective sanctions when necessary. Thus Hart's idea of legal order not as essentially coercive, but as involving 'Voluntary co-operation in a coercive system' can be endorsed, albeit within a framework that departs some distance from his.[43]

To conclude: this institutionalist way of looking at legal and political order opens up possibilities about pluralism. It makes possible, though not necessary, a degree of opposition to traditional centralizing theories about sovereignty, its absoluteness and its essential quality for securely established law. In place, we can put ideas about subsidiarity, negotiation, balance between different forms and levels of government and self-government. This is not necessarily an easy way of looking at law, or of running a society. The problems about societal insecurity that lie at the heart of Hobbes's vision of the human condition, and that continue to animate Bentham and Austin, are real problems. The diffusionist picture is a happy one from many points of view, but its proponents must show that the Hobbesian problems can be handled even without strong central authorities, last-resort sovereigns for all purposes.

By personal disposition and political conviction, I am a diffusionist. I do not claim that the case for this view can be established simply by advancing the 'institutional normative order' conception of law. What I hope to have shown or suggested is, however, that such a theory of law has a certain persuasiveness as a descriptive account. It is not incompatible with a sovereigntist approach to constitutional politics. Maybe some institutional normative orders do just have to enshrine all-purpose territorial supremacy. But the present theory differs from voluntaristic positivism in not loading the dice for sovereigntism from the outset. We live in times of exciting and profound constitutional debate, here and throughout Europe. No less than in the past have we need of legal philosophies that open up practical possibilities without begging the question of where in politics lie the things of ultimate value, and what these are.

---

[43]   Hart, *Concept*, 193; Lagerspetz, op. cit. 198–207.

6

A Very British Revolution?

Introduction: the sovereignty dispute

Was there a revolution in Britain in 1972? Was the constitution then overthrown, not by violence but by stealth, when the Heath Government procured the enactment by a narrow majority of the European Communities Act 1972? Was the referendum of 1975 a belated democratic legitimation of a revolution already accomplished? Or did the revolution remain on hold until the House of Lords finally decided in *Factortame v Secretary of State for Transport*[1] that traditional parliamentary sovereignty had been abandoned, and a later Act of Parliament might be disapplied to honour a commitment to European Community law confirmed by the earlier? Or is there some other way to account for what happened when, in accordance with the provisions of section 2 (1) and (4) of the European Communities Act 1972, and in the light of the ruling of the European Court of Justice concerning the incompatibility of the fisheries provisions in the Merchant Shipping Act 1988 with Community law, the House set aside the 1988 Act's provisions? Is talk of revolution exaggerated, overdramatic? Did the United Kingdom succeed in joining the European Community[2] without undergoing a revolution in the process?

The present chapter is a contribution to a debate already under way. Sir William Wade has put his high authority behind the 'revolution thesis', but his argument has been countered in vigorous fashion by Trevor Allan. Sir William, of course does not wish to portray bloodshed and violence and tumbrels rolling to the guillotine, but only a 'technical revolution' in the legal sense.[3] A change, he points out, was made in the fundamental rules of the constitution of a kind that the constitution as understood in 1972 could not have authorized. For in 1972, the constitution had as its

---

[1] See *Factortame v Secretary of State for Transport* [1991] A. C. 603; Lord Bridge's dictum at pp. 658–9 has been noted as particularly significant: 'If the supremacy within the European Community of Community law was not always inherent in the E.E.C. Treaty, . . . it was certainly well established in the jurisprudence of the European Court of Justice long before the United Kingdom joined the Community. Thus, whatever limitation of its sovereignty Parliament accepted when it enacted the European Communities Act 1972 was entirely voluntary. Under the terms of the Act of 1972 it has always been clear that it was the duty of a United Kingdom court, when delivering final judgment, to override any rule of national law found to be in conflict with any directly enforceable rule of Community law.'

[2] Notwithstanding the continued existence of the three 'communities' referred to in the European Communities Act, I shall in this chapter follow the popular simplification of terms achieved in the European Union Treaty of 1992, the Maastricht Treaty, and refer to the 'European Community', the Community being now (together with the ECSC and Euratom) the first of the three 'pillars' of the European Union. European Community law, and the jurisdiction of the Court of Justice (hereinafter, the 'ECJ'), is confined to this 'first pillar', the other two being of an essentially intergovernmental character.

[3] See Sir W. Wade, 'Sovereignty—Revolution or Evolution?', *Law Quarterly Review*, 112 (1996), 568–75 at p. 574

fundamental rule that Parliament is sovereign, in the sense that Parliament at any time can enact any norm it chooses as valid law, save a norm that would bind a successor Parliament. Dicey[4] says that as a 'merely legal conception', sovereignty is 'the power of law-making unrestricted by any legal limit'. Wade says that 'the rule was that an Act of Parliament in proper form had absolutely overriding effect, except that it could not fetter the corresponding power of future Parliaments'.[5] For the sake of the subsequent argument, I shall re-express this in the present tense and in Hohfeldian categories as follows: 'Parliament has an unrestricted and general power to enact valid law, subject to only two disabilities, namely, a disability to enact norms disabling Parliament on any future occasion from enjoying the same unrestricted and general power, and a disability to enact laws that derogate from the former disability.' This rule, according to Wade, existed as a practice of the judges, and was itself changeable only through decision by the judges.

Wade's thesis is that the House of Lords in its *Factortame*[6] decision in 1991, especially in the account given of it in the speech of Lord Bridge of Harwich, connived at overturning that fundamental constitutional rule, since it treated the legal change made by the Parliament that enacted the 1972 Act as one which imposed a restriction on the later Parliament that enacted the 1988 Act. If the decision did not itself overturn the fundamental rule, it indicated that the rule had already been overturned. Either way, a change of a fundamental kind had occurred in the way in which judges interpreted the legislative power of Parliament after accession to the European Communities. Judges now interpret Parliament's powers in terms different from those that were previously in use among the judiciary.

This change was one that could not have been itself legally warranted under the former understanding of the constitution. Accordingly, it could only have come about by a judicial decision to change the constitution or to acquiesce in a change made by the 1972 Parliament, despite the fact that the decision to make the change lacked authority in or under the constitution as that had long been understood up to the moment at which the change was made. Had the legislation been differently drafted, it might have been possible to achieve continuity, but given the terms of the 1972 Act, no pretence that a mere change in statutory interpretation was all that had happened could disguise the radical breach that had in fact occurred. Adopting terminology from H. L. A. Hart (himself a prior debtor to Professor Wade), Wade characterizes the revolutionary change he detects as a change in the 'rule of recognition' that lacked the authority of the rule of recognition in use prior to the change.[7] What rule of recognition the judges subscribe to is a question itself of political fact.

---

[4] A. V. Dicey, *An Introduction to the Study of the Law of the Constitution*, 10th edn., ed. E. C. S. Wade (London: Macmillan, 1960), 27.　　　　　　　　　　　　　[5] 'Sovereignty', at p. 574.

[6] [1991] A. C. 603 at pp. 658–9.

[7] See 'Sovereignty' at p. 574 '[The rule quoted above at n. 5] is a rule of unique character, since only the judges can change it. It is for the judges, and not for Parliament, to say what is an effective Act of Parliament. If the judges recognize that there must be a change, as by allowing future Parliaments to be fettered, this is a technical revolution.'

Since the facts have changed in a fundamental way, not derivable from the previously observed rule, a revolution must simply be acknowledged to have occurred. Hart himself had argued, partly by reference to a justly celebrated contribution by Wade[8] to an earlier debate about sovereignty, that the existence of an 'ultimate rule of recognition' cannot itself be validated by any other rule or norm of law, but can only exist through a 'complex and normally concordant practice' among judges and other officials. Its existence can thus only be a matter of social fact.[9]

Trevor Allan's response shows that there is no escape in such a debate from the deepest questions of legal philosophy. He criticizes Wade's approach as one based on a thin conception of the ultimate rules of constitutional law, for it suggests that the development of these rules is a process not subject to arguments of fundamental legal principle, but only to the influence of political considerations.[10] Ultimate constitutional rules belong to common law not to statute law. This does not diminish, but reinforces, the need for recourse to arguments of legal principle, including the principles necessary to and inherent in democratic constitutionalism. Such principles become decisively important when fundamental questions arise for decision in the light of developments such as the (ultimately political) decision of the United Kingdom to join the European Communities. The House of Lords may indeed have failed to explore such reasons as fully as it might and should have done in the *Factortame* decision. But the deficiencies of the decision in any event 'suggest the influence of an inadequate positivist jurisprudence'.[11] In the light of his own Dworkinian interpretivist approach to constitutional questions, developed in *Law, Liberty and Justice*,[12] it can fairly be inferred that Allan sees the baneful influence of 'inadequate positivist jurisprudence' as pervading also Sir William's argument for the conclusion that the old constitution has been overthrown by acts of an essentially, albeit technically, revolutionary kind.

The foundations of a constitution

The debate is one that goes to the fundamentals of an understanding of law. It poses sharply the issue of how it is possible to change a constitution in its fundamentals, while still acting in a constitutional and lawful manner and spirit. It thus demands some satisfactory account, necessarily a theoretical account, of what the foundations of a legal-constitutional order are, and how it is possible for these foundational

---

[8] See H. W. R. Wade, 'The Legal Basis of Sovereignty', *Cambridge Law Journal* (1955), 172–94.

[9] See Hart, *The Concept of Law*, 2nd edn. (Oxford: Clarendon Press, 1994), chs. 6 and 10; the acknowledgment of Wade's piece is at p. 295.

[10] See T. R. S. Allan, 'Parliamentary Sovereignty: Law, Politics, and Revolution', *Law Quarterly Review*, 113 (1997), 443–52, arguing that the emergence of judicial review of Acts of Parliament for conformity to European Community law is an evolution within constitutional law, justifiable by an appropriate interpretation of the relationship between democracy and sovereignty.

[11] Ibid. 448.

[12] Allan, *Law, Liberty, and Justice* (Oxford: Clarendon Press, 1993).

elements in some way to regulate their own amendment or change. Wade having pitched his argument on the ground of Hart's theoretical account of these funda-mentals, we do well to start there. As will be seen, particular attention must be given to the two Hartian ideas of 'rules of change' and 'rules of recognition'.

To put these in context, let us recall that according to Hart any viable human community must live under shared rules that regulate at least interpersonal violence and some administration of the things that are necessary for human survival. These essential 'primary rules' establish mutual obligations of mutual forbearance and limited mutual assistance. A simple regime of pure 'primary rules of obligation' would, however, be too static and inefficient for large-scale technologically innova-tive societies. Such societies must by some means have developed institutions that can change the law legislatively and that can administer it judicially. These institu-tions depend more on power-conferring than on obligation-imposing rules. In summary, law in such societies takes the form of a 'union of primary and secondary rules'.[13] Primary rules concern the obligations imposed by law on persons in society in favour of others or in the public interest. Secondary rules concern the institutional organization and regulation of the making and enforcement of other rules. The secondary rules can be summarized (in alphabetical order) as:

1. 'rules of adjudication', the substantial cluster of rules that constitute courts and empower judges to hear and determine trials and disputes, concluding them by the issuance of enforceable orders;
2. 'rules of change', being (*a*) rules that constitute legislators or legislative bodies with power to enact general rules for the guidance of the population, and (*b*) rules that enable private persons to vary their rights and duties, by varying the inci-dence or application of primary rules that impose obligations;
3. a 'rule of recognition'[14] that establishes criteria for identifying which rules are valid members of the legal system maintained by the legal officials whose roles are regulated by rules of adjudication and rules of change. This rule depends on a complex but normally concordant practice of those officials whereby they appeal to the same rules as the rules of law that must be used and observed in their soci-

---

[13] The essential reference for all this is *Concept of Law*, ch. 5; for my own prior reflections, see MacCormick, H. L. A. Hart (London: Edward Arnold, 1961,) 103–20, esp. at 108–12.

[14] Hart's usage is not absolutely consistent, for sometimes he seems to envisage a single 'rule of recog-nition' establishing an obligation to apply the rules that satisfy one or other of several 'criteria of recogni-tion' or 'criteria of validity', while at other times the suggestion appears to be that there might be several rules of recognition. Moreover, as Dr John Gardner has reminded me, Hart also envisages the possibility of 'permissive sources of law' to which recourse may be had when the 'mandatory sources' covered by the rule of recognition as a duty-imposing rule are non-existent or in need of interpretative clarification. I believe that the 'single rule' version is the one more consistently and convincingly deployed by Hart, for the key to the single rule is that it can internally to itself rank different criteria in order of priority. If the permissive sources are brought in, the rule is partly duty-imposing and partly permissive, for it states that judges must apply rules satisfying the mandatory criteria, and may when necessary apply rules or other standards satisfying the permissive criteria. Those who prefer the idea that there may be more than one rule of recognition must acknowledge that there then must be an ultimate rule that ranks these rules in some priority order. Nothing in the present argument would be defeated if that option were preferred.

ety. In healthily democratic societies, this shared practice also engages the active assent of citizens in general, but this is not necessary as a minimum condition for the existence of a legal system.

This idea of law as a 'union of primary and secondary rules' has a pleasing simplicity and clarity, at any rate at first sight. Yet there are problems concerning the relationship among secondary rules of the three kinds. In particular, it is difficult in a concrete situation to see just what is the difference between a 'rule of change', at any rate that concerning the highest acknowledged power of change, and the 'rule of recognition', at any rate, that part of it which states the highest recognized criterion for the validity of law. This point has particular significance in the context of the present debate. Earlier, I summarized Wade's understanding of the doctrine of parliamentary sovereignty (pre-1972) in these terms:

Parliament has an unrestricted and general power to enact valid law, subject to only two disabilities, namely, a disability to enact norms disabling Parliament on any future occasion from enjoying the same unrestricted and general power, and a disability to enact laws that derogate from the former disability.

Wade considers this to be, in Hartian terms, a 'rule of recognition' for the United Kingdom; more cautiously, one might say that it is or was the 'supreme criterion of validity' within the rule of recognition. This seems at first sight to put Hart's idea quite properly to use, for indeed when Hart applied his own theory to the British constitution as an illustrative example he stated that in England (*sic*) the 'supreme criterion' of recognition within the 'rule of recognition' recognized by English lawyers and in particular by English judges was this: 'Whatever the Queen in Parliament enacts is law.'[15]

The two formulae apparently say almost exactly the same thing. Looked at one way, they state or assume that Parliament has (unrestricted) power to enact any rule into law. Looked at in the other way, they state that a rule is a rule of law if it is enacted by Parliament (and, as the Wade formula brings out, not superseded by any rule enacted by Parliament at a later date). On closer inspection certainly, the formula I ascribed to Wade is explicitly about the power to enact laws (the power to change law, that is), whereas the Hartian formula puts it the other way round, and is explicitly about ascribing the status 'law' to whatever (in the way of a rule) Parliament enacts, or has enacted. It is perhaps a little uncertain whether Wade himself intends to express his point in terms of the power of Parliament to enact rules in an unrestricted way, or in terms of the overriding effect that the courts recognize to be inherent in whatever Parliament enacts. However that may be, for present purposes we may take it that there are on either Wade's or Hart's view two aspects of

---

[15] *Concept of Law*, 148. There are in English law (to which Hart confines his remarks) other subordinate criteria: what is established by way of delegated legislation is also law, and so are precedents of the higher courts. As between these other criteria, there are some priority rankings to settle which prevails in case of conflict; but necessarily rules authenticated by reference to the supreme criterion override all others.

the situation. Parliament has unrestricted power of enacting laws; the laws it enacts have to be recognized as binding by the judges.

If there really is a difference between a rule of change and a rule of recognition, the Wade formula as I stated it seems to be a rule of change, the Hart formula, of recognition. But is there a difference? Are we not simply dealing with two ways of saying the same thing? If there is a difference, there may also be a question why in Hart's scheme of things the rule of recognition is said to be the ultimate rule of a legal system. One might on the face of it argue as well that constitutions are ultimately about power and about any limits to which power can be subjected. The present popular concern is surely about the power question. Are not the deepest constitutional questions, indeed, those of law-making power? That is what is really at stake in the issue of the survival of sovereignty. Who has the final say? Parliament or Brussels? Why turn this round and look for the last answers in practices of recognition?

To see why it might be of value to differentiate two faces of essentially the same idea, postulating a distinction between rules of change and of recognition, two rules rather than one, it is necessary to reflect further on the idea of a constitution in which powers of legislation and adjudication are separated. This separation of powers is, of course, an idea that belongs to the framework of a constitutional state, to one species, we have seen, of institutional normative order rather than to the whole genus 'law'. But clearly it is the framework relevant to the present debate. Wherever such a constitution exists, by deliberate adoption at a foundational moment or by the curious process we see to have been involved in the United Kingdom, there has to be some way of ensuring that the different powers the constitution confers are exercised in a coherent way over time. For this, there has to be some reciprocal understanding among those who exercise different powers about the conditions and effects of their exercise.

A legislature in a constitutional state would fail to fulfil the function of making laws if those who administer the law fail to regard and to use as law the output of the legislature in the form of enacted rules of law. The judiciary in a constitutional state would fail to function as such if there were no executive arm ready to enforce and implement their judgements and decrees. And yet commonly, at least in their details, the organization and powers of the Courts are laid down in legislation, as are the details of the administrative law through which the executive arm has to operate. So there is a mutual interdependence. This is inevitable given that, although such a constitution achieves a certain (at least partial) separation of powers, the powers so separated are the powers of the same state that has to act with at least a minimal degree of coherence and integrity to be a functioning state at all.

In short, contemplating such a state, we need to differentiate those aspects of a constitution that confer powers, including conditions and restrictions on powers, and those that regulate the exercise of powers conferred. According to the model of a democratic, constitutional state, there have to be rules that confer powers of legislation on a legislature with a defined composition and structure elected by citizens through the use of voting rights enshrined in the constitution. There have to be rules that confer power to conduct the executive government, with power under appropriate legislation to raise (by taxation), and to spend, public money for public purposes. And there have to be rules that establish courts and empower the judges who sit in them to determine controversies of right and to preside over the trial of persons accused of crimes.

Explicitly or implicitly, those who hold the power to judge and decide cases according to law, must be provided with, or must develop through constitutional interpretation, norms that quantify their obligation to determine cases 'according to law'. What counts as law, and what is the rank order, or hierarchy, of validity-criteria? The point is that there must be a shared sense of its being obligatory to implement valid laws, and a shared understanding of what counts as valid law, and of the circumstances in which rules valid under higher-ranking criteria of validity override other rules.

An appropriate understanding or adaptation of Hart's structural account of 'legal system' does thus differentiate the power-conferring 'rules of change', 'rules of executive empowerment' (omitted by Hart) and 'rules of adjudication' from the duty-imposing 'rule of recognition', with its structured hierarchy of legal sources, alias 'criteria of recognition'. Here then we have identified a necessary condition for coherence in a workable constitution for a law-state. There has to be reciprocal matching between the criteria for recognizing valid law, and the criteria for validly exercising the power to enact law (including any special procedures required for validity of a legislative change that changes provisions of the constitution itself). This necessary reciprocal reference belongs to what some consider the inevitable self-referential quality built into systems as such.[16] It is partly dependent on convention and inevitably subject to a process of evolution over time. It involves discussion and interpretation by journalists, scholars, and citizens as well as by legislature, executive, and courts over time, the courts' interpretations carrying the especially authoritative stamp characteristic of states that abide by the rule of law. The evolutionary character of constitutional law and doctrine is particularly marked where, as in the United Kingdom, there is no single written instrument (perhaps with an appendix of valid amendments up to date) that contains the fundamental empowering rules and such limits on the powers.

So it is not only possible but necessary to draw a distinction between the rule of recognition and the rule(s) of change in a constitution. The doctrine of the sovereignty of Parliament is not itself a 'rule', but indeed a 'doctrine' with two aspects. On the one hand, it concerns Parliament's power of change. According to the doctrine in question this is a power conferred by [a rule of] common law, the power being unrestricted except under the two conditions (the two 'disabilities') noted above. On the other hand, it either concerns or cross-refers to the judges' obligation (also a

---

[16] See G. Teubner, *Law as an Autopoietic System*, trans. A. Bankowska and R. Adler, ed. Z. Bankowski (Oxford: Blackwell, 1993), 19–24.

common law obligation) to implement any validly enacted Act of Parliament as a highest source of law. But when we think of a constitution, or of the British constitution analytically, in the manner of Hart's conception of law, the 'doctrine' reappears in our ideal reconstruction of the constitution as two distinct 'secondary rules'. And it is arguable, though only on one reading of his text, that Wade has conflated the two, thereby generating the problem of the apparent constitutional impossibility of the process of accession by the UK to the EC.

Changing the rule of recognition

Having brought matters to this stage, we can now face up to one critical question about the interaction and reciprocal referencing of the 'rule of change' that empowers a supreme legislature and the 'rule of recognition' itself. The question is: can the legislature amend the rule of recognition by adding to it new criteria of recognition of valid law? Must the courts recognize and give effect to legislation that purports to bring this about? Is any special legislative process called for in this case?

There can be no all-purpose theoretical answer to this question. Certainly, nothing in the general theory of law should exclude the possibility of such change. If the rule of recognition is a central part of constitutional law, and if constitutions are amendable, then surely it is a question for the interpretation of any particular constitution whether amendment of the rule of recognition is permitted (empowered) and, if it is, by what process and procedure. Assuming the United Kingdom constitution to have at its centre the elegant simplicity of the doctrine of parliamentary sovereignty (in tandem, perhaps, with the Rule of Law), the answer would seem obvious. 'Yes. Parliament's powers include power to enact changes to the rule of recognition, but they do not include the power to change it in such a way as to disable Parliament from reversing in the future any such change that it makes.' With great respect to Wade, it cannot be true that only the judges can change the rule of recognition, though certainly they have the last word on the question whether and how any change that Parliament may purport to make should have effect.

If we looked at historical precedents such as those involved in the Reform Acts and the Parliament Acts, we would note that changes connected with the power of change, concerning the composition of Parliament and of the electorate, have always required express legislative change. For example, *Nairn v University of Saint Andrews*,[17] upheld the proposition that a major and controversial change in the composition of the electorate, admitting women to the vote, could not be deemed to have been achieved merely by implication. So legislation that enabled Universities to adopt schemes for admitting women to degrees did not impliedly confer voting

---

[17] *Nairn v University of St. Andrews* [1909] A. C. 147, 1909 S. C. (H. L.) 10; see A. C. at p. 161: 'It would require a convincing demonstration to satisfy me that Parliament intended to effect a constitutional change so momentous and far-reaching by so furtive a process' (*per* Lord Loreburn L.C., [1909] A. C. at 161).

rights on women graduates, even though, at that time, University graduates as such were entitled to a vote in the University constituencies. This decision has been sharply criticized from a feminist standpoint, but the proposition that major changes require express enactment has a certain rough common sense about it.

Bearing that in mind, let us now examine the provisions of section 2(1) of the European Communities Act 1972:

All such rights, powers, liabilities, obligations and restrictions from time to time created or arising by or under the Treaties . . . as in accordance with the Treaties are without further enactment to be given legal effect or used in the United Kingdom shall be recognised and available in law, and be enforced, allowed, and followed accordingly; and the expression 'enforceable Community right' and similar expressions shall be read as referring to one to which this section applies.

Coupled with that is the provision in section 2(4) that such obligations take effect so as to override 'any enactment passed or to be passed' by the UK Parliament.

One should not impute to the draftsman or to Parliament intimate acquaintance with Hart's jurisprudence, far less an intent to refer to it, but one may nevertheless linger a little on the word 'recognized' in section 2(1). Here Parliament instructs all persons and all officials of the state, and plainly not least the judiciary, that a new source of law is henceforward to be recognized. This is the force of: 'obligations [etc. that are] created . . . by . . . the Treaties and that in accordance with the Treaties are without further enactment to be given legal effect.' How obligations so recognized are to be ranked in competition with other sources is stated in 2(4). They have a ranking superior to Acts of Parliament passed or to be passed. Parliament in so enacting clearly envisages that its own powers (derived from what Hart calls a 'rule of change') do extend to making a change in the criteria of what are to be recognized as legal rights and obligations in the United Kingdom constitution (that is, in what Hart calls the 'rule of recognition').

This is done without conferring a new power of legal change on any agency internal to the constitution. The power of legal change with which this criterion of recognition meshes is not itself a power conferred by or in the United Kingdom constitution, however elastic the concept of 'unwritten constitution' may be. It is (explicitly) the 'Treaties' that confer the power of legal rule making (the power of change) whose output the Act obligates all and sundry in the United Kingdom to recognize.

Obviously, section 2(1) is not itself an entire 'rule of recognition' as Hart intended the term.[18] A rule of recognition may, and usually does, contain more than one criterion of validity of law, though when more than one criteria are included they are then ranked in priority. Clearly, section 2(1) inserts a new criterion of recognition into an already functioning rule of recognition, and section 2(4) indicates its ranking above other criteria. Previously, the recognized sources of law for the UK were, in rank

---

[18]   But cf. again note 14 above.

order, Acts of Parliament, acts of delegated legislation so far as interpreted to be *intra vires*, and precedents of the higher courts, themselves ranked hierarchically. Henceforward they are to include 'enforceable Community rights' in the sense defined, and these are to supersede the provisions of Acts of Parliament 'passed or to be passed'. So the criterion of being obligatory under the Treaties assumes hierarchical superiority over parliamentary enactment (perhaps one ought to expand the phrase, 'being obligatory under the Treaties within the domains of legitimate activity of the Communities as interpreted by the European Court of Justice').

The issue raised by Wade therefore transforms itself. Had Parliament power to amend the rule of recognition as it purported to do by section 2 of the 1972 Act? On the prevalent reading of the constitution as of that date, to which of course Sir William Wade speaks with high authority, Parliament could enact into law whatever it thought fit to do, except for any provision that would bind its successors. Clearly, that would have ruled out any attempt to make a change in the rule of recognition that would itself be entrenched against future repeal by Parliament. On one interpretation of the 1972 Act, it achieved or purported to achieve just this impermissible effect. If we read section 2(4) as extending the superior validity of Community obligations over Acts of Parliament 'to be passed' in future so as to rule out legislation expressly repealing sections 2(1) and 2(4) of the 1972 Act, this would clearly amount to an irrevocable transfer of power. That would convert Parliament into a subordinate legislature within some larger sovereign entity.[19]

But the very fact that this interpretation would carry such an implication is a reason for rejecting it and seeking an alternative interpretation consistent with Parliament's decision to enter the European Community by a constitutionally legitimate process, given the understanding of the constitution that was prevalent in 1972. The alternative, and preferable, interpretation is that the 1972 Act made a valid change in the rule of recognition, as it purported to do, but with the implied condition that Parliament retained its power to reverse that change. That is, there is an implied condition that it could repeal section 2(1) and 2(4) if in future it should choose to do so. This is in fact generally held to be the case. The constitution remains a customary constitution, and one can say with reasonable confidence that this power of repeal, that is of unilateral and valid secession from the EC, subsists in the constitution of the United Kingdom and is exercisable by an Act of Parliament expressly enacted to that end.

This cannot blind one, however, to the magnitude of the change that was brought to light through the drawn-out soap-opera of the *Factortame* case. The pre-1972 doctrine of parliamentary sovereignty entailed as an unquestioned corollary a doctrine of implied repeal expressible in terms of the brocard *lex posterior derogat priori*, or 'Where two laws are incompatible, the later repeals the earlier to the extent

---

[19] Dicey, of course, thought such a transfer was possible. Indeed, he considered it to have occurred historically to each of the former Parliaments of England and of Scotland when in 1707 they transferred their separate sovereignties to a new sovereign, the Parliament of Great Britain.

of the incompatibility.' Acts of Parliament being supremely valid law, if there were an incompatibility between any two Acts, or parts of them, the more recent expression of Parliament's will necessarily cancelled the earlier. If the change to the rule of recognition has been validly enacted in the sense suggested, the *lex posterior* principle must be considered overridden in relation to matters of Community law.

If this were not so, the upshot would be remarkable. Any post-1972 Act found on proper interpretation to be in conflict with any enforceable Community right would have to be held to have repealed section 2(1) to the extent necessary for the validity of the legislation in question. A case in point would be the provisions of the Merchant Shipping Act 1988 that were attacked in *Factortame*. The position would yield the following dilemma. Either the attacked provisions are valid in Community law, in which case the Spanish fishermen lose their case alike in UK law and in EC law; or the attacked provisions are invalid in Community law, in which case, because they conflict with an enforceable Community right, they impliedly repeal section 2(1) of the 1972 Act. In the latter case, they are valid for the purposes of domestic law after all, and the Spanish fishermen lose their case so far as concerns any United Kingdom court. But the UK will be found to be in breach of its Treaty obligations, that is, in breach of Community law. No doubt Parliament could and perhaps would subsequently enact laws to rectify the British breach of Community law, possibly making retrospective provision to secure the Spanish fishermen the fruits in the UK of their enforceable Community right. But that would involve precisely the kind of process that the doctrine of 'direct effect' in EC law is supposed to eliminate. It would fail to square with the arrangements to which Parliament resolved to sign up in 1972.

In the light of all that, we face some incentive to discover an alternative interpretation of the constitution that will make more reasonable sense of the decision taken by Parliament in 1972, confirmed by referendum in 1975, and subsequently upheld in the teeth of quite determined 'Euro-sceptic' opposition. Can such an interpretation be found? I believe so. What this interpretation says is that Parliament did in 1972 have the power it then exercised to amend the rule of recognition by adding a new criterion of validity at the highest sub-constitutional level. By doing so, it excluded future application of the '*lex posterior*' principle in relation to sections 2 (1) and (4) of the 1972 Act. That did not, however, involve disabling Parliament, or purporting to disable Parliament, from repealing in future the change then being made to the rule of recognition. It would follow that Parliament has power to re-amend the rule of recognition, but is only to be interpreted as exercising this power if it enacts legislation with that express purport. That is, it requires legislation expressly repealing sections 2(1) and 2 (4).

Why might the second interpretation be preferable? First, it might be said that changing a fundamental article of the constitution is a weighty matter, not lightly undertaken. Here one might indeed point to the circumstances of the passage of the 1972 Act, with the attendant controversy that led up to and was only finally dispelled or at any rate stilled by the referendum of 1975. Then further, one might point to the fact that the 1988 Act was enacted on the understanding, by no means unreasonable, that it did a lawful thing. That is, in relation to the fisheries issue, it provided a means (contravening no enforceable Community right) to protect the domestic fisheries industry by upholding the rights of the United Kingdom in respect of Fisheries Quotas allowed within the Common Fisheries Policy. This understanding turned out false because of the European Court of Justice's interpretation of the Common Fisheries Policy in the light of the Four Freedoms, according to which the Spanish fishermen did suffer infringement of an enforceable Community right on account of the material sections of the Act. It would be a perverse conclusion indeed if an Act passed with the intention to implement Community law must be assumed to have impliedly repealed the 1972 Act just as soon as it turned out that the scheme devised to protect British fishermen did not implement but contravened Community law.

Taking the opposite line on this does not involve denying that Parliament has both right and power to decide that the issue of fisheries is a make-or-break issue, and thereupon to resolve by explicit legislation to revoke wholly or in part the United Kingdom's reception of enforceable Community rights as binding and applicable domestically. Of course, this could not be done without provoking a major crisis in the Community (and Union), and most probably the European Court of Justice would hold any unilateral legislation to this effect invalid and of no effect in the perspective of Community law. In turn, the courts in the United Kingdom would then face the question whether to uphold European law at the cost of a revolution in United Kingdom law, or to uphold United Kingdom law at the cost of a revolution in Community law. These are grave choices, and it is possible to envisage circumstances in which by deliberate political decision and with a clear democratic mandate a parliamentary majority would force just such a choice by deliberate legislation directed to that very end. What would be extraordinary, however, would be if the doctrine of implied repeal, coupled with the principle that later acts derogate from earlier ones, were judged to have forced this choice upon Parliament through a concatenation of unforeseen judicial decisions in 1989–91.

There can be no doubt of the magnitude of the legal and constitutional change that was involved when the UK acceded to the European Community. So long as that accession remains in force, the legal systems of the United Kingdom interact with a 'new legal order' of a supranational kind, and incorporate into their own legal order(s) norms that are valid in that other legal order and accordingly (under section 2(1)) valid domestically as well. These norms are themselves subject to highest-level interpretation by the European Court of Justice, with its doctrine of the 'primacy' or 'supremacy' of Community law over the several laws of the member states. While the jurisprudence of the ECJ has been subjected to considerable controversy, and the United Kingdom government has sought to attack the Court's position,[20] it ought to be acknowledged that the crucial decisions about 'new legal order' and 'direct

---

[20]   See the White Paper, *A Partnership of Nations*, Cm. 3181, 1996.

effect' were all in place prior to the UK's accession. To impute to Parliament in 1972, or to the electorate in the 1975 referendum, ignorance of the EC constitution as elaborated through the Court's decisions is to suppose a quite astonishing ineptitude on the part of those who led the Parliamentary and Referendum campaigns against accession. Such an imputation cannot be squared with any reasonable practice of ascertaining legislative intent against a background of known (in this case, notorious) contemporary circumstances.[21]

Given the system that is now in place, with the parallel existence and interaction of domestic and Community law, the interpretation proposed above secures for the overall system both coherence and integrity.[22] It achieves this far better than if we adhered to the alternative that says there can be piecemeal amendment and alteration to the rule of recognition in respect of enforceable Community rights, casting doubt on the extent of their domestic enforceability on a case-by-case basis. This would be all the more deleterious given the normative framework within which the European Court of Justice operates. That framework would require it to hold that all community obligations remained binding within the UK notwithstanding the opinion of British judges that inconsistent Acts of Parliament enacted after 1972 must prevail as a matter of domestic law.

Pedigree, principle, and grundnorm

Trevor Allan has written slightingly of 'an inadequate positivist jurisprudence'. By implication, he suggests that any attempt to build a better understanding of constitutional law and theory on foundations constructed from Hart's theory of legal system is foredoomed to failure. He works from within a similar intellectual framework to that of Ronald Dworkin, and Dworkin in turn has doubted the whole idea of a legal theory that judges what counts as a valid proposition of law by reference to its 'pedigree'.[23]

The present chapter exhibits, I believe, the weakness as well as the strength of the attack on positivism and its concern with 'pedigree'. In any question about the effects of the UK's accession to the European Community, we are bound to consider what is to be the status so far as concerns the Courts of the UK of enforceable community rights. (To be exact, what is the status of any 'such . . . obligations . . . from time to time created . . . by . . . the Treaties . . . as in accordance with the Treaties are without further enactment to be given legal effect or used in the United Kingdom'?) When the UK resolved to accede to the Community, its decision had to entail that such obligations were to be 'recognized and available in law, and be enforced, allowed, and followed accordingly', for that was the very character of the Community to which the country had decided to accede.

---

[21] This is the very point that Lord Bridge of Harwich made so forcefully in *Factortame* (see n. 1 above).

[22] On 'integrity', see R. Dworkin, *Law's Empire* (London: Fontana Books, 1986), ch. 7.

[23] See R. Dworkin, *Taking Rights Seriously*, rev. edn. (London: Duckworth, 1978), ch. 2.

In turn, the character of that decision requires it to be accompanied by a decision on the issue how obligations with that 'pedigree' (in general, 'enforceable Community rights') are to stand in relation to legal norms with the distinct pedigree of being contained in Acts of Parliament. Again, the character of the Community to be joined entails that they must override provisions in Acts of Parliament to the extent of any inconsistency. And then the question arises whether it lies within the power of Parliament to enact legislation that will effect this fundamental alteration to pedigree-ranking of legal sources in the United Kingdom. Whatever be the merit of any one or another answer to that question, the question cannot be posed, let alone answered, without inquiry into what one might call the institutional rules of the constitution. These in turn are made intelligible through some general theory of legal systems and the constitutional framework of a state within the rule of law. There certainly were and are flaws in Hart's account of legal structures and in Sir William Wade's deployment of that account in relation to the present controversy. But the answer is not to abandon the enterprise on which they embarked, nor to indulge in put-downs about 'inadequate positivist jurisprudence'. It is to try to achieve a more thorough and satisfactory analysis that gets to the root of the problem about 'pedigree tests', that is in more sober language, 'criteria of recognition', and the extent of constitutional power to change those criteria within this legal system as it exists now.

On the other hand, it would be absurd to engage in some kind of a mock battle with the interpretive approach advocated by Allan and Dworkin, on the ground of some factitious —and factious—clash of schools or camps within jurisprudence. It is obvious that one can make no headway whatever with the attempt to understand a constitutional order in terms of the Hartian or similar structural accounts unless one engages in interpretive argument. That has to draw on what one takes to be the implicit principles of a constitutional order of the kind in question, interacting with a supranational community whose constitution is likewise to be interpreted in the light of the principles one takes to animate it. Our understanding of the kind of enterprise Hart was embarked on, and to which he made so large contributions, is indeed transformed when we reconsider it in the light of lessons taught by Dworkin, Allan, Guest,[24] and others of their cast of mind. But this is not, in my view, a transformation that makes redundant the foundational work that went before. The present debate brings this point out with remarkable clarity.

A further remark is necessary with a view to associating the name and achievement of Kelsen with the attempt to reach a synthesis of competing juristic tendencies at this apex-point of legal deliberation. He, after all, gave much thought to identifying the highest point in constitutional order, and the processes (if any) of constitutional change to which it is subject. The foregoing discussion of the reciprocal interaction of the highest-level 'rule of change' with the 'rule of recognition'

---

[24] See S. Guest, *Ronald Dworkin* (Edinburgh: Edinburgh University Press, 2nd edn., 1997).

suggested a way of reading, or rationally reconstructing, actual constitutions, whether written or unwritten, in a theoretically intelligible way. The upshot is that it seems difficult to acquiesce in the idea that, however you look at it, any constitution can be identified with, or said to yield a single highest-level rule to which all else is in some way subordinate.

From some points of view, most crucial is the dynamic aspect of a constitution, and the way it both empowers and yet sets conditions on legitimate change up to and including change in the constitution itself at its highest level. From other points of view, the question may be one of attempting to make sense of changes that have been made or at least attempted. Here, the critical questions focus on the 'rule of recognition', that is on new criteria of validity and how they mesh with pre-existing ones, and, in particular, what are now the obligations of the courts as they seek to do justice 'according to law'. Understanding a constitution is not understanding any single rule internal to it as fundamental; it is understanding how the rules interact and cross-refer, and how they make sense in the light of the principles of political association that they are properly understood to express. If there is a fundamental obligation here, it is an obligation toward the constitution as a whole. It is the obligation to respect a constitution's integrity as a constitution, an obligation that has significance both in moments of relative stasis and in more dynamic moments. These are moments when, in response to changing circumstances, legislators or the people in a referendum make amendments, or judges engage in interpretative adjustment of principles and doctrines in a way that may produce great constitutional change but that does not thereby amount to radical or revolutionary discontinuity.

This, I think, shows that Kelsen was right in thinking that any fundamental norm underlying the whole of legal order has to be conceived as external to the constitution itself. The constitution is a totality of interrelated rules or norms that is historically given and yet dynamic in providing for the possibility of its own change by processes for which it itself makes provision. As was argued in Chapter 2, however, there is no reason to follow Kelsen in treating this as a mere presupposition or transcendental hypothesis. Surely a working constitution requires this to be the kind of shared custom or convention held among those who treat the constitution as foundational of normative order. That is, then, a common social practice, and it is a practice that necessarily involves shared membership in what Dworkin calls a 'community of principle', not a mere chance overlap of practical attitudes among those who hold power.[25] The idea of a *Grundnorm*, it is submitted, should be adapted to this sense. It is rewarding to see that out of the fierce dialectic of thesis and counter-thesis, a rewarding synthesis can be created from ideas developed by three of the most powerful and insightful jurisprudential thinkers of the century now ending.

[25] See *Law's Empire*, ch. 6.

Sovereignty now

The conclusion of this chapter, in relation to its opening question, is in the negative. There was not in 1972 a revolution in the United Kingdom, not even in a technical legal sense. The constitutional changes that were made in 1972 are capable of being read as changes that involved the use of the 'power of change' to add a new 'criterion of recognition' to the rule of recognition. Unless this were interpreted as precluding later re-amendment of the rule of recognition by the same process, there would be no constitutional objection in terms of the constitution of 1972. Nothing forces such an interpretation, and it ought not to be accepted. There is therefore no legal discontinuity, no usurpation of power under the guise of legality.

In a less technical usage, the change made in 1972 was momentous enough to invite the label 'revolutionary', and *Factortame* does indeed dramatize the point. For the time being, sovereign power has effectively been transferred in relation to certain matters to the European Community and its organs. It nevertheless remains true, when one examines constitutional questions solely in the perspective of English law or (at least *pro tempore*) Scots law, that one can say this with confidence: The power of unilateral reversal of the change of 1972 remains vested in Parliament by the constitutional law of the United Kingdom. Yet at the same time, the very transfer of powers achieved in 1972 introduces a new player into the interpretative scene, the European Court of Justice. So far as concerns obligations arising under the Treaties, the ultimate power of interpretation of the powers transferred by the UK and other member states, and of interpreting what counts as their valid implementation, rests with the European Court of Justice.

Under the constitutional case-law developed by the ECJ, the law of the European Community is a distinct legal system of a new type, neither international law nor state law, that enjoys 'primacy' or 'supremacy' over the laws of the member states. As Lord Bridge noted, this was an established doctrine before the United Kingdom resolved to join the Community. It carries the implication that Community law as a distinct system applies to all member states, and thus to the United Kingdom, and that in the perspective of this law the obligations of the member states to respect Community institutions are determined by Community law, not national law. It is therefore a question of Community law whether the overriding effect of Community norms over norms of national law includes or does not include fundamental constitutional provisions including those that could be interpreted as preserving a unilateral power of secession.

This very issue of the extent to which Community law and the jurisdiction of the ECJ can reach into fundamental constitutional principles in the member states is one of concern in all member states, and has issued in controversial judicial decisions and juristic opinions. Perhaps it will be resolved by a deliberate declaration of Community law in terms that avoid conflict by indicating the extent to which that law holds that constitutional questions remain in the unfettered discretion of the states.[26] Or perhaps it will remain a matter without final decision, with conflicting tendencies in the judgments of state courts and the ECJ, but with an avoidance of any outright collision. In such a condition of studied indeterminacy, there remain in being two sets of interlocking and interacting legal systems that have the potential to answer the same question in mutually contradictory ways. So the answer to the question whether the states have irrevocably transferred part of their sovereign power to the Community, or have done so in a merely conditional and revocable way, may for the moment depend on whether you raise the question in the perspective of the law of a member state or the law of the Community.

In the meantime, as I shall argue in Chapter 8, the condition of the various interacting entities might be best characterized as one of 'post-sovereignty'. The Community is a non-sovereign polity or commonwealth comprising no-longer-fully-sovereign states, and the relationships of the various parts will depend in the long run on a still-to-be-elaborated principle of subsidiarity, rather than on the zero-sum game of competition for sovereignty. Alternatively, this post-sovereignty may turn out to have been a mere phase, after which either the Community or the states or regions or nations within them will emerge or re-emerge as fully sovereign entities in the classical sense. This outcome is by no means inevitable. If we in Europe do succeed in transcending the old order of sovereignties and statehoods, the process will involve abandoning through constitutional custom and in the debate of constitutional principles those 'rules of change' that preserve powers of unilateral secession from the Community. That would be a revolution indeed; but down that road no one as yet appears to have reached a final point of no return.

---

[26]   For a suggestion to this effect, and a scholarly discussion of the controversies noted above, see D. Rossa Phelan, *Revolt or Revolution: the Constitutional Boundaries of the European Community* (Dublin: Round Hall/Sweet and Maxwell 1997), discussed in Ch. 7 below.

7

Juridical Pluralism and the Risk of Constitutional Conflict

Introduction

In the context of American federalism, it is remarkable how long it took for the Supreme Court to become a really significant organ of the Union. From the very beginning the President's office was a working reality, and Congress also assumed effective legislative powers. The Court certainly laid down a marker in 1803[1] concerning the powers it was to exercise, with a significance later generations have come to appreciate well. But the decisive interventions of the Court in policing the constitution against encroachments either by states or by federal government were not part of the original making of the American union.

It has been otherwise with the forging of union (now 'Union') in Europe. Lawyers are well warned not to over-state the role of the European Court of Justice in making the various community treaties into a working reality.[2] Yet it is true that the Court's role was a decisive one. For it took key decisions on the juridical character of the European Economic Community (now known simply as the 'European Community') at a time at which there was severe tension among member states between 'supranational' and 'intergovernmental' approaches. This tension even for a time paralysed the Council of Ministers, and was more acknowledged than solved by the Luxembourg compromise of 1965. In applying legal theory (and, in particular, the conception of law as institutional normative order) to understanding the 'new legal order' that exists in Europe, the decisions on the juridical character of Community and Union have particular importance, though always with regard also to the political character of the whole, and the significance of institutions other than the Court.

Certainly, the Court's initiative was a decisive one when it interpreted the juridical character of the entity brought to birth through the foundation treaties as being a distinct legal order. This was an order of a new and hitherto unique kind, one whose norms were directly applicable and directly effective both against and in favour of natural and juristic persons within the states as well as against and in favour of the states themselves. It was the Court, moreover, that decided these directly applicable and directly effective norms were to be accorded supremacy in each state over national law. These decisions necessarily imply that the foundation treaties, as subsequently amended by further treaties, each careful to conserve the cumulative

---

[1] See *Marbury v Madison* (1803) 1 Cranch 137

[2] See P. Craig and G. de Búrca, *EU Law: Text, Cases and Materials*, 2nd edn. (Oxford: Oxford University Press, 1998), 78–9.

acquis communautaire, amount effectively to the constitutional framework of a quite special entity, this 'European commonwealth' as I later suggest calling it. What is more, the Court has elaborated the doctrine that it is the Community constitution, the normative order that the treaties establish by their own force and without the aid of international law, that confers the interpretative as well as the decisional powers that the Court exercises.

This position has been established chiefly in cooperation with the courts of the member states. Joseph Weiler has pointed out that litigation involving companies and private individuals in European law has almost invariably (and necessarily) started and finished in national courts, so that any decision handed down has had the backing of these courts, with the weight of legitimacy implied in that.[3] At any rate in the developing years of the Community, citizens of member states considered themselves unthreatened by a body of law that their own courts handed down to them. This was so, even if the domestic courts relied for their decisions on crucial interpretations provided by the European Court of Justice under the procedure for reference under Article 177 of the Rome Treaty. Hence there was a lack of any perceived imposition from without. If national courts were ready to go along with integrationist European interpretations of the law of the Community, why should citizens balk at that?

A high-water mark of this loyal acceptance of the integrationist logic of Community law was, one might suggest, the *Factortame* decision in the UK, discussed in the preceding chapter. Here, the price of judicial loyalty to integrationist doctrine in Community law was a high one, but the House of Lords was ready to bite the bullet. Norms that had hitherto been considered central to the basic doctrine of UK constitutional law, the doctrine of parliamentary sovereignty, turned out to be defeasible in favour of a weak reading of Parliament's incapacity to be bound by its own prior decisions. Injunctions ran against a Secretary of State to prevent his acting on a contested Act of Parliament, and the Act itself was in due course disapplied. After twenty years of UK membership in the Communities, the chicken wrapped up in the European Communities Act 1972 came home finally to roost.

The move from 'Community' to 'Union', or, rather, the incorporation of Communities into Community within Union, was to give rise to a weightier reaction. The Maastricht Treaty on European Union, with its adoption both of the concept of subsidiarity and yet at the same time of the concept of 'European citizenship', though initially well received, did not take long to provoke a reaction. Where other states initially ratified without too much difficulty, making any necessary constitutional amendments, the Danes, against their Parliament's advice, said

---

[3] J. Weiler, 'The Least Dangerous Branch: A Retrospective and Prospective of the European Court of Justice in the Arena of Political Integration', *Journal of Common Market Studies*, 31 (1982); cf. E Stein, 'Lawyers, Judges, and the Making of a Transnational Constitution', *American Journal of International Law*, 75 (1981), 1; for a highly critical account of the Court's approach and the problems to which it can give rise, see Hjalte Rasmussen, *European Court of Justice* (Copenhagen: GadJura, 1998), 314–50.

'No' in a referendum.[4] Following the Danish referendum, John Major's Government in the UK found itself, even after a decisive election victory in April 1992, in deep trouble with the 'Eurosceptics' in the governing Conservative Party. The government had to drag its feet for a year before enabling legislation could be carried, and then only by a pretty narrow margin. There was an Irish referendum that approved Maastricht by a reasonable majority. In France the Conseil Constitutionnel held that a constitutional amendment was required to ratify the Treaty on the ground that its provisions involved derogation from national sovereignty. The referendum required for the amendment was carried by only a narrow majority, and finally the Conseil Constitutionnel held that the decisions involved were a direct expression of the sovereignty of the French people and were not subject to further constitutional review.[5] A similar decision was reached by the Constitutional Court in Spain on the necessity for a referendum to amend the constitution and to authorize a transfer of sovereign rights by the authority of the sovereign people.[6]

Most telling of all, perhaps, was the judgment of the Federal Constitutional Court of the German Republic in response to a challenge mounted by Mr Manfred Brunner and several German members of the European Parliament to their country's purported accession to the Maastricht Treaty by due process of constitutional amendment. The Constitutional Court, the supreme constitutional tribunal of Germany, rejected the argument that the German constitution contained no power to make legitimate an accession to a European Treaty that would violate the principles of democratic government. According to the argument, the German constitution requires the German federation to conduct itself as a *soziale Rechtsstaat* organized in accordance with federal and democratic principles. Since the European Union, and within it the Community, were not properly democratic, any transfer of powers to the Union involved a transfer from democratic to non-democratic authorities, and was accordingly *ultra vires* and of no effect in law. The Constitutional Court rejected this line of reasoning, but on the rather narrow ground that no fundamental state powers were in fact transferred under the Treaty.[7]

That was all very well, and satisfactory to the Treaty's supporters. They found more troubling, however, further holdings by the Court, of which two are of special importance to the present argument. *First*, it was held that any future transfer of sovereign powers to a Community lacking in adequately democratic institutions would breach the constitution and would hence be null and void judged against the German Basic Law. *Secondly*, it was held that Community organs necessarily had restricted competence assigned by them by the Treaties, and this competence could not include a competence in any Community organ to have the power to determine

4 See A. Oppenheimer (ed.), *The Relationship between European Community Law and National Law: The Cases* (Cambridge: Grotius/Cambridge University Press, 1994), 275.

5 See Decisions Nos. 92-308 DC, 92-312 DC, 92-313 DC, English translations in Oppenheimer, *Relationship*, 385–409.

6 Case No. 1236/92; Oppenheimer, *Relationship*, 712–30.

7 Case Nos. 2 BvR 2134 and 2159/92; Oppenheimer, *Relationship*, 527–76.

the limits of its own competence. This second point, denying the existence of 'competence-competence' goes to the root of the issue about sovereignty. In German theory, the critical issue of sovereignty concerns competence-competence. Whoever has the competence to determine the limits (if any) on their own competence is truly sovereign. All other competences are necessarily subordinate or derivative.[8]

Much of the controversy concerning the Constitutional Court's judgment is directed at the second holding, and the implicit or indeed explicit assertion of a continuing sovereignty in the German people, with corresponding restriction of the powers of the organs of the European Community or Union. Particularly noteworthy was the denial by the Court that the European Court of Justice, or any other European organ, could legitimately be held to have competence over its own competence. This extended to denying that the Union as a whole could be said to have competence-competence corporately. It followed therefore that the competence to determine the competence of European organs must lie somewhere other than in these organs.

From a German point of view, the Court effectively held that it itself had this competence. The Court itself would have the final power of decision over any future question concerning the outer limit of European competence in respect of matters concerning Germany, or concerning any of the fundamental constitutional rights or powers of the German federation. It would be for the Court to uphold the fundamentals of German constitutional law, and reciprocally to determine the limits of competence over Germany of the European organs. It would not in such a setting consider itself bound to respect the opinion of the ECJ. Indeed, its own constitutional obligations would preclude it from acknowledging a competence of the ECJ so to interpret EC law that it trenched upon fundamentals of the German constitution reserved to the ultimate democratic control of the German people.

Although Mr Brunner's particular challenge to the validity of Germany's ratification of the Treaty failed, the Court thus left a marker, a line drawn in the sand, indicating that there might be future challenges that it would uphold if European organs should adopt an unduly expansionist view of their competences. There is an interesting contrast with the UK's position as analysed by the House of Lords. The Lords' holding appears to imply that, so long as the UK Parliament continues to uphold British membership of the Community, this implies upholding the supremacy of Community law and with it the interpretative competence of the European Court of Justice. This does not elide the power of the UK Parliament to decide upon a total repeal of the European Communities Act, with the effect of unilaterally seceding from the Community. An Act of Parliament to that effect would be valid in the perspective of UK law, whatever the Community organs might at that hypothetical future date think, say, or do. So, while there is a greater flexibility concerning the recognition of Community law and the extensive competence of Community organs

    [8] Cf. N. MacCormick, 'The Maastricht-Urteil: Sovereignty now', *European Law Journal*, 1 (1995), 259–66.

during the subsistence of British membership, there is again an assertion of last-resort supremacy of the United Kingdom constitution. From the Lords' point of view as from that of the Federal Constitutional Court of Germany, the reason for the binding character of Community law is the provision of domestic constitutional law that made valid the acceptance of Community membership and Community law through accession to the relevant treaties.

The same goes for other member states. For example, in Ireland the question has arisen concerning the implications of Community law on the issue of rights to obtain information about the provision of abortion within the legal régimes of other member states. Freedom to provide services might after all be presumed to carry with it freedom to provide anywhere in the Community information about services lawfully available in any member state. Freedom to provide services is, of course, one of the fundamental 'four freedoms' of Community law. On the other hand, Ireland has taken a different line about the lawfulness of abortion than that which has prevailed in the other member-states. By the eighth, twelfth, and thirteenth amendments to the Irish Constitution, Article 40.3.3 stipulates that the human right to life includes the right to life of the unborn foetus. Suppose that the validity of Community law in Ireland depends on its recognition under the Constitution, through specific amendments to the effect of adopting Community norms and competences. In that case, it is a question of Irish constitutional law whether the right of life of the foetus (or indeed other rights) would take priority over contrary provisions of Community law. The Irish Supreme Court has indicated its opinion both that this would be the correct interpretation of the Irish constitution, and that the Court's recognition of the validity of Community law is, from its point of view, required by that very constitution, expressly amended for this purpose.[9]

This is the point at which it becomes blindingly clear why the issue characterized by the Germans as that of 'competence-competence' is of such vital importance. For the point of view of the European Court of Justice does not match that of the courts in the member states. The ECJ has been author of a long line of decisions that have effectively asserted the constituent (and thus constitutional) character of the foundation treaties for the 'new legal order' that they brought into being. The large and complex body of law and practice that at any given time comprises the *acquis communautaire* is (in the ECJ's perspective, at least) valid primarily on account of the higher law of the Communities in its character as constitutional law. Hence the European Court is committed to a different conception of the basis of the 'supremacy' of Community law than that which the states' courts acknowledge, to the extent that they do reciprocally acknowledge the 'supremacy' doctrine. For them, the ultimate validating ground is found in domestic constitutional law, whereas in the view of the ECJ, the Community has its own constitutional charter to whose

---

[9] *S.P.U.C. v Grogan* [1990] I.L.R.M 350; discussed, with other relevant cases, D. Rossa Phelan, *Revolt or Revolution: The Constitutional Boundaries of the European Community* (Dublin: Round Hall/Sweet & Maxwell, 1997).

validity in its own right the ECJ is necessarily committed according to its own long-standing doctrine.

This interlocking of legal systems, with mutual recognition of each other's validity, but with different grounds for that recognition, poses a profound challenge to our understanding of law and legal system. The resources of theory need to be enhanced to help deal with a challenge full of profound and potentially dangerous implications for the successful continuation of European integration. We come to the frontier of the problem of legal pluralism, and have to reflect on solutions to the difficulties for practice implicit in the very idea of pluralism.

Groundwork: 'Law', 'Constitution', 'Constitutionalism', 'Pluralism'

The remainder of this chapter will therefore consider the character and implications of the kind of legal pluralism that institutional theory admits. The context is one in which we see ongoing challenges along the interface between the state-law systems of member states of the European Community, and the Community legal order as interpreted by the European Court of Justice.

The starting point is one of embracing pluralism. By this, is meant the idea that there can coexist distinct but genuinely normative legal orders. Two such distinct legal orders can generate different answers to the same question, for example, the question whether Henry is married to Mary and therefore not free to marry Anne, or divorced from Mary and therefore free to marry Anne. This, of course, diminishes the utility of law as a determinate guide to conduct at least in the area of conflict, for Henry must now decide whether to marry Anne or not, knowing that if he does he acts legally and validly in the perspective of one legal system, but wrongfully and without validity in the perspective of the other. Which shall he respect, which flout?

The supposition is that law in all its species belongs to the genus 'institutional normative order'. This is widely prevalent among humans, by no means confined to the context of states and their agencies. Institutional normative order, or 'law', is certainly to be discerned in the European Union, both in respect of its member states and in respect of the 'Community Pillar' of the Union, arguably also of the Union as a whole. The 'constitution' of any such order can best be defined in terms of the establishment and empowerment of the agencies ('institutions' in one sense) that perform the roles of enunciating, executing, administering or judging about the norms whose institutional character is established by the very exercise of those powers. Such establishment or empowerment is itself achieved by institutional acts, that is acts guided by norms. To avoid an infinite regress, it is necessarily the case that some ultimately empowering norms be informal and customary or conventional in character. Of course, it may be that norms originally customary or conventional in character can be reduced to writing and formally enacted; but there is always a last-line question what authorizes any such enactment. That can only bring you back either to a conventional or customary normative basis, or to first-person assessment of the rightness of upholding the order in question from the viewpoint of autonomous morality. A normative system as an element in an institutional normative order can be self-referential, and so it can happen that powers originally exercised through empowerment by custom and convention are subsequently confirmed and redefined through formal legislation, whether or not in the form of a comprehensive 'written constitution'. In a similar way, those who are called upon to act as judges under conventional or written norms can by their authoritative interpretation of their own powers and of other constitutional norms transform the character of the original empowerments involved. The reading of the Rome and related Treaties that produced the conception of European Community law as a 'new legal order' is one remarkable illustration of this, but the process is by no means out of the ordinary.

Formal empowerment of institutionalized agencies like executive, courts, legislature, depends, then, on norms either conventional or institutionally articulated. An appropriately self-sufficient cluster of such norms of empowerment is a constitution, or at any rate is the central element in a constitution. A constitution in this empowering function always and necessarily imposes conditions on the powers it confers. For the constitution, however skeletal, is always 'above' the powers it confers. Constitutionalism as a minimal virtue involves duly respecting the conditional quality of powers conferred in this way and involves observing faithfully the (interpreted) conditions of the respective agencies' empowerment. Since the example set by the first ten amendments to the US Constitution in 1789, so soon to be followed by the *Déclaration des droits de l'homme et du citoyen*, there has been a tendency to hold that constitutions do not merely (perhaps do not mainly) empower the main arms of a government, but also lay down or state the fundamental rights of those who stand before government. Sometimes, constitutionalism is taken to be specifically the virtue of respecting those rights.[10] To my mind, this is too absolutist a view concerning the type of conditions a constitution sets upon the powers it confers. Constitutions may set genuine conditions of validity without including an entrenched charter of rights. It remains a virtue to uphold these weaker validity conditions. Clearly, a charter of rights sets quite strong conditions (in my view, desirably strong ones) on the powers the constitution confers. But without conferment of those powers, nothing would be constituted nor could the rights condition any lawful governmental power, for there would be none. It is better, then, to say that the conditions of valid exercise of governmental power may be weaker or stronger, and hence constitutionalism can have weaker or stronger senses. Only in the stronger sense does it involve the strong conditions, embodying rights of human beings as well as other restrictions and restraints on the powers conferred by the constitution. For any speculation about constitutionalism in the European Union, this is the conceptual frame supplied by the institutional theory of law.

---

[10]   See L. Ferrajoli, 'Il diritto come sistema di garanzie', *Ragion pratica*, 1 (1993), 143–61, discussed in G. Pino, 'The Place of Legal Positivism in Contemporary Constitutional States', *Law and Philosophy*, 19 (1999) forthcoming.

Constitutional pluralism is relevant here, given my earlier more general remarks about normative pluralism. There are obviously contexts in which the constitution of one body can be, or be represented as, a subordinate offshoot of a 'higher' constitutional order. For example, a public University might have a constitution wholly encapsulated in, or validated by reference to, an Act of the state Parliament. Then (assuming it agreed that the University has a 'constitution' at all) it is clear that the University has a dependent and delegated constitution, dependent on the state constitution. Much more questionable would be the issue of the constitution of, say, an international church operating within a given state. No doubt such a church would have reasons of prudence (at least) to ensure that its activities conform to the state's laws, including any provisions in the state's constitution about churches and religious observations in general, or about this church in particular. But it would be problematic to represent the church in its world-wide aspect as validated by a single state (any single state). Yet as a single international or universal church it must surely have a single constitution as 'constitution' has been defined here (not as many constitutions as there are states in which it operates), and surely also it must be acknowledged to have law, 'canon law', or 'church law'. The church might well and might reasonably hold the validity of its constitution to be not conditional upon state approval in any particular state. The states in turn would be no less likely to consider themselves self-sufficient. All those within which such a church operates are most likely to consider the existence and legitimacy of their own constitution and lawfully constituted legal order to be independent of any conferment of power, or even acknowledgement or legitimation of power, by the church. That is not to say that there are not also states whose constitutional conception of their own legitimacy expressly depends on some form of ecclesiastical or religious confirmation.

So it would seem reasonable to say that here there are two sets of constitutions, each of which is acknowledged valid, yet neither of which does, or has any compelling reason to, acknowledge the other as a source of its validity. Where there is a plurality of institutional normative orders, each with a functioning constitution (at least in the sense of a body of higher-order norms establishing and conditioning relevant governmental powers), it is possible that each acknowledge the legitimacy of every other within its own sphere, while none asserts or acknowledges constitutional superiority over another. In this case, 'constitutional pluralism' prevails.

Applying the analysis

It must be obvious how the stated conceptual approach bears upon the contemporary European scene. At least on the face of it, constitutional pluralism obtains among the member states of the European Union, and certainly between them and non-members. The validity of Germany's constitution is not conditional on any grant of power by or under the Danish constitution, nor vice versa, and so on for the other member states. Certainly, in so far as each of the states is constitutionally committed to respect for international law, each at least implicitly acknowledges the legitimacy of every other, since all are legitimate and effective entities in international law. But it is open to question whether this implies a common constitutional (and thus power-conditioning) foundation for each state in international law. Here, a different view might be held from the viewpoint of the Netherlands, to the extent that the Dutch constitution grants overriding effect to all international obligations, including treaty obligations.

The European Court of Justice has declared the law it administers to be a new legal order, an order of a new kind, and has declared that this law enjoys 'primacy' or 'supremacy' over the state law of the member states (the 'high contracting parties' to the foundation treaties). In its guise as new legal order, European Community law seems at least potentially worthy to be noted as a further instance confirming the theory of constitutional pluralism. The idea of its being constitutionally dependent on the member states or any one of them is at the very least put in question by the claim of 'primacy' or 'supremacy'. The converse possibility of the states now being constitutionally dependent on the Community is difficult to square with constitutional doctrine and constitutional jurisprudence in the states themselves such as was briefly reviewed above. At this stage, one should not prejudge the question whether in the end some form of pluralistic analysis is the correct one. Certainly, any approach that precluded this possibility a priori would seem unreasonable. There is an open question here, to be answered after further due and careful consideration.

Clearly enough, we can make little progress in understanding this legally polycentric, pluri-systemic, multi-state legal order (or conglomerate of legal orders, perhaps) without some reasonably articulated theoretical framework. Yet just as the theorists have tended to neglect the problems and opportunities posed by the development of the European Union and within it European Community law, so on the other side the approach of doctrinal scholars in Community law has seemed somewhat defensive toward the need for theory.

Despite the challenge of a claim that here we have law in what is somehow a new form, maybe a new sense of the term 'law', not many scholars seem to have been stirred into deep consideration of the theoretical underpinnings of doctrinal study in European Community (hereinafter 'EC') law. Even outstandingly insightful and provocative work like that of Diarmuid Rossa Phelan seems sometimes almost aggressively anti-theoretical. The following passage from his *Revolt or Revolution* is (with respect) symptomatic:[11]

Wider perspectives are not considered, whether they be questions of justification in the sense of evaluation by, or soundness in respect of, any extra-order principles or values, comparative federalist perspectives, or legal theories. [The] 'order approach' [taken in *Revolt or Revolution*] is an extension in the context of relations between legal orders of the internal approach to law, and is humbler than considering the other approaches listed but has the advantage of trying

---

[11] Phelan, *Revolt or Revolution*, 3–4. I have omitted the author's footnote citations in the quoted passage.

to avoid the debates which surround the perspectives of justification, the mutually disputed positions of federalism and states' rightists, and legal theories.

Phelan on the whole chooses to ignore the extent to which his own position and approach belong firmly within theory. His way of dealing with the situation is not really to abandon theory, but to abstain from argument with theoretical positions other than his own. His own position is a qualified positivism. He believes that there are legal systems, and that they can each be understood from the inside, in their own terms ('hermeneutically', one might say, though he does not). A doctrinal under-standing of the rules and principles of a system so understood gives a genuine though partial picture of a social reality.

Phelan's positivism does however exhibit a qualified character only. This becomes clear when, in discussing the fundamental rights enshrined in the Irish constitution, he exhibits himself as willing to ascribe these to a source in natural law that guarantees their validity despite the presence or absence of confirming norms of enacted law. And it seems that he wishes not only to say that agents within the system think they are uphold-ing natural rights, but to give it as his own opinion that they are in fact doing so.

The 'institutional theory' gives no ground for objection to this internal-to-the-order way of approaching questions. One should, however, be careful to avoid begging the question of how many distinct orders there are; and the issue of the ontological character of natural rights had better be laid to one side at least for the moment. Subject to modest caveats of this kind, there is no reason to doubt that Phelan's theoretical approach can be thoroughly helpful for pursuit of the inquiry on which we are at present embarked. But the theoretical issue will have to be pursued more deeply than Phelan envisages. In particular, as has been said several times, deeper thought needs to be given to the question how we are to understand systems and linkages or interrelationships between them.

Community jurisprudence on Community law

From early in the history of the Community, previously 'Communities', and particu-larly in the development of the European Economic Community, the European Court of Justice ('ECJ') took a strong line in the development of the law through interpretation of the Rome Treaty and related Treaties. Critical decisions in the formative period of the Community held that the Community constituted a new legal order. First, this was characterized as a new legal order of international law. But later the concept of 'international law' was dropped, and there was said to be simply a new legal order, or an order *sui generis*.[12]

---

[12] The sequence of cases is well known: see particularly case 26/62 *Van Gend en Loos v Nederlandsie Aministratie der Belastingen* [1963] E.C.R. 1, case 6/64 *Costa v ENEL* [1964] E.C.R. 585, case 106/77 *Amministrazione delle Finanzie dello Stato v Simmenthal* [1978] E.C.R 629; for a lucid but critical exposi-tion, see Phelan, *Revolt*, 98–120.

The norms of this order include express treaty norms, norms made under powers conferred by the Treaties, and norms explicated as tools to assist interpretation of the Treaties, under the guise of fundamental legal principles applicable in EC law. These principles are founded on an appreciation of the values implicit in the Treaties and on the values of legal order inherent in the common juridical experience of the member states. All such norms have been held directly applicable and directly effective (in appropriate cases) so as to confer rights and obligations on citizens of the member states (now also 'citizens of the Union'). This law of the Community has been held to enjoy 'supremacy' over domestic law. Correlative with this assertion of supremacy has been the doctrine that the member states in acceding to the Community necessarily transferred to it a part of their 'sovereign rights'.[13]

As often happens with developed bodies of law, the path that Community law has taken now seems to have a kind of retrospective inevitability. When we see what the makers have wrought, we are apt to think, 'But how could they have done otherwise?' It is difficult indeed to imagine things having developed differently. Yet it is worth trying to exercise the required feat of imagination. What if the ECJ had held from the outset that the Treaties merely constituted a body of regional international law with specialized organs established to secure observance of it?[14] The obligations arising under this law would have been obligations of states to maintain their law in such a condition as to satisfy their international obligations. The resultant rights and obligations of individual legal persons would have been mediated through national law, adjusted by one means or another to achieve conformity with the said international obligations.

It is not inconceivable that this could have worked as a successful legal basis for achieving the economic and political aims envisaged by the states at the time of adopting the Treaties. The parallel case of the European Convention on Human Rights and Fundamental Freedoms helps make the point. That states are obligated to observe certain norms in favour of their citizens and others within their jurisdiction does not entail that these norms must have direct effect so as to be enforceable *ipso jure* in a domestic context by parties who hold their rights have been infringed. The UK's Human Rights Act 1998 indicates that there even exist ways of domesticating obligations undertaken through an international convention that leave the ultimate constitutional authority of the state's own legislative and judicial organs unimpaired thereby. For the Courts are charged with the task of so interpreting the domestic laws of the United Kingdom that they avoid, so far as possible, conflict with Convention rights (as British Courts interpret these in light of the jurisprudence of the European Court of Human Rights). In the case of any Act of the UK Parliament that the Courts find impossible to interpret as compatible with Convention rights, they are to issue a 'declaration of incompatibility'. It will then be for Government and Parliament to decide how, if at all, to amend domestic law to eliminate the incompatibility, and a simplified legislative process is available to this end.

---

[13] See *Costa* [1964] E.C.R. 585 at pp. 593–4.
[14] See the writers and writings cited by Rossa Phelan at *Revolt*, 23, and the discussion pp. 26–7.

However that may be, the European theatre exhibits two different ways of achieving common legal standards among a diversity of states, the 'Community way', the '*sui generis* interpretation' involving a 'new legal order', and the 'Convention way', the 'internationalist interpretation', where state legal orders interact with standards binding in public international law. There does not seem to be any evidence that levels of compliance with the Human Rights Convention have been spectacularly or at all lower than levels of compliance with Community law, so from that point of view one way might be considered quite as good as the other.

Would an 'internationalist' interpretation of Community law, had it prevailed, have been worse than the actually prevailing '*sui generis*' view? As of 1958, say, was one or other clearly the better answer in strictly legal terms. Even now, could one say that the view taken by the ECJ in *Costa*, *Van Gend*, and the other cases of the famous series was, after all, the wrong or a mistaken view? Or was it always right, or has time made it so? These are puzzling questions.

Plainly, the issue is not a merely arbitrary one. There are solid and reasonable arguments either way. A persuasive case can be made for the view that the implicit needs of a 'common market', an 'economic community' include a need for the same law to be in force with direct effect throughout the community, and therefore to override any conflicting or competing local law. Whoever signs up to a common market signs up to exactly such an enterprise, and the Court in determining in favour of the *sui generis* view simply draws out the implicit assumptions of the enterprise. But there is a persuasive counter-case that lays stress on the initial and continuing recourse to international treaties as the basis for the foundation and subsequent enlargement, modification, and reform of the Union. This counter-case argues that a more natural interpretation of the whole ensemble would be one rooted in international law, especially in the principle *pacta sunt servanda*.

Reasonable views reasonably stable come into conflict over an issue like this, and there will be more than two or even a few possible formulations of points in issue. That being so, we are perhaps inclined simply to say: 'Well, somebody must settle the issue, choosing among reasonable alternatives.' And this, we might further reflect, is just what happened. The ECJ did settle the matter. Starting with quite skeletal provisions in the foundation treaties, and working incrementally over time, the ECJ has built up a substantial jurisprudence in which is enshrined the *sui generis* view and a series of subordinate and satellite determinations which give body to the view. It is characteristic of such an incremental process to find that the scope for determination in later cases becomes steadily more constrained the larger the body of case-law and doctrine has grown. As the materials for interpretation expand, so the scope for acts of interpretation contracts. Question by question, the 'right answer' thesis gathers momentum, and the air of retrospective inevitability thickens.

Yet how can it be said that the ECJ has settled the matter? To say its decisions ought to be accepted as settling the question is to impute to it a normative authority to decide this and like matters. But to justify such an imputation would be to re-enter the discussion of the proper interpretation of the Treaty-constituted order, and thus to reopen a version of the question that the ECJ is being said to have authoritatively closed. There is an obviously paradoxical quality in the answer that the ECJ necessarily has this authority because it has interpreted its own authority in just this way, an obviously question-begging argument whose conclusion is already assumed in its premises. Such paradox, such question-begging, such circularity of reasoning, is perhaps built into our very understanding of system. The highest authority in any normative order can appeal to no higher positive confirmation of its own authority than that enshrined in its own jurisprudence.[15]

But the very situation we study is one in which the issue of highest or ultimate authority is itself at stake. The ECJ is not the sole actor here with pretensions to ultimate authority. The highest tribunals of the member states also belong within normative orders in which they claim ultimate authority to adjudicate, and are accustomed to approval, or at least acquiescence, in their doing so. What if they characterize the legal order of Community law in terms different from those used by the ECJ? Could they take the line that the ECJ (and other organs of the Union and Community) exercise powers delegated by the states through the Treaties, and are therefore not ultimate authorities after all, but mere delegates? Certainly, the delegation is complicated by the fact that each member state is under an obligation of international law to every other to respect on the same terms the decisions of the delegated authorities. These obligations, however, cannot logically be interpreted as including an obligation to accept as binding a decision taken under delegated authority that goes clearly beyond the proper range of the delegated power.

In *Revolt or Revolution*, Phelan poises the problem of European politico-legal development on just this deliberative fulcrum. He critically scrutinizes the jurisprudence of the ECJ in relation to the doctrines of *sui generis* legal system, supremacy, direct effect, transfer of sovereign rights, and the rest of it. He sees these as highly contentious, tendentious even; he considers them to be doctrines determined by the will of the court not by the will of the high contracting parties to the Treaties (for the Treaty texts are silent on many of the key points). He roundly rejects any notion of retrospective inevitability. The argument above concerning the tenability of the 'internationalist' conception of Community law is indeed little more than a pallid summary of an argument developed colourfully, trenchantly, and at some length by Phelan. The ECJ, he contends, could have taken a less federalist line, one less corrosive of the sovereignty of the member states, less tending towards an assertion of sovereignty for the Community, that is, of the competence of its organs to determine their own competence.

The conclusion to which the argument drives is that Europe has reached, or is teetering on the brink of, a crisis. The problem is that of a conflict of obligations. Constitutional courts, or regular supreme courts in some cases, exercise a vital

---

[15] For a valuable discussion of self-referentiality within systems, See G. Teubner, *Law as an Autopoietic System* (Oxford: Blackwell, 1993), 3–12, and see also I. Maher, 'Community Law in the National Legal Order: A Systems Analysis', *Journal of Common Market Studies*, 47 (1998), 237–54. Ms Maher kindly let me study her paper prior to its publication.

responsibility to uphold constitutional norms and in particular constitutional rights, human rights as guaranteed in constitutions. Constitutions (where not the product of custom and statute in mosaic) represent the ultimate exercise of popular sovereignty, the self-constitution of a territory's inhabitants into an organized state whose organs act under the restrictions agreed by the people, most significantly restrictions in favour of individual rights. Where a state has acceded to the Community and Union, making appropriate constitutional amendments to that end, the constitutional tribunal must undertake its task in the light of the constitutional empowerment of Community law. This will include a duty to have regard to authoritative interpretations of Community law supplied by the ECJ.

Can it, however, include a duty to accept without question the ECJ's conception of the constitutional responsibilities of the national court under the national constitution? One quite natural interpretation of the doctrine of legal order *sui generis* yields the implication that the ECJ may and must do this very thing. For the ECJ considers the obligation of the state court to be one arising directly under Community law. Yet, setting aside the case of the Netherlands, and the special place the Dutch constitution gives to treaty obligations, including the Community treaties, state constitutional or supreme courts, by an equally natural interpretation of the domestic constitution, reach a different conclusion. They hold, as we have pointed out, that their obligations derive from the national constitution, including such amendments validly made as have rendered domestically effective and applicable the norms of the Community legal order, including the norm that authorizes Article 177 references to the ECJ.

The dilemma: revolt or revolution?

National courts which implement Community law thus find themselves doing so on a ground different from that which the ECJ regards as mandating their doing so. The ECJ considers the implementation of Community law by national courts to be directly required by an EC constitution, and considers the doctrine of primacy or supremacy as applying (above all) to that constitution. The national Courts consider Community law, constitution included, as applicable only in virtue of national constitutional law. Herein lies Phelan's dilemma of 'Revolt or Revolution'. He warns that the present legal situation cannot last forever. Key test cases are bound to arise, if, indeed, they have not already arisen. The highest court in some state (or in more than one) will be driven, he suggests, to the point where one or other of two paths must be taken. Either loyalty to Community law will force them to sanction a revolution in their own state, a constitutionally unauthorized change of the constitution that will effectively transfer the people's sovereignty to organs of the Union. (According to Sir William Wade, this has already happened in the United Kingdom.)[16] Or loyalty to the constitution as expression of the people's sovereign

---

[16]   See the discussion in Ch. 6 above.

mastery of their state will sanction a revolt against the constitution of the Community, and the decisions of the ECJ that have created it.

Phelan's case for his thesis is laid out in three phases. First there is a lucid account of the evolution of the Community legal order. The author sees this as attributable mainly to acts of will of the ECJ, which have developed norms well beyond the scope of the foundational Treaties. Secondly, there is an account of French constitutional law and of the jurisprudence of the *Conseil Constitutionnel*, together with a shorter account of the posture of the *Conseil d'Etat* and the *Cour de Cassation* towards Community law as developed by the ECJ. Throughout, there is a contrast between questions of ultimate competence posed in the French constitutional perspective and similar questions viewed in the perspective of the ECJ. Direct conflict has so far been avoided, but the rationale whereby the French courts treat it as constitutional to implement Community rights and obligations is in clear contrast with the ECJ's rationale for this. There is therefore serious potential for a conflict where the difference of rationale yields contrariety of practical decision.

Thirdly, Phelan gives an extensive treatment of Irish constitutional law, and particularly the Irish constitutional jurisprudence of fundamental rights, which in turn includes the theory that these are pre-constitutional natural rights transcribed into the constitution rather than invented by its drafters. The abortion decisions have already been mentioned. Through a sequence of highly newsworthy and controversial decisions, the Irish Court and the ECJ succeeded in avoiding a direct conflict. It remains the case, however, that the Irish constitution recognizes as a human right the right to life of the human foetus, and requires its judges to uphold this. By contrast, most of the other systems within the European Union reject this, taking the more restrictive view that rights commence at birth, not at conception, and permitting abortion in various legally determined circumstances. In some states at least, there are grounds in turn for considering the legal regime in question to be one that embraces respect for a woman's right to privacy and control of her own fertility. Believers in (rival versions of) fundamental rights can find themselves here in a deep conflict over the proper interpretation of conflicting rights. If the condition of European law is not such as to leave different state-societies, different sovereign peoples, to reach their own conclusions on such issues, intolerable pressures will build up. Yet the hitherto evident ambition of the ECJ to forge a judge-made constitution for Europe points inevitably, according to Phelan, in the very direction of settling a Community-wide resolution of this and other similar issues one way or another.

Is there then a remedy? The author believes so, and puts forward a proposal in the following terms:[17]

[A] European Community law constitutional rule [ought to be] adopted to the effect that the integration of European Community law into national law is limited to the extent necessary to avoid a legal revolution in national law. The extent to which such limitation is necessary is

---

[17]   *Revolt*, 417; for supporting argument, see pp. 417–28.

to be finally determined by national constitutional authorities (such as the Supreme Court [of Ireland] or the *Conseil Constitutionnel*) in accordance with the essential commitments of the national legal order, not by the Court of Justice.

He argues that already within EC law and jurisprudence there exist adequate warrants for a development of this kind. Clearly, there may be differences of 'essential commitments' in different national systems, and these cannot but generate some lack of uniformity in the law across the community as a whole. However, this would be rendered tolerable from a Community point of view if the decisive step were taken by a ruling of the ECJ aimed at establishing a rule of EC law that protects fundamental commitments even when these are in opposed senses in different states.

This is an interesting and suggestive possibility. There is, however, one potential weakness internal to Phelan's argument, whether or not other objections can be mounted from outside of it. The author's critique of the ECJ's development of the *sui generis* view with the associated doctrines of supremacy, direct applicability, and direct effect, is firmly premised on an absence of explicit member-state consent to any such doctrines. For states such as the United Kingdom and Ireland, which acceded to the communities only some time subsequently to such decisions as *Costa* and *Van Gend*, this is not at all convincing. For these states signed up to the law of the Community as it was understood at the time of their joining. Even for original founder members, there have been several occasions of Treaty-revision which have provided the opportunity, had anyone taken it, to set out the terms of a new view that would partially repeal the jurisprudence of the ECJ and radically cut back the *acquis communautaire*. This has not been done. So one part of the case against the legitimacy of the *sui generis* view seems to be seriously flawed.

Certainly, the difficulty of defining a reduced *acquis communautaire* would be formidable, so it is not to be wondered that no Intergovernmental Conference appears seriously to have attempted such a task. In effect, the Community and its law have evolved as they have evolved. There have been controversial landmark decisions, such that at particular points in history a different (and perhaps more cautious) trajectory of development could have been traced for the Community. But these are not matters of a kind that permit the turning back of a clock to an earlier moment of decision and deeming a different trajectory then to have been traced. In some measure, the choice at any moment is thus an all-or-nothing one—to keep with the evolved system you have, or to abandon it forthwith. No state has yet raised the latter course as a serious possibility. The former is not incompatible with trying to develop new norms that set a more cautious course for the future, and a pointer in that direction may indeed be found in the provisions about subsidiarity in the Maastricht Treaty.

However that may be, it seems better to consider the character of EC law as being now settled in the general direction of the 'new legal order *sui generis*', rather than to raise the possibility of some such radically different approach as would be involved, say, in trying to restart conceptually on the basis of a purely public-internationalist reading of the treaties and sub-treaty decisions, regulations and directives. The only real question posed by Phelan's proposal is whether it could itself be reasonably accepted as a new principle developing current EC law so as to settle in a fresh way the boundary between EC law and national law. The question is one about how to settle boundaries between interacting systems on the assumption of non-hierarchical ranking between them. In the spirit of the theoretical position stated in the second section of this Chapter,[18] I shall now to take up this issue.

Constitutional pluralism or constitutional monism?

Legal systems are not solid and sensible entities. They are thought-objects,[19] products of particular discourses rather than presuppositions of them. Certainly, their existence has effects in the ordinary world. For much that people do, especially when acting in governmental roles, is guided by law or at least by beliefs about law. These beliefs include belief in the idea of law as a systemic enterprise, focused on an ordered, self-consistent, and coherent body of norms. To postulate the existence of the 'legal system' as a kind of 'regulative ideal'[20] is a way of making this intelligible. A closely connected idea is that of 'legal order', which is the kind of, or aspect of, social order that we consider imputable to the fact that people, especially when acting in official roles, orient their conduct to satisfying norms of the legal system.

The idea that there are 'governmental roles' supposes some structure of government. For this, we have to imagine that there is some kind of systematic normative conferment of competences of the kind that was earlier characterized as 'constitutional'. Hence it is a truism that those holding governmental roles must, at least in part, orient their conduct towards norms that they impute to a legal system which they represent to themselves and others as binding, that is, as one they are duty-bound to accept and implement. Legal system and government within a modern territorial state have certain distinctive features. Such a state is a coercive association, its legal order making provision for physically coercive enforcement of its norms, through forcible implementation of punishments and civil remedies for breaches of primary norms. Organized defence forces are maintained to protect against external violations of the internal order, and these may contribute also to repression of internal disorder.

---

[18] See N. MacCormick, 'Beyond the Sovereign State' (1993) 56 MLR 1–18; 'The Maastricht-Urteil: Sovereignty Now' (1995) 1 *European Law Journal*, 259–66, 'Liberalism, Nationalism, and the Post-Sovereign State' (1996) 44 *Political Studies*, 553–67; the present essay is in very similar terms to the 1995 paper, but in the meantime I have been substantially influenced by Catherine Richmond's powerful 'Preserving the Identity Crisis: Autonomy, System and Sovereignty in European Law', in (1997) 16 *Law and Philosophy*, 377–420, also in MacCormick Constructing Legal Systems: 'European Union' in *Legal Theory* (Dordrecht: Kluwer, 1997), 47–90; cf. also my own 'Democracy, Subsidiarity and Citizenship in the "European Commonwealth"', id. 1331–56 and 1–26 respectively, or see Ch. 9 below.

[19] The phrase and the concept are Ota Weinberger's. See MacCormick and Weinberger, *An Institutional Theory of Law* (Dordrecht: D. Reidel, 1986), 35–7.

[20] See J. Bengoetxea, 'Legal System as a Regulative Ideal' (1994), *Archiv für Rechts- und Sozialphilosophie, Beiheft*, 53, 66–80.

But state-law is not the only kind of law that there is. There is also law between states, international law, and law of organized associations of states such as the EC/EU, law of churches and other religious unions or communities, laws of games, and laws of national and international sporting associations. Non-state law has also the character of being institutional normative order, but not that of being physically coercive (except for rare cases of sanctions taken under the auspices of the United Nations). In general, they are not directly so, though they may become so indirectly, through the action of organs of a state-system.

The coercive and non-voluntary character of the state as an association adds urgency to the demand that it be governed according to the rule of law, and that the exercise of governmental power in the state be restrained by respect for fundamental rights. Constitutionalism is a condition of legitimacy. Among its implications are that a constitution contain both a clear allocation of powers, and a reasonable separation of them. The state has to have both legislative and judicial organs constitutionally empowered. The existence of institutions with powers of law-making, of adjudication, or of law-enforcement depends on constitutional and sub-constitutional norms of competence. These norms are themselves properly regarded as elements of the system. Yet the functions of the institutions that these norms empower include those of legislatively determining, and those of adjudicating upon and interpreting, the very norms that constitute the system, including its empowering norms. So it is both true that the laws make the institutions, and yet also true that the institutions make the laws, or make them determinate in the process of applying them. Again,[21] we note how legal systems in modern states, but also in the *sui generis* system of European community within European union, exhibit the apparently paradoxical character of being self-referential.

Yet this is not too paradoxical, for their institutional existence is only 'in part' dependent on their own norms; it is also dependent upon at least some measure of efficacy. They do not exist just because laws say who are judges and judges say what laws mean and how they are to be implemented. They exist because, and to the extent that, legal propositions are widely treated, for a bewilderingly wide range of reasons, as proper and even compulsory grounds for action and inaction, and are openly acknowledged as such, and invoked in myriad ways in all the business of life. Efficacy in this sense depends both on legitimacy in the eyes of those whom the putative norms of the system regulate; and on state organs' power or influence over the conduct of the human beings to whom the norms are addressed. The sources and forms of legitimacy, power and influence are, of course, characteristically different as between different forms of legal order. In the case of the state, with its pretension to physical coercion, coercive civil power and military power are important in securing state-institutions and obedience to norms constituting or constituted by those institutions.

The 'rule of law' element in legitimacy requires at least that laws be reasonably clear and that they be reasonably identifiable. The rule of law is not khadi-justice,

---

[21] Cf. n. 15 above.

however enlightened might be the principles on which the khadi acts in coming to particular decisions. There must be interpersonally acknowledged and reasonably determinate criteria for testing what counts as a norm (rule or principle or individual norm) of the system in question. Where there is a constitution in a formal sense, the constitution itself will contain norms that belong to law and are justiciable by the courts established in or under the constitution. Constitutional power to legislate, and to grant delegated powers of legislation, entails the validity of norms enacted by way of primary or secondary legislation, within whatever limits there are on the power of legislating. Constitutional or sub-constitutional validity is a criterion of recognition of norms as binding norms, 'laws', within a given legal system. Systems of precedent can also, but do not necessarily,[22] generate criteria of recognition of case-law rules as norms of law within a system. Where there is a multiplicity of criteria of recognition, they have to be ranked in some order of priority. H. L. A. Hart's celebrated idea about the 'rule of recognition' is nothing other than that of a judicial practice of acknowledging a common rank order of criteria of recognition, and treating as obligatory the judicial implementation of norms that are binding according to the criteria in question.[23]

Clearly, the constitutionally given power to legislate, to change law, is a mirror-image of the relevant criterion of recognition. A practice would not be one of legislation, of law-making within a system, if it did not yield norms that were acknowledged to be applicable as binding norms by the judges of that system. Validity as an enacted law is the defining consequence of a valid exercise of a power of legislation. It is a necessary condition of the binding character of an enacted norm for a judge or court.

Classically, state-law was home-made. Even when norms had an extraneous history through a reception or an inheritance from colonial rule, the mark of sovereign independent statehood was that the power to change received or inherited law was fully autochthonous, exercisable within state territory by organs established for that very state by its own constitution. The development of European Community law has wrought a profound change in this for the Member States. The Treaties, and norms validly made under the Treaties, and interpretative principles acknowledged by the ECJ, are all now recognized as part of the law of each of the member-states. Each state has amended its criteria of recognition to include validity-in-EC-law as a criterion of validity domestically. Moreover, the concept of the 'supremacy' of EC law has entailed its being a high-ranking criterion, ranking above legislation and all subordinate forms of law locally. Without such recognition, it does indeed seem doubtful whether the process of creating a common market could really have come successfully to fruition.

What is much more contestable is whether validity in EC law could be made a

---

[22] Cf. D. N. MacCormick and R. S. Summers (ed.), *Interpreting Precedent: A Comparative Study* (Aldershot: Ashgate/Dartmouth, 1997), ch. 15.

[23] H. L. A. Hart, *The Concept of Law* (Oxford: Clarendon Press, 1961), ch. 6.

criterion superior to a state's constitution itself. The norms of a constitution that facilitate its own amendment can properly be held to allow of amendment up to the point of subordinating even constitutional provisions to EC law in a hierarchy of criteria (of 'sources of law'), to the extent that a constitutional amendment expressly provides for this. But it would indeed make no sense in the perspective of a member state's legal order to hold that accession to the Community or Union necessarily entails subordinating the state's constitution as a whole package to Community law. For that would amount to holding that the criterion of EC-validity outranked the whole constitution among the criteria of validity. This would be a manifestly absurd and unacceptable interpretation of the processes of unification of Europe under the Treaties.

If the Community is to be a community of states interacting on equal terms, whatever answer is given to the question of the validity-ranking of EC law for one state system, the same will indeed have to hold good for every other. Moreover, one main purpose of the EC-system is to establish a single market on common terms among all member-states. It is therefore necessary that the common EC-norms override all rival local norms within the relevant 'material sphere of validity',[24] namely that of market-regulation. Once we have established this doctrine of the supremacy of Community law, however, the question inevitably to be posed is whether there is any need at all for an elaborate theory about interaction of distinct systems. If system X enjoys supremacy over system Y, why trouble to have a theory about separate systems, rather than a theory which acknowledges the fact that Y belongs to X as a sub-system of it? Applied stringently, this leads to the view that in the Europe of the European Union there is but a single legal system, with as many sub-systems as there are member states. This has echoes of Kelsen's theory of legal monism,[25] one reading of which holds that there is essentially one legal order in the World, that of international law together with the totality of national systems that are, in effect, sub-systems of the international system. For contemporary Europe, this could hold good only with the added complexity that the Community legal order alone is a sub-system of international law, validated by the international law norm *pacta sunt servanda*, while the state systems, validated by Community law, would constitute sub-sub-systems. Other readings could suggest, for example, that international law continues to be the ground of validity of member-state law, while these systems jointly validate community law, which is then the sub-sub-system. Perhaps most credibly of all, it might be held that in a coordinate way, international law functions as a common ground of validity both of member-state systems and of Community

---

[24] The idea of a 'material sphere of validity' is Kelsen's. See H. Kelsen, *The Pure Theory of Law* (trans. M. Knight) (Berkeley and Los Angeles: University of California Press, 1967), 316–17.

[25] See H. Kelsen, *The Pure Theory of Law* (trans. M. Knight) (Berkeley and Los Angeles: University of California Press, 1967), 328 ff.; and compare Richmond, above n. 17 for a brilliant analysis, appreciation, and deployment of Kelsen's idea. My own account here remains considerably less thorough than Richmond's. For a broader discussion, cf. S. L. Paulson and B. L. Paulson (ed.), *Normativity and Norms* (Oxford: Clarendon Press, 1998), 525–81 (papers by Kelsen, J. G. Starke, and H. L. A. Hart).

law, neither being therefore a sub-system of the other, but both cohering within a common legal universe governed by the norms of international law. Since this position involves pluralistic relationships between the law of the Community and the member-states (and among the states *inter se*), albeit within a 'monistic' framework of international law, I shall in subsequent discussion refer to this position as that of 'pluralism under international law'.

What is not convincing in relation to the EC is the picture that holds the legal orders of the member-states to retain validity only through the mediation of EC law. This does not square well with the fact that the effective legislature for the Community is the Council of Ministers, whose members are identifiable only by reference to the place they hold according to state-systems of law. So Community powers of legal change and criteria of validity presuppose the validity of competences that are conferred by state-systems but not otherwise validated by EC law. Nor does it square with the fact that the process of constitutional amendment for both Union and Community remains a process of treaty-making among member-states. Yet more generally, the institutional theory of law insists on a degree of sociological realism, hence is not in the Kelsenian sense a pure theory. From this point of view it is clear that institutions of state law look to the state legal order for confirmation of their competences. They do not treat this as contingent upon ulterior validation or legitimation by the Community. And in turn Community institutions look to the foundation treaties as sufficient for their validation, without further reference to member-state constitutions.

A pluralistic analysis is in this instance, and on these grounds, clearly preferable to the monistic one that envisages a hierarchical relationship in the rank-order International law—Community law—Member-state law. Accordingly, the doctrine of supremacy of Community law should by no means be confused with any kind of all-purpose subordination of member-state-law to Community law. Rather, the case is that these are interacting systems, one of which constitutes in its own context and over the relevant range of topics a source of valid law superior to other sources recognized in each of the member-state-systems. Moreover, the power that the ECJ exercises of interpreting Community law as binding in member states entails in its exercise a competence to interpret the norms conferring this interpretative competence, and thus an interpretative, as distinct from a norm-creating, competence-competence.

There seem to be only two reasonably arguable analyses of the situation that obtains among the states and the Community and Union. I shall call these respectively 'pluralism under international law', and 'radical pluralism'. Both are pluralistic in the sense that they deny the constitutional dependency of states on each other or of states on the Community. No state's constitution is as such validated by that of any other, nor is it validated by Community law. For each state, the internal validity of Community law in the sense mandated by the 'supremacy' doctrine results from the state's amendment of constitutional and sub-constitutional law to the extent required to give direct effect and applicability to Community law. On the other hand, the Community's legal order is neither conditional upon the validity of any particular state's constitution, nor upon the sum of the conditions that the states might impose, for that would be no Community at all. It would amount to no more than a bundle of overlapping laws to the extent that each state chose to acknowledge 'Community' laws and obligations. So relations between states *inter se* and between states and Community are interactive rather than hierarchical. The legal systems of member-states and their common legal system of EC law are distinct but interacting systems of law, and hierarchical relationships of validity within criteria of validity proper to distinct systems do not add up to any sort of all-purpose superiority of one system over another. It follows also that the interpretative power of the highest decision-making authorities of the different systems must be, as to each system, ultimate. It is for the ECJ to interpret in the last resort and in a finally authoritative way the norms of Community law. But equally, it must be for the highest constitutional tribunal of each member-state to interpret its constitutional and other norms, and hence to interpret the interaction of the validity of EC law with higher level norms of validity in the given state system.

Where then lies the difference between pluralism under international law and radical pluralism? The answer depends on the relationship between the Community systems and international law. Granted that the relationships between the states and the Community are 'interactive rather than hierarchical', does the same obtain as between states and Community on the one hand and international law on the other? According to pluralism under international law, the obligations of international law set conditions upon the validity of state and of Community constitutions and interpretations thereof, and hence impose a framework on the interactive but not hierarchical relations between systems. According to radical pluralism, these obligations simply give a third perspective on the relationships in question, a further non-hierarchical interacting system. Which view is preferable?

Whatever answer is given to this question, it has to be sensitive to the weight attached to the *sui generis* interpretation of Community law in the jurisprudence of the ECJ. Community law is self-interpreted as being something other than a mere regional subset of norms of international law, and unless this were to be shown untenable or absurd, a theoretical account of the totality of juridical relationships in Europe should seek to accommodate it. We should therefore presume a distinctness of legal systems between international law and Community law. The constitution of the Community commenced as an international treaty, but became internalized into a self-referential legal system. There are precedents for this, for example, the United Kingdom, which was founded by a treaty between the Kingdoms of England and of Scotland, but which became through this process a single state, not an international community. The Community is of course a polity or commonwealth different in kind from a state, so the analogy is imperfect. But it is not on that account irrelevant.

The imperfection of the analogy lies, of course, in the fact that within the Community (by contrast with internal relations in the UK) the 'High Contracting

Parties' remain distinct parties in international law, and that is part of the difficulty with which we are wrestling. It does follow, though, that they are subject to obligations of international law among themselves in respect of the treaties they have agreed. The treaties in question have had the effect of constituting a new legal order *sui generis* that could not now be lawfully repudiated by any of the members, though it could be dissolved or radically changed in character by treaty amendment. The good reasons that we have for conceptualizing the relevant relationships in favour of a coordinate rather than a hierarchical interaction between EC legal order and member-state legal order are not reasons for denying that this coordinate relationship is itself subject to norms of international law. Hence the validity and partial mutual independence of EC law and member-state law is authorized by (public) international law. If international law were assumed as conditioning the validity of the legal orders respectively of member states and of Community, the same thesis as to the coordination without subordination of legal orders would be available within pluralism under international law as under radical pluralism. (Here, one should note again that 'pluralism under international law' would be an instance of 'monism' in Kelsen's sense, though he was never able himself to contemplate the kind of *tertium quid* between international and municipal law that the Community constitutes according to the '*sui generis*' interpretation here endorsed.)

A pluralistic analysis in either of these senses shows the systems of law operative on the European level to be distinct and partially independent of each other, though also partially overlapping and interacting. It must then follow that the constitutional court of a member-state is committed to denying that its competence to interpret the constitution by which it was established can be restricted by decisions of a tribunal external to the system. This applies even to a tribunal whose interpretative advice on points of EC law the constitutional court is obligated to accept under Article 177. Conversely, the ECJ is by the same logic committed to denying that its competence to interpret its own constitutive treaties can be restricted by decisions of member-state tribunals.

Under radical pluralism, that is all that is to be said as a matter of law. Acceptance of a radically pluralistic conception of legal systems entails acknowledging that not every legal problem can be solved legally. The problem in principle is not that of an absence of legal answers to given problems, but of a superfluity of legal answers. For it is possible that the European Court interprets Community law so as to assert some right or obligation as binding in favour of a person within the jurisdiction of the highest court of a member state, while that court in turn denies that such a right or obligation is valid in terms of the national constitution. The problem is not logically embarrassing, because strictly the answers are from the point of view of different systems. But it is practically embarrassing to the extent that the same human beings or corporations are said to have and not have a certain right. How shall they act? To which system are they to give their fidelity in action?

Resolving such problems, or, more wisely still, avoiding their occurrence in the first place, is a matter for circumspection and for political as much as legal judgment.

The ECJ ought not to reach its interpretative judgments without regard to their potential impact on national constitutions. National courts ought not to interpret laws or constitutions without regard to the resolution of their compatriots to take full part in European Union and European Community. If conflicts despite this come into being through judicial decision-making and interpretation, there will necessarily have to be some political action to produce a solution.

In this light, there seems much to be said for Phelan's proposal about the future development of European law at the junction point between Community law and member-state law. The radical pluralist thesis suggests that neither can or should claim all-purpose supremacy over the other. It would therefore be of value for all participants to make this explicit in some way. Something along the lines suggested in *Revolt or Revolution* might do the trick admirably.

But pluralism under international law suggests that we need not run out of law (and into politics) quite as fast as suggested by radical pluralism. The potential conflicts and collisions of systems that can in principle occur as between Community and member-states do not occur in a legal vacuum, but in a space to which international law is also relevant. Indeed, it is decisively relevant, given the origin of the Community in Treaties and the continuing normative significance of *pacta sunt servanda*, to say nothing of the fact that in respect of their Community membership and otherwise the states owe each other obligations under international law. A part of the legal considerations that ought to bear upon the deliberations of both state courts and the ECJ is regard for these mutual obligations. To take account of this would lead one to qualify in an important way any proposition along the line suggested by Phelan. Simply to remit to state courts an unreviewable power to determine the range of domestic constitutional absolutes that set limits upon the domestic applicability of Community law would seem likely to invite a slow fragmentation of Community law. Yet it is a clear mutual international obligation of states not to fragment the Community by unilateral decisions either judicial or legislative (or, for that matter, executive).

Phelan's proposal if adopted raw would give an unsatisfactorily unbounded discretion to state courts in permitting, for the sake of the domestic constitution, limitation of the local effectiveness of Community law. The terms in which he suggests this are:

The extent to which such limitation is necessary is to be finally determined by national constitutional authorities (such as the Supreme Court [of Ireland] or the *Conseil Constitutionnel*) in accordance with the essential commitments of the national legal order, not by the Court of Justice.

Surely this is much too strong, and ought at least to carry the qualification 'in accordance with international obligations to other member states and in accordance with essential commitments of the national legal order including the commitment to good faith observance of international obligations'. What that signals in the first instance is that state Courts have no right to assume an absolute superiority of state constitution over international good order, including the European dimension of that good order. This is not the same as saying that they must simply defer to whatever the ECJ considers to be mandated by the European constitution. For its reading of that constitution and the state Court's reading of its own constitution ought both to have regard to the international obligations which still subsist notwithstanding, or indeed because of, the fact that Community law is a 'new legal order *sui generis*'. Such an approach would help to diminish the risk of normative collisions. But in the event of an apparently irresoluble conflict arising between one or more national courts and the ECJ, there would always on this thesis be a possibility of recourse to international arbitration or adjudication to resolve the matter.

At one time, I was on the whole persuaded by the position that I have here called 'radical pluralism'. For the reasons here indicated, it now seems that the thesis of 'pluralism under international law' is contextually more persuasive and appropriate. Although this is a kind of 'monism' in Kelsen's sense, I remain of the opinion that the correct understanding of the interaction between different normative systems is a contingent matter, not one that flows from the very concept of normative order. This chapter has considered whether, in conditions of pluralism, collisions are inevitable. The answer is that they are possible, but not inevitable. How likely they are depends on the wisdom with which interested parties approach problem-situations, and the theoretical resources available to them in approaching them. Under the approach suggested, they are not incurable in the event that they do occur, and there are ways of actively avoiding them by advance precautions that fall well short of forcing an amalgamation of plurality into flat unity.

8

On Sovereignty and Post-Sovereignty

Introduction

The world of modernity owes much to the epoch of reformation and religious wars in sixteenth- and seventeenth-century Europe. Elizabeth Tudor won it a certain insular safety in her long reign in England, but the Sweden of the Vasa dynasty was its first and founding guarantor in Northern Europe. Not until the Peace of Westphalia in 1648 was it settled that the new order would prove durable. At a conference on argumentation in Lisbon some years ago, Stephen Toulmin made a remark that left a great impression with me. He remarked how significant was the date of birth of Gottfried Wilhelm Freiherr von Leibnitz—in 1646. So Leibnitz was just 2 years of age as the Peace of Westphalia was being signed. It is from Leibnitz, perhaps second only to Descartes, who died in Uppsala in 1650, that what is now known and often criticized as 'foundationalism' in philosophy descends. Foundationalism seeks a starting point in something interpersonally certain and indubitable from which to carry forward the search for reliable forms of knowledge. Toulmin found it only too natural that a Europe weary with thirty years of religious war should be hospitable to philosophies offering some common ground of indubitable certainty, above or below the level of all the religious controversies. The persuasive character of Cartesian or Leibnitzian foundationalism was, he suggested, the outcome of that longing.

Toulmin's speculation is a pleasing one. Yet however tempting it is in relation to metaphysics, all the more plausible would be its analogue in relation to politics. Immediately, Leibnitz's older contemporary Thomas Hobbes springs to mind as candidate founding foundationalist for political theory. It is difficult to be sure whether we would better call him an absolute foundationalist or a foundational absolutist. For Hobbes, absolute state-power, absolute sovereignty, was (as remarked in Chapters 2 and 5) the necessary condition for stable politics and indeed for human safety. The fundamental question is about the founding of absolute state-power. Although this power has to be founded on the common agreement of all who are subject to it, the sovereign constituted by the foundational compact cannot be limited by its terms. For the sovereign is not one of the parties to the bargain, but the one who stands over it guaranteeing it with the power of the sword. 'Covenants without swords are but words', we recall.

Religion, in Hobbes's view is simply an adjunct of state-power, not a coordinate base of, far less a higher source for, state authority. Uppsala, with the castle on the hill addressing its cannonry towards the Cathedral in the valley might almost have been designed to illustrate the Hobbesian thesis on church–state relationships.

Perhaps Gustavus Adolphus and his clan would have found little in Hobbes's work with which to disagree.

To be sure, the odd thing about Hobbes's version of the original social contract is the way he turns it into the basis for absolute royal or parliamentary-oligarchical authority. Here, he went against contractarian predecessors, such as George Buchanan, who derived limits on the kingly power from the myth of a foundational compact. *In De Iure Regni apud Scotos*,[1] Buchanan argued that in the Baltic countries and in Scotland there uniquely survived kingdoms based on the choice and consent of the populace rather than on external conquest. In such polities, he argued, royal or governmental power is always subject to the limits expressly or impliedly put upon it by the people as, generation by generation, they confirm the title to rule of the next representative of the same old royal line.

The basic idea in Buchanan's account has had influence on posterity only via the distorting mirrors first of Locke and subsequently of Rousseau. Distinctively, it accords true sovereignty ultimately to the people on whose will depends the legitimate authority of constitutional rulers and Parliaments. In Locke's version, though, the people act to protect their natural rights to life, liberty, and estate. These rights are derived from a higher law of reason, and that higher law in turn places restrictions on the absoluteness of any claim to legislative sovereignty, even, we must suppose, the sovereignty of the people acting collectively against any individual of their number.[2]

On the whole, and certainly in Britain, state practice seems to have owed more to the doctrine of Hobbes, through his successors such as David Hume, Jeremy Bentham, or John Austin or, in constitutional law, A. V. Dicey, than to the Lockean school. Elsewhere in Europe, Hegelian versions of state absolutism, however unfaithful to the original thought, tended to prevail in the nineteenth century and into the twentieth. In Sweden, the influence of the Uppsala school[3] no doubt brought about the abandonment of Hegelian voluntarism as well as Hegelian idealism. But the residual idea of law and indeed of morality as conformity to settled patterns of behaviour upheld by power of an ultimately physical kind was no less hospitable to the idea of an unchallengeable sovereignty in the state.

In all these traditions, the modern state has been portrayed as the stark alternative to anarchy at home and abroad. The absolute power of the sovereign state has been the foundational doctrine for political theory and practice. No doubt the French revolution was one defining moment in this process. But in the North the

---

[1] See G. Buchanan, *The Art and Science of Government among the Scots* (trans. D. H. MacNeill, Glasgow: William Maclellan and Co, 1964); there is a surprising lack of scholarly editions and translations of Buchanan's work.

[2] This is discussed in a more elaborate way, and with citation of source, in Ch. 2 above.

[3] This is the group of philosophers and jurists who took their intellectual lead from Axel Hägerström, best known in English language sources through Karl Olivecrona's *Law as Fact*, 1st edn. (London: Humphrey Milford/Oxford University Press, 1939; 2nd edn. London: Stevens, 1971); see also Hägerström, *Inquiries into the Nature of Law and Morals*, trans. C. D. Broad, ed. K. Olivecrona (Stockholm, Almqvist & Wiksell, 1953).

origins are, I suspect, older. We might not go far wrong if we located them in the form of post-reformation kingdoms that emerged with Leibnitz into the light of day at the end of the Thirty Years War.

Whenever we should date the emergence of the sovereign state, and wherever we may locate its first emergence, it seems that we may at last be witnessing its demise in Europe, through the development of a new and not-yet-well-theorized legal and political order in the form of the European Union. If that were so, would it be a cause for concern or for satisfaction? On the side of concern, even alarm, there are two lines of thought, one nationalistic and the other democratic. The nationalistic one deplores the erosion of national independence and self-determination. The democratic one recalls the point made by contractarians about the popular sovereignty that may be taken to underlie the sovereignty of the state. In truth these two run together, for the relevant version of democracy locates the ultimate source of legitimacy in a people as in principle a pre-political entity. National self-determination similarly alludes to the people as a pre-political body, and asserts each people's right to determine its own destiny through its own processes of decision-making. The great revolutions, particularly in America and in France, gave dramatic expression to these basic ideas. The overthrow of misruling monarchs restored sovereignty to the people, who constituted themselves into a state or union of states through adopting a constitution by common consent. The sovereign state or union asserted itself as a nation state, the property of its sovereign people.

So if the sovereign state is a democratic state, concern about sovereignty is also concern for democracy. Can sovereignty be lost without abandoning popular self-government? Can it be lost without breaking the democratic faith? This fear is held in common among those Europeans, perhaps more numerous in the Nordic countries and the UK than farther south, who are sceptical of the possibility of democracy being realizable in a Europe that is not a super-state. Yet these same people are all the more repelled by the idea of such a super-state. In the same vein was the argument of the German petitioners who challenged the Maastricht treaty, in the manner discussed in the preceding chapter, as requiring an illegal abandonment of the democratic form of government guaranteed in the German constitution.

The Court did not agree that the Maastricht treaty had that effect, but one of the theses it stated, not hitherto taken into account, was that there could not be a democratic European Union without the emergence of a self-determining European *demos* or *Volk*. Pending further evolution of popular European consciousness, there could not lawfully be any further radical transference of power to European organs.[4] The powers already transferred must be confined within the carefully delimited spheres marked out by the Union Treaty and its predecessors. In line with this, the Constitutional Court declared itself ready to

---

[4]   See J. H. H. Weiler, 'European Neo-constitutionalism: in Search of Foundations for the European Constitutional Order', *Political Studies*, 44 (1996), 517–33 at pp. 522–5.

draw lines beyond which decisions of the European Court of Justice would be unacceptable for implementation in Germany. In short, the Court asserted a continuing German sovereignty, and did so in the light of its particular constitutional duty to uphold the democratic character of the state constituted by the Grundgesetz, the German 'Basic Law' of 1949.

Perhaps we should not be too ready, then, lightly to embrace the demise of sovereignty either as already accomplished fact or as consummation devoutly to be wished. Yet we cannot be so sure, for there is another side. The international order of sovereign states has been a bloody one, marked by struggles over the establishment and maintenance of empires. Sweden and Switzerland practically alone succeeded in holding aside from interstate violence on a catastrophic scale during the two most recent centuries. It is easy to understand a special reluctance in such countries to give up an independence so prudently exercised. Yet the example from all around does not make it seem that mere nostalgia for lost sovereignties, or zeal for establishing new ones in the old mode, is necessarily a happy posture. It is a serious issue whether it is possible to envisage a world 'beyond the sovereign state' in which new types of legal and political interaction come into being that exclude claims of out-and-out sovereignty either from old states or from new communities devised to reorder economic and political coexistence. Could we advance in peace and prosperity without losing popular democracy?

The key question becomes whether there can be a loss of sovereignty at one level without its inevitable and resultant re-creation at another. Is sovereignty like property, which can be given up only when another person gains it? Or should we think of it more like virginity, something that can be lost by one without another's gaining it—and whose loss in apt circumstances can even be a matter for celebration? This book is dedicated to the latter view. The case to be made here is one welcoming the prospect of Europe beyond sovereign statehood. The idea of subsidiarity points us to better visions of democracy than all-purpose sovereignty ever did. There is a possible future reality preferable to the past of nostalgic mythology.

My argument depends on a careful analysis of basic ideas. Much of the argument up to this point has been posited on the distinction drawn between political and legal forms of power. If that distinction holds, and if sovereignty is a form of power, then there is merit in the old idea that sovereignty has both a political and a legal form, which are not necessarily the same thing. A related, but not identical, distinction is that between sovereignty internal to a country and that same country's external sovereignty *vis-à-vis* other states or relevant international entities. This distinction between external and internal sovereignty is what makes it possible to contemplate division or limitation of sovereign power. Armed with these distinctions, we can reflect on the reasons why neither member states nor the European Union of which they are members can strictly be said to enjoy sovereignty at the present time. Finally, reflection upon subsidiarity and democracy will help assuage any alarm the conclusion about sovereignty may have aroused.

Sovereignty, legal and political

What is 'Sovereignty'? Let me recall an earlier quoted remark by A. V. Dicey:[5] whereas as a 'merely legal conception', sovereignty is 'the power of law-making unrestricted by any legal limit', by contrast 'that body is "politically" sovereign or supreme in a state the will of which is ultimately obeyed by the citizens of the state'. Power without restriction is on this view the key idea. Power of one kind, normative power or 'authority', is conferred by law. This may be a power of law-making in a certain territory conferred by a certain constitutional order that is effectively observed in that territory. Sovereign power is that which is enjoyed, legally, by the holder of a constitutional power to make law, so long as the constitution places no restrictions on the exercise of that power (though, necessarily, the constitution must define what counts as a valid exercise of the power, and judges may have to satisfy themselves in problem cases that the validity-conditions have been satisfied, and this may involve problematic interpretation of the constitutional validity-conditions).

If the constitution then confers such a power but contains no limit upon the power (other than the discretion and judgement of those who exercise the power) we may say that sovereignty is vested in the holder of the law-making power.

But what of political sovereignty? By parallel reasoning, one would be inclined to define it as political power unrestrained by higher political power. We recall the elucidation offered of political power. Political power is interpersonal power over the conditions of life in a human community or society. It is the ability to take effective decisions on whatever concerns the common well-being of the members, and on whatever affects the distribution of the economic resources available to them. The taking of such decisions has important bearing on the reasons that guide the actions of people in their social intercourse with each other.

As between human beings, power of one over another, or over others, is the ability within some determinable context to take decisions that affect that other's (or those others') interests regardless of their consent or dissent. When one has power so defined, one is also able to affect the other's reasons for action. Someone who has power over another is able to impose on that other reasons for action or inaction that would not otherwise have existed. Since people often act in accordance with the reasons they have for acting, it follows that having power means being able to get people to do things, to act as they might not otherwise have acted. Exercises of power affect the way in which it is rational for people to act.

Sovereign power is, then, territorial in character, and is power not subject to limitation by higher or coordinate power. It is material to consider which of the two species identified, political or legal sovereignty, has priority. Is ultimate political power a precondition of ultimate legal authority, or vice versa? The tradition

---

[5] *Law of the Constitution,* 27, discussed above, Ch. 5.

of Hobbes, carried on by Austin,[6] reconceptualized in the Germanic tradition by Carl Schmitt, unhesitatingly ascribes primacy to the political. However it comes about that one person or group is habitually obeyed by others, thereby acquiring the power to enforce physical sanctions over any recalcitrant elements, the person or persons who hold this position are able to issue commands to others within their society, and those commands are laws.[7] Legal authority established by such commands is evidently secondary to political power. Law is then dependent on political sovereignty. Only a sovereign person or group, absolutely sovereign at home, independent of any purported external power, can be an authentic source of law. In Schmitt's version, the key to the ultimate basis of law lies in the question who can exercise effective power on behalf of a whole community in states of emergency or 'states of exception' when ordinary legal provisions break down or prove inadequate.[8]

Persuasive and illuminating though such accounts may be for some types of politico-legal order, they have been found wanting in respect of those situations in which there is a standing constitutional tradition. Under such a tradition, the powers of state are effectively divided according to a constitutional scheme that is respected in the practical conduct of affairs. There is then a difficulty in identifying any sovereign being or sovereign entity holding power without any legal limitation. Confronted with the example of federal states, Austin in particular was driven back to analysing such cases, in particular the USA, in terms of the sovereignty of the people (or, at least, of the actual electorate whose members can amend the constitution). The difficulty is that the account then becomes circular, since one has to assume the validity of the constitution in order to explain how the people can carry out an act of amendment as a binding and effective legal act.

For the case of the *Rechtsstaat*, law has to be explained in terms that do not presuppose the prior existence of an absolute political sovereignty. I am happy to suggest such terms. Law, as stated above, is an institutional system of rules or norms involving both duties which are required of legal subjects and powers vested in legal institutions holding legislative, executive, or judicial power. Legal systems so understood do not only and do not necessarily exist in states. There are non-state systems of law, such as for example Canon law, public international law, the specialist international law represented by the European Convention on Human Rights, and the law of the European Union, and other less presently relevant forms of law as well. But the point of the *Rechtsstaat* is that it is a state which has law, and in which law regulates and restricts the conduct of political officials as well as citizens, presupposing no monolithic political sovereign power outside or above the law. Where a 'law-state' in this sense exists, it is presumably explicable in terms of a political practice

---

[6] J. Austin *The Province of Jurisprudence Determined*, ed. H. L. A. Hart (London: Weidenfeld & Nicolson, 1954), chs. 1 and 6.   [7] Ibid., as cited.

[8] C. Schmitt, 'Was bedeutet der Streit um den Rechtsstaat?', *ZStW* 95 (1935), 189; cf. D. Dyzenhaus, *Legality and Legitimacy: Carl Schmitt, Hans Kelsen and Hermann Heller in Weimar* (Oxford: Clarendon Press, 1997), chs. 1 and 2, esp. at p. 54.

and tradition within which a constitution and a broadly shared approach to constitutional interpretation are accepted.

This seems to show that sovereignty is neither necessary to the existence of law and state nor even desirable. A well-ordered Law-State or *Rechtsstaat* is not subordinated to any political sovereign outside or above the law, nor is it necessarily constructed around some constitutional organ which enjoys sovereignty conferred by law. Certainly, the classical theory of the British constitution ascribed sovereignty to the monarch in Parliament, or, more summarily, to Parliament itself. This was held to be a doctrine of the common law, and to be advantageous as a legal dispensation on the ground that it secured the political sovereignty of the electorate. But such supreme legal power ascribed to a single organ is not necessary even in a unitary state, and is incompatible with the very frame of government of a federal state.

Nevertheless, before dismissing sovereignty out of hand, we need to reflect on a further distinction, that between internal and external sovereignty. As was stated above, sovereignty is power not subject to limitation by higher or coordinate power, held independently over some territory. It is clear that this could apply in two different ways. If we look at a state in terms of its internal ordering, we may ask whether there is any person who enjoys power without higher power internally to the state. Either in the political or in the legal sense, we may discover that all power holders are subject to some legal or some political checks or controls. In that case, there is no single sovereign internal to the state, neither a legal nor a political sovereign.

On the other hand, we might survey the same state from the outside, considering its relations with other states and international or religious or commercial organizations. We might conclude that in this perspective a state, whatever its internal distribution of legal or political power, is a 'sovereign state' in the sense that the totality of legal or political powers exercised within it is in fact subject to no higher power exercised from without. What we shall therefore call 'external sovereignty' characterizes a state which is not subject to superior political power or legal authority in respect of its territory.

Politically, this enables us to distinguish a fully or substantially independent state from a mere satellite or client state which, even if legally independent, has no effective independent power of decision. In a legal sense, external sovereignty is the authority granted by international law to each state to exercise legal control over its own territory without deference to any claim of legal superiority made by another state or organization. This is coupled with the right under international law to be free from the exercise of military power or political interference by other states.

External sovereignty is thus distinct conceptually from internal sovereignty, and may be present even when in the strict sense internal sovereignty is absent.

These distinctions make it possible to account for the concept of 'divided sovereignty', which some theorists, such as Austin and Schmitt, have taken to be a contradiction in terms. They were anxious to argue that nothing which has supreme power can coexist with a rival supreme power in any stable way within a single legal or political order. From their point of view, it was certainly misleading to say that the organ or institution which has the ultimate power of decision over a certain range of topics is sovereign over those topics, while other organs and institutions are sovereign for other purposes. The doctrine of sovereignty was a doctrine of the unity of states and of the unity of governmental functions within them. As such, it was a significant element in the drive towards modernization and the development of unified territorial states in place of the more fragmentary feudal forms of ancient kingdoms and empires. For the same reason and in the same way, they were unenthusiastic both analytically and politically about the idea of limited sovereignty.

Nevertheless, the distinction of external and internal sovereignty shows that even a strict definition of sovereignty permits a sense of divided or limited sovereignty. The point is this. A state that is sovereign in the external sense may have a constitution under which no full sovereign power is possessed by any organ of state. The external sovereignty of the state may be, so to say, internally distributed among organs of state in such a way that none legally exercises plenary power, or competence finally to define its own competence. Each such organ is effectively limited by checks and controls exercised by another. Where that is so, and where constitutional stability has engendered a political system in which the limits laid down in the constitution are well respected, we can predict that there will be no internal political sovereign. Yet externally, the state may be as sovereign as it is possible to imagine. The United States, Canada, Australia, and Switzerland, all provide rather good examples of this.

A final conceptual point to be made about sovereignty concerns the issue of 'popular sovereignty', 'the sovereignty of the people'. There are various constitutional and political traditions that promote this idea. The idea goes back at least as far as to the constitutional writings of George Buchanan. Its appeal is to the principle that all political and legal power ought to rest on the will and consent of those among or over whom power is exercised. This is a principle of political morality. It has two applications. One is in the context of an established constitutional order, and here the claim is that the constitution must always be subject to adoption, confirmation, or revision by processes involving the whole people. The other is where a group or community of people seeks to exercise self-determination by constituting itself into a legal and political rather than simply a cultural or ethnic or religious community. In either application, the principle belongs to the theory of democracy as a basis for ideal constitution-making, to some greater or lesser extent achieved in the actual constitutional experience of different states or polities.

In terms of the differentiation of external and internal sovereignty, we can now properly add that where a state is sovereign in the external sense, it makes perfect sense to say that this sovereignty belongs to the whole people of the state. Especially in the context of a *Rechtsstaat* enjoying a democratic form of internal government, there would be significant truth in the idea that the people as a whole exercises self-government independently of higher power. Popular sovereignty in this sense does not imply or presuppose the existence internal to the state of any constitutional or political organ enjoying either legal or political sovereignty in the internal sense.

Indeed, it is the absence of any such organ—king, president, party, or Parliament or whatever—that forces us to identify the people as the ultimate possessor of the sovereignty of their state. This does not mean that there is an entity 'the people' that has an existence distinct from or prior to their constitution. On the contrary, they count as 'a people' by virtue of the constitution that makes them so.

Beyond the sovereign state

The argument so far has tried to elucidate the ideas of sovereignty, legal and political, and of the sovereign state and sovereign people. The next point is to discuss the relevance of contemporary developments to these concepts. I particularly wish to consider their relevance and usefulness in the context of the developing European Union evolving from the Paris and Rome Treaties, and through to the Union Treaty of Maastricht, the Treaty of Amsterdam, and beyond.

As was discussed at some length in Chapter 7, since at least 1964,[9] it has been the doctrine of the European Court of Justice that the Community (as it now is) constitutes a new legal order, neither a subordinate part of the laws of the member states nor simply a sub-system of International law. From the point of view of a soundly pluralistic theory of law as institutional normative order, there is no difficulty about accepting this self-characterization of Community law as a distinct legal order. It owes its origin, certainly, to treaties binding under general International law. Further, from the point of view of member-state legal systems, the ground of validity of provisions of Community law is located within the state-system. Community law's validity as a high level source of law is traceable to the acts of ratification or adoption of foundational or amending treaties by appropriate modes of decision-making. The appropriateness to this end of a mode of decision-making is determined by the state constitution in question. But there has been an institutionalization of a legal order under the foundation treaties and the treaty amendments have elaborated this, always preserving the *acquis communautaire*. There are now long-established Community organs for law-making, for executive action, and for judicial law-application. That these have operated in a largely efficacious way over a substantial period of time makes it both proper and necessary to recognize that here we have a full-blown instance of an institutional normative order, and thus to confirm the Court's representation of it as a distinct legal order.

Within that legal order and from the point of view of Community organs and persons working within Community law, the criteria for recognition of the validity of Community legal provisions are now internal to this legal system. The system has acquired what Niklas Luhmann or Günther Teubner would characterize as self-referentiality.[10] As a system, it differentiates itself from other systems by whose

---

[9] See *Costa v ENEL*, case 6/64.

[10] See N. Luhmann, 'Law as a Social System', *Northwestern Univ. Law Rev.* (1989), 136 at 141–3.; G. Teubner, *Law as an Autopoietic System*, trans. R. Adler and A. Bankowska, ed. Z. Bankowski (Oxford, Basil Blackwell 1993), 13–24.

distinct criteria of validity Community legal provisions are also valid and applicable. This is the case within the legal orders of member states, each of whose organs acknowledge Community provisions as valid and applicable in relevant situations, in a manner coordinated with, and justifiable by, reference to the member state's own internal criteria of validity. 'Community-validity' is a relevant fact when it comes to assessing member-state validity. 'Member-state validity' is a relevant fact for some purposes of Community law. The situation is one of differentiation of systems subject to mutual overlap and interaction. There are institutional arrangements to resolve potential conflicts of norms or of their interpretation.

The application and enforcement of rights and obligations under Community law remain, to a considerable extent, matters for implementation by the authorities of member states, though remedies can now be awarded against states by the European Court to compensate for damages arising from state action found to have been in breach of Community obligations. Community law is and remains to a considerable extent both normatively and politically dependent on law and practice in member states. So far as concerns the validity of national legislation, legislators within state systems are now limited by the requirement to avoid conflict with valid Community law. Community decisions of various kinds can change law within state-systems regardless of the operation of the normal internal legislative process. Yet the making of Community decisions depends at the highest level on the joint action of state authorities of member states acting in the Council of Ministers of the EC. Politically and economically, there are powerful reasons deterring states from large-scale unilateral defiance of Community norms or (*a fortiori*) unilateral renunciation of membership (which would clearly be invalid as a matter of Community Law, though possibly valid or subject to being validated by the law of the member state).

Given that, and given our earlier discussion of sovereignty whether as a legal or as a political concept, it is clear that absolute or unitary sovereignty is entirely absent from the legal and political setting of the European Community. Neither politically nor legally is any member state in possession of ultimate power over its own internal affairs. Politically, the Community affects vital interests, and hence exercises political power on some matters over member states. Legally, Community legislation binds member states and overrides internal state-law within the respective criteria of validity. So the states are no longer fully sovereign states externally, nor can any of their internal organs be considered to enjoy present internal sovereignty under law; nor have they any unimpaired political sovereignty. The Community on the other hand is plainly not a state. Nor does it possess sovereignty as a kind of Federation or Confederation. It is neither legally nor politically independent of its members. The German Constitutional Court in its decision on the Maastricht Treaty denied that the Union or Community and their organs of decision have the ultimate legal competence to determine their own competence. If so, this precludes sovereignty.

In one highly important sense, sovereignty has not been lost in this process. In International law, no state or other entity outside the Union has any greater power over member states individually or jointly than before, except to the extent that a similar process on a global level has brought about the formation of the World Trade Organization. Thus there is a kind of compendious legal external sovereignty towards the rest of the world; and politically it seems that the scale of the Community enhances the independence of action of its members collectively and perhaps even individually for some purposes. To the extent that the terminology of 'divided sovereignty' is found valuable either rhetorically or analytically, it can be applied here—the sovereignty of the Community's member states has not been lost, but subjected to a process of division and combination internally, and hence in a way enhanced externally. But the process of division and combination has taken us 'beyond the sovereign state',[11] indeed, well beyond it. Despite the rhetoric of politicians, it cannot be credibly argued that any member state of the European Union remains politically or legally a sovereign state in the strict or traditional sense of these terms. Yet it is to their traditional sense that the political rhetoricians make implicit appeal when they harangue party conferences.

Democracy and subsidiarity

Western Europe's successful transcendence of the sovereign state and of state sovereignty is greatly to be welcomed. It has been and will be a condition for the security of peace and prosperity among us. Yet many are conscious of a residual unease concerning popular sovereignty. At least, in a sovereign state, with its own organs of executive and legislative government, the target for democratic activism is clear. Provided there is real popular control of sovereign government, with fair conditions for full and equal participation by all citizens, or all citizens who wish to involve themselves, democracy can be realized. There is no room for relapse into rule by a virtuous few, whether a bench of supreme court judges, or a council of ministers deliberating in private, or a bureaucracy of highly trained experts.

British Euroscepticism has in effect posed in just such terms the democratic challenge to what Eurosceptics consider the onward march of an unacceptable federalism at the European level. The British Parliament for them is the repository of legal sovereignty under the constitution, and through that legal sovereignty is secured the political sovereignty, internal and external, of the British people. European organs of legislation are immune to direct democratic control, and the European Parliament has been belittled for having neither adequate legislative power nor control over those who do have it, nor ability effectively to make accountable the members of the executive branch at Community level. To them, combined and divided state-and-community sovereignty seems the enemy of popular sovereignty, and strengthening the position of the European Parliament, as has happened in the past decade, may be as much a part of the problem as of the solution. The grounds for their concern are evident and real.

---

[11] See N. MacCormick, 'Beyond the Sovereign State', *Modern Law Review*, 56 (1993), 1–18.

On the other hand, the record of the sovereign unitary state is not so very bright either. The highly centralized version of sovereign state presented by the United Kingdom in its classical phase itself deserves scrutiny. Here we had a proclaimedly sovereign Parliament dominated by a system of political parties with strong internal party discipline, and with an absence of proportional representation in the electoral system. This certainly did not foster anything approximating to an ideal system of popular government with fair equality of participation for all citizens or all points of view. Nor did it prevent the growth of an extensive bureaucracy, nor the enhancement of power of the executive branch of government in the modern period. So far as democracy depends not only on formal allocation of voting power to each adult citizen, but some guarantee of civil and political—perhaps also economic and social—rights to each person, to ensure continuing opportunity of participation on fair terms with others, the UK's accession to the European Human Rights Convention was a decisive step, and yet one which diminished external sovereignty. The growth of a pluralism of law and institutions in Western Europe has been in some ways problematic for democracy, but in other ways advantageous; and, to the extent that the Union Treaty formally adopts human rights standards, the advantage is enhanced.[12]

There is another potential advantage. Concentrations of power can create opportunities for what might be called monolithic democracy. That is, if all legal or political power is concentrated at the level, say, of a single assembly with complete power over all matters in a large territory, then decisions affecting localities within the whole are as much subject to majority decision by the totality as decisions which have a broader, or even a holistic, scope. But the majority of the totality may be at odds with the majority in any particular locality. The traditional theory of internal sovereignty considers any decision-making power at local level to be the mere creature and delegate of central sovereign power. Hence it is a matter of political choice for the central power, and behind that for the holistic majority, whether to allow local-level democracy on the basis of local majority opinion, or to override local opinion and impose the solution favoured by the holistic majority.

In this light, if there is a sense of popular sovereignty ('sovereignty as self-determination', perhaps) which calls for recognition of the rights of significant groups or communities within larger wholes, the state-sovereignty version of popular sovereignty can be itself an enemy of other democratic rights. In general, any form of popular government or majoritarian democracy inevitably poses the questions: 'Who are the people? Of what group must the majority be a majority?'

The great problem of nationalism in the modern world is perhaps revealed at just this point. It is graphically and tragically revealed by the strife and slaughter in former Yugoslavia. If the sovereign state is taken as the self-evident and only available framework for democracy, it becomes vital to struggle over boundaries

---

[12] Cf. the excellent discussion in P. Craig and G. de Búrca, *EU Law: Text, Cases, and Materials*, 2nd edn. (Oxford: Oxford University Press, 1998), 155–9.

and membership, vital to define the 'nation' as possessor and master of the sovereign state, the nation-state. Inevitably there are minorities, even 'national minorities'. In Spain there are Catalunya and the Basque Country and others; in Belgium there are Flanders and Wallonia; in the United Kingdom, there are England, Scotland, and Wales, and the itself internally contested province of Northern Ireland. In the UK, the English majority is normally the majority of the whole.

The end of the sovereign state creates an opportunity for rethinking of problems about national identity. The nation as cultural, or linguistic, or historical, or even ethnic community is not coextensive with the (former) sovereign state, the traditional 'nation-state'. The cases I have mentioned all make this obvious in the highest degree. The suppression of national individualities is wrong in itself and almost inevitably a cause of bitterness and strife. But if the ideological unity of the traditional sovereign state is abandoned, new possibilities are opened.

At least one reading of the already-contested concept of 'subsidiarity' points the way here. If the idea of a pluralistic legal order advanced here is an acceptable one, then it is capable of generalization and extension to what is sometimes called the 'regional' level within Europe, although many people in some of the so-called regions find it important to characterize their own region and others as 'nations'. There can then be a basis on which to recognize further levels of system-differentiation and partial mutual independence. The doctrine of subsidiarity requires decision-making to be distributed to the most appropriate level. In that context, the best democracy—and the best interpretation of popular sovereignty is one that insists on levels of democracy appropriate to levels of decision-making. And the tendency to over-centralize at the level of member states is as much to be countered as is any over-centralization towards Brussels. The demise of sovereignty in its classical sense truly opens opportunities for subsidiarity and democracy as essential mutual complements. It suggests a radical hostility to any merely monolithic democracy.

It also suggests a need to reconsider some issues about democracy, or at any rate, about representative government. For the moment, at least, it is obvious that Heads of Government of Member States of the European Union enjoy considerably greater power and standing than do Governors of States in the USA. Their standing in the domestic politics of their countries remains of high significance, and electing or rejecting governments remains the basic currency of democratic politics in European States. The composition of the Commission and the Court, and their method of nomination and confirmation preclude some of the abuses of respectively party-power and presidential or governmental Court-packing that can occur in other states or federations. And yet none of what is done falls outside of some real possibility of democratic scrutiny.

It is not only our theories of law, but also our theories of democracy, that are challenged by the new forms that are evolving among us in Europe. A commitment to principles of democracy and of subsidiarity calls us to ensure the vitality of decision-making processes at many levels and in a polycentric way. It calls on us to reflect on forms of popular control that are effective at given levels, and on ensuring that those we adopt for 'higher' levels do not become inimical to the vitality of politics at 'lower' levels. These are questions that call for further reflection and discussion; they shall receive this in the next chapter.

9

Democracy and Subsidiarity in the European Commonwealth

Introduction

When one contemplates the dreadful conflict that engulfed first Europe and then practically the whole world from 1914, with no more than a partial cessation of hostilities between 1918 and 1939, it is no wonder that the years since 1945 have been years in which Western Europeans have sought to make war among themselves unthinkable. The project to create a new order in Europe is one that has gripped the imagination of many. There really is a common good among the people of the whole of this continent, and certainly among those of western, northern and southern Europe currently brought together in the Europe of the European Union. That common good includes first of all the avoidance of war and obtaining peace and prosperity and cooperation by other means. In that context it seems more than worthwhile to raise a discussion of 'democracy and subsidiarity' as defining frameworks of cooperation in the construction of a better ordered Europe.

The present discussion has five parts: the first is about 'post-sovereign Europe'— is this already in some sense a lawfully constituted commonwealth? The second is about democracy—is this a democratic commonwealth? The third concerns the question 'democracy or what?' and goes into the idea of a 'mixed constitution'; the fourth is about values—what is good about democracy or about subsidiarity?; the fifth is about the persistent contemporary worry concerning the 'democratic deficit' in the organs of European government as at present constituted—is there indeed a democratic deficit, or a subsidiarity deficit?

Post-sovereign Europe: a constituted commonwealth?

People talk from time to time about 'constitutional moments', the fleeting junctures of opportunity for radical redesign of a polity, an idea borrowed from Bruce Ackerman's study of the transformations of American constitutional order at great moments of opportunity.[1] Is there such a moment here in Europe in the closing years of the twentieth century? Is this a time when there is need for a European constitution, or a radically transformed one? If so, how can such a thing be achieved? Do we have one already? Is this thing (to use no more definite a term) that is Europe, or the

---

[1] See B. Ackerman, 'The Storrs Lectures: Discovering the Constitution', *Yale Law Journal*, 93 (1984), 1013–72.

Europe of the European Communities and European Union, something that actually does already have a constitution, in however imperfect a form? There have been debates about drafting a constitution for Europe, rather on the assumption that there is no constitution here now. But this view is, as to its underlying assumption, rather implausible.

In the European Union, there are established law-making and executive organs, a directly elected Parliament with considerable (and growing) powers in relation to legislation and to executive action, and a Court that can rule authoritatively on the powers of the other organs, and on the powers, rights, and Community obligations of member states and their citizens. It would seem, therefore, that there must be somewhere some set or cluster of norms that define these organs and confer their powers, while at the same time constituting, or authorizing the creation or conferment of, rights and obligations. With various enlargements, reforms, adjustments, and restatements there has been such a set of norms for practically forty years. This started with the Paris and Rome Treaties, and wound up with the compendious version contained in the Treaty on European Union agreed at Maastricht in 1992, with further provisions made in the Treaty of Amsterdam of 1997.

These treaties themselves are in the first instance, and uncontroversially, binding among their parties as a matter of international law. But they do not merely confer rights and obligations on states; they establish institutions or organs as noted a moment ago. These organs can create further norms by way of directives and regulations. The court can recognize and apply these along with the treaty norms themselves, interpreted in the light of the purposes and principles implicit in the order that they constitute, and in the light of the principles of legality that are considered fundamental in the laws of the member states. It was held from quite early in the life of the European Court of Justice that the treaties had constituted a 'new legal order', distinct both from general international law and from the laws of the member states. This law had direct effect in conferring rights and obligations directly on citizens of the member states, not only on the states and their organs. Within the spheres covered by the treaties, the law so constituted necessarily had supremacy over the law of the member states, for otherwise there would not be a common body of European Community law that would have the same impact everywhere where it was binding.[2]

What confers on this new legal order the genuinely normative quality it has to have if we correctly qualify it as 'law'? One ground of its normativity is certainly the *pacta sunt servanda* ('treaties are to be kept') principle of international law. Those who ought to keep to their treaties ought to keep to whatever is validly mandated by or under these treaties. The Community and Union Treaties being pacts among states, the states ought to keep them. If the pacts create norm-creating organs, then the norms they create within the power conferred ought to be observed by the states.

---

[2] Cf. P. Craig and G. de Búrca, *EU Law: Text, Cases and Materials*, 2nd edn. (Oxford: Oxford University Press, 1998), chs. 2 and 4.

But there is more to it than this. The institutions and organs have had a continuous existence over several decades and through many changes of personnel. They have become central institutional facts in the thinking of Europeans. Citizens and officials throughout Europe have interpreted the norms of and under the treaties as having direct effect on private persons and corporations as well as on states. Over more than four decades this has proceeded with impressive continuity and one might say solidity, with a quite high degree of compliance, never perfect, of course, and somewhat variable from field to field. This has led participants in the purported 'system' of Community law to treat it with very little dispute as constituting a new legal order of just such a kind as the Court of Justice has pronounced it to be. This has received confirmation more than once in the kind of self-referential way that is arguably characteristic of systems in operation. Each time there has been an accession of further states to the original six, then nine, then twelve, and so on, there has been a new Treaty of Accession agreed between existing member states and postulants for membership; and there have been major amendments and consolidations, particularly the Single European Act of 1986, the Maastricht Treaty of 1992, and the Amsterdam Treaty of 1997. It has been suggested earlier in the present book that every viable legal order requires the underpinning of what Kelsen called a 'basic norm'. This, however, is not a mere juristic hypothesis; rather it is a norm rooted in custom and convention, the common acknowledgement of mutual obligations of respect for the framework of an institutional normative order. The evidence of many years is that this obtains in Europe.

It is not surprising that it should be so. Implementing the various treaties has called for debate and decision, frequently constitutional amendment, sometimes referendums, whether constitutional in character or technically only advisory in character (as in the United Kingdom). These processes have been necessary for ratification of new treaties or as enabling measures to give them full effect within member states. In effect, those who have taken these measures have either themselves or through their governing authorities, taken their decisions in full knowledge of the European Court's doctrines about direct effect, supremacy, and 'new legal order'. It would not therefore be deniable that these doctrines have been confirmed as part of the packages confirmed at each stage of enlargement and consolidation of the Community and now the Union. The states have confirmed an order whose own competent judicial organ has affirmed it to have a certain character. Yet hitherto no substantial reservation or derogation has been attempted from the legal doctrines so affirmed, though in the process of treaty making there have been quite legitimate attempts to express principles aimed at steering the Court's development of the law into narrower paths.[3] There has in this way been, substantially, a democratic endorsement of these key doctrines concerning the standing of Community law as a distinct system interlocking with the laws of member states but overriding them for some purposes.

---

[3] Cf. Hjalte Rasmussen, *European Court of Justice* (Copenhagen: GadJura, 1998), 328–9.

It is possible to argue from a purist democratic position that this is not in itself enough. Such democratic assent as has occurred has been achieved state-by-state, and bit by bit, without at any one time a whole compendious measure being put to the European people as such in order that they may, acting together, confirm or reject it. Can this argument be taken too seriously, though? The United States Constitution of 1787 purported to be issued by 'We the people . . .', but its actual ratification and implementation was by a process of state-by-state decision in constitutional conventions called in each of the states. If state-by-state was good enough for the USA as a paradigm case of the classical Lockean approach to constitutional legitimacy, it is not clear why a similar process should be less acceptable now. This is an age of far more effective media of communication and information and far wider franchises in the states than could possibly prevail in the early United States. More people know, and more have been consulted, and had their say, than was ever the case then. This is not a matter of superior virtue, but of different circumstances.

There are solid grounds for assenting to the 'new legal order' theory, and for claiming it to have undergone at least a fair measure of democratic legitimation. In this context, it seems reasonable therefore to scrutinize the whole body of the law contained in the Treaties, including the principles and purposes imputed to them by the Court, and consider whether these do in fact amount to a 'constitution'. Perhaps better: we should ascertain how far there are constitutional norms for a European legal order discoverable within the available body of normative material. It is fairly clear, and unsurprising, that there is in fact a coherent body of norms allocating powers and functions and imposing certain basic duties that are correlative with the four freedoms fundamental to the community as 'common market'.

Looking at this in theoretical terms, one may reflect again upon Hans Kelsen's theory about the way in which state legal systems link up to international law under the 'monistic' theory.[4] In accordance with the custom that grounds the norms to be observed among states, we can assert as binding the norm *pacta sunt servanda*, 'treaties are to be kept'. In that light, it is clear that the norms that have instituted the organs of the Community and endowed them severally with a mutually coherent scheme of powers, and that regulate the exercise of these powers through basic principles such as 'the four freedoms', have a root in international law that gives them normative validity from that point of view. The same applies to states, whose constitutional legitimacy can also be imputed to international law. Yet those who pass judgement internally to states do not in all or even in many cases yet treat the validity of state-law as somehow dependent on international law. What in one perspective appear to be only conditional grounds of validity can from another point of view be treated as ultimately validating. It is at least far from uncommon that nation-states

---

[4]　See H. Kelsen (M. Knight trans.), *The Pure Theory of Law* (Berkeley and Los Angeles: University of California Press, 1967), ch. 9. Cf. C. Richmond, *Law and Philosophy,* 16 (1997), 377–420, also in MacCormick (ed.), *Constructing Legal Systems: 'European Union' in Legal Theory* (Dordrecht: Kluwer Academic Publishers, 1997), 47–90, sect. III.1 for a more thorough analysis, allowing that the 'international law' perspective is not the only possibility here. See also Ch. 7 above.

treat their own constitutional framework as a self-sufficient ground of the validity of all that is done under it, without treating the fact of its legitimacy in international law as conferring on it the normative quality it has.

This is now true of European Community law too. The original legitimation through international law is very plain and visible in the case of a legal order dependent on treaties, and from time to time adjusted by amending treaties. But from the 'internal point of view' (to switch momentarily into Hartian terms of reference)[5] of those who operate the system of Community law, it has come to be considered a self-referential and independently valid legal order. There is accordingly no less reason to treat the Community's foundational norms as constitutional in purport than there is reason so to treat the foundational norms of national law. What is a constitution in a legal-logical sense is a different thing from what is a constitution in a popular-political sense; namely a concise document headed 'The Constitution'. Even where such a document more or less exists, for example, in the United States of America, it is trite knowledge that the really operative constitutional law goes far beyond the original text, even with its listed amendments, and includes many fundamental doctrines nowhere stated in the text.

To summarise: there are legal norms that constitute and empower the Community's organs, and there are basic doctrines and principles—the four freedoms, and those parts of European Human Rights Law that enter into the Community sphere of competence, and fundamental principles derived from the common experience of member states. This amounts to a fairly thick body of law that is thoroughly and fully constitutional in any reasonable interpretation of 'constitution'. It cannot reasonably be disputed that the Community is a lawfully constituted entity, nor that it conducts itself, as a 'law-community', a *Rechtsgemeinschaft*, albeit not a *Rechtsstaat*, for it is not a state.

But within the geographical space wherein the Community legal order functions, it is not alone. There are here other, no less robust, legally constituted entities which are states, that is to say, of course, the member states. They retain their own fundamental laws, their own basic norms in one or another of the senses of that elusive phrase. While they may have ceded sovereign rights to the Community for certain purposes, they retain such rights for other purposes. However it may be as between member states among themselves, or as between member states and the Community considered corporately, the status of each of these states towards other states external to the European Community and Union has not changed in the way of any diminution of their independence and 'sovereignty' in an external sense. This is a fact which does not conflict with the equal truth that, in the internal perspective of the Community and the relations of member states, each has ceded fundamental powers pertaining to sovereignty, with the effect that none remains in the full classical sense a sovereign state, as was argued in the preceding chapter.

---

[5] See H. L. A. Hart, *The Concept of Law* (Oxford: Clarendon Press 1961), 54–6, 86–8; cf. N. MacCormick, *Legal Reasoning and Legal Theory*, rev. edn. (Oxford: Clarendon Press, 1994), 273–92.

Here then we have a 'post-sovereign' Europe. It is a Europe of no longer absolutely sovereign states interacting with and through a Community with an independent legal order of its own. The Community, or the Union in which it is now embedded, is in turn not, and not within measurable distance of becoming, a sovereign federal union such as we see in the United States or Canada or Australia, or, more doubtfully, Switzerland. This chapter started with a reminder of dreadful wars. Post-sovereignty seems from that point of view a very welcome development in diminishing the probability of recurrence to the barbarisms of time recently past. This evolution beyond sovereignty has not occurred by a process whose result has been that the powers formerly vested in a sovereign state no longer exist or are exercisable in Europe. But they are no longer exercisable by a single power-structure with a single normative frame. They still exist but have been diffused or parcelled out in a new and distinctive way.

Europe's new way of parcelling out powers opens the door to a conception of subsidiarity that could gradually acquire real teeth. That is to say, once a process of sharing out powers is seriously undertaken, one can ask the question where it is best for the common good that a particular power be exercised. How far should things be done locally on a basis of local knowledge and understanding, how far centrally in a way that equalizes the situation, at any rate the normative situation, in a very wide-reaching way but with a cost in the overriding of local knowledge? It is, after all, desirable as far as possible for people to be masters of their own destiny at the level of individual and local-communal life, without losing the power to operate in a large-scale economy that can create the conditions for a decent prosperity and thereby a durable peace.

Thus it can be said that there now coexist these two entities or sets of entities, the states of Europe, now not-fully-sovereign states, and the European Union, still a non-sovereign Union. One of the things which gives rise to a difficulty of comprehension is the absence of a satisfactory terminology to talk about such entities. It is all very well to say that the EU or EC is an entity '*sui generis*', 'of its own special kind'. But this does not take us far in the way of constructing a reasonable account of what this thing-of-its-own-kind is. The proposal that I repeat[6] here is that we should revive an eighteenth-century usage of a term which has developed one specialized sense in the twentieth century, but which can easily accommodate another. The term I propose is that of a 'commonwealth', used along something of the lines intended by David Hume in his utopian *jeu d'esprit*, 'The Idea of a Perfect Commonwealth'.[7]

---

[6] Previously suggested in the annual European lecture in Queen Mary and Westfield College, London, on 11 Nov. 1996, and published as 'Democracy, Subsidiarity and Citizenship in the "European Commonwealth"', *Law and Philosophy*, 16 (1997), 331–56, and MacCormick (ed.), *Constructing Legal Systems: 'European Union' in Legal Theory* (Dordrecht: Kluwer Academic Publishers, 1997), 1–46, of which the present chapter is a considerably revised version.

[7] See D. Hume, *Essays Moral Political and Literary* (London: Oxford University Press, 1963), 499–516 (part II, Essay 16); cf. R. Goodin, 'Designing Constitutions: the Political Constitution of a Mixed Commonwealth', *Political Studies*, 44 (1996), 635-46. See also R. Bellamy and D. Castiglione, 'Building the Union', *Law and Philosophy*, 16 (1997), 421-45, and N. MacCormick (ed.), *Constructing Legal Systems: 'European Union' in Legal Theory* (Dordrecht: Kluwer Academic Publishers, 1997), 9–115, esp. at 441–5 (111–15), on Europe as 'a mixed commonwealth'.

The particular point of what we can call a 'commonwealth' is that it should comprise a group of people to whom can reasonably be imputed some consciousness that they have a 'common weal', something which really is a common good, and who are able to envisage themselves or their political representatives and governing authorities realizing this or striving after it through some form of organized political structure, embodied in some common constitutional arrangements. In this sense, both member states and the Union are commonwealths, one more intensive and localized, more strongly rooted in a sense of tradition and of personal identity and loyalty, the other more extensive and broadly inclusive. Here in Europe we have something which is a constituted order, which does have however imperfectly a legal constitution, whose members have certain vital interests in peace and prosperity that they can best pursue as common interests through policies oriented towards this common good. 'Commonwealth' seems a natural term here to use.

A democratic constitution: what kind of demos?

The next question, even were the above terminological proposal accepted, must be whether it is in any sense a *democratic* commonwealth. The very term 'commonwealth' has implicit in it some suggestion of popular belonging and popular self-management, so that 'commonwealth' stands in contrast to 'tyranny' or 'autocracy'. Perhaps commonwealths have to be at least democratic in spirit and aspiration even if not absolutely or perfectly so in constitutional frame. If so, there is a certain matter for concern about the line the argument is taking. For there is high authority in support of the view that the European Union is not, and indeed lacks any present capability to become, a validly democratic entity.

This has been held by the Constitutional Court of Germany, the highest court of the German federal republic. At the time at which constitutional amendments were undertaken to bring into effect the Maastricht Treaty, Mr Manfred Brunner and others challenged the legislation embodying the amendments as unconstitutional. Among other points, this was argued to the Court: since Germany is by its constitution constituted to be a democratic federal republic, and the requirements for democracy are absolutely fundamental constitutionally, it must follow that no constitutional amendment can validly subordinate the democratic republic to a non-democratic supranational entity, nor transfer to it the vital powers of a state or federal union; the purported transfer of powers to the European Union was exactly such a transfer, hence it could not be valid. In its opinion, the Court upheld the validity of the amendment on the ground of the non-essential character of the powers that were transferred, and the fact that the Union as distinct from one of its pillars, the Community, was essentially a framework for intergovernmental collaboration, not self-governing entity. But it did hold that there would be fundamental barriers to transfer of vital state functions to the European Union while it retained a non-democratic constitutional order, and it expressed doubts concerning the possibility of democracy in Europe, certainly for the foreseeable future.[8]

Democracy, the Court argued, requires a common sense of belonging to one polity expressed in such things as common press and other media, shared political parties and a common political debate. But this does not exist in Europe. Elections to the European Parliament are in each state concerned primarily with intra-state politics, there are not European parties with European manifestos. There is not a common sense of belonging to or of constitutional loyalty towards European institutions or the constitutional norms that create them. Democracy is rule by the *demos*, the people, *das Volk*. Where no *demos* exists, no democracy can exist; no *demos* exists in Europe, hence further transfers of power to the Union would be unlawful and ineffectual, and any claim by European organs to have competence to settle the extent of their own competences ('*Kompetenz-Kompetenz*') would be illegal and not recognized as valid in German law. In this view, the defects of European government are not merely technical, not to do with erecting better representative institutions more answerable to the whole electorate. The democracy-deficit is fundamental, since Europe has not yet become, even if it one day might become, the kind of entity within which there is enough of a holistic self-conscious *demos* for there to be a real popular will controlling the commonwealth and hence a real opportunity for real democracy.[9]

There is a possible answer to this. We need not overstress the requirements of culture or common ethnicity or language as essentially constitutive of a *demos* in the sense required for the concept of democratic government. I should like to suggest the possibility of our conceiving such a thing as a 'civic' *demos*, that is, one identified by the relationship of individuals to common institutions of a civic rather than an ethnic or ethnic-cultural kind.[10] People can have a civic identity constituted perhaps by what Habermas has dubbed 'constitutional patriotism', *Verfassungspatriotismus*. This is a common loyalty to a common constitutional order, regardless of differences of language, ethnic background, and the rest. People are sometimes willing to sink differences of culture, of language, of heritage, of history for the sake of their common participation in a lawfully constituted polity or commonwealth.

If there is, however deficiently, a lawfully constituted commonwealth of Europe, then that makes it possible (not inevitable) that we can orient ourselves toward this,

---

[8] See BvR 2134/92 and for an English translation of the case report, see [1994] 1 CMLR 57; discussed Ch. 7 above, and in MacCormick 'The Maastricht-Urteil: Sovereignty Now', *European Law Journal*, 1 (1994), 259–66.

[9] See BvR 2134/92 and [1994] 1 CMLR 57; here, I am expanding somewhat the argument in Ch. 8, and again do so with a large intellectual debt to Joseph Weiler. See J. H. H. Weiler, 'European Neo-constitutionalism: in Search of Foundations for the European Constitutional Order', *Political Studies*, 44 (1996), 517–33 at pp. 522–5.

[10] For a discussion of 'civic' versus ethnic nationalism in relation to this concept, see MacCormick, 'Liberalism, Nationalism, and the Post-Sovereign State', in *Political Studies*, 44 (1996), 553–67 at 562–3. (Special issue *Constitutionalism in Transformation: European and Theoretical Perspectives*, ed. R. Bellamy and D. Castiglione); also Ch. 11 below.

and regard this as something of ours, a common possession and achievement of the peoples of the states that participate in the commonwealth. That gives us a basis for acknowledging each other as fellow members in the same enterprise, and makes sense of the admittedly thin, even etiolated, citizenship provisions included in the Treaty of European Union. That we do now have an acknowledged European citizenship, defined within this constituted order, in itself creates an opportunity for, though not necessarily the immediate realization of, a sense of European civic identity, and therewith a European civic *demos*. The citizenship is doubtless a 'thin' citizenship, the *demos* a 'thin' *demos*, for each depends upon pre-existing statehood and membership of the Union only via the member states. It does not cancel, but presupposes, the distinct peoplehoods of the different peoples of the member states.

It is not to be supposed that many people as they go about their daily tasks feel conscious of or glad about or loyal towards the constitution and the various constituted organs of the European commonwealth. 'Brussels' may be as much a target of impatience, hostility, even a kind of contempt, as it is a focus for loyal self-identification. But if we remind ourselves of the imperatives of peace and decent prosperity, then so long as people are aware of European integration (up to some point) as preconditions for these, there exist sufficient conditions for some thin but effectual sense of community in Community. At least, we have solid grounds for seeking identification, and something with which to identify, beyond state, state-nationality, state loyalty. There is enough of a *demos* here to make democracy possible, if democracy is what we want.

Democracy or what? the character of a mixed constitution

So is democracy what we want? Clearly, it is a tall order to make a thriving democratic entity out of a commonwealth of nearly four-hundred million people, distributed among states with relatively thick and deep institutional and cultural identities. If this great mass of individual persons is excluded from any say in the conduct of their commonwealth's affairs, we have indeed a serious democratic deficit.[11] Yet finding ways of including them all on fair and equal terms seems vastly difficult. Perhaps this is just not the sort of thing that can be run democratically, and therefore has to be reckoned a kind of political entity to which may be entrusted only those functions in relation to which non-democratic governance seems acceptable. Essentially, this seems to be the thought of the German Constitutional Court. But, if so, can it become democratic by any means short of turning it into that old-fashioned kind of a commonwealth, a sovereign state or sovereign federal union, with one person one vote and power exercised over the whole by officials elected after open competition on a universal franchise?

---

[11] On the concept of a 'democratic deficit', see, e.g., J. Weiler, U. Haltern, and F. Mayer, 'European Democracy and its Critique', in J. Hayward (ed.), *The Crisis of Representation in Europe* (London: Frank Cass, 1995), 32.

This question challenges us for a moment to reflect upon the question, 'Democracy or what?' What do we take to be the relevant rivals of democratic rule? It is now almost universally taken for granted that democracy is a precondition of the legitimacy of any large-scale system of government. This has not always been taken for granted. Aristotle started a tradition, one that ran for many centuries, of comparing constitutional types, and the types of human character that tended to flourish in each. Classically, there was a three-way choice: monarchy, where one person rules; oligarchy, where a few rule over the many, benignly in case the few represent the best and wisest of the community, in which case we have aristocracy in its strict sense of 'rule by the best'; and democracy when all the people participate in rule over the whole commonwealth to which they belong. Either one rules, or some rule, or all rule. Each of these ways of governing has its own characteristic strength, monarchy because a single person decides and hence there can be clarity and decisiveness; oligarchy because in its best form, aristocracy, it brings together the greatest wisdom and procures policies best tailored to the common good; democracy, because it unites the energies of the whole people and calls for their commitment to the business of the *polis*, forming it into a cradle of civic virtue. But each can degenerate, respectively into the tyranny of a despot, or into corrupt minority rule, or into faction-ridden anarchy. The trick of statecraft is accordingly to find combined forms of government that achieve the characteristic virtues of the distinct forms but provide effective checks and controls upon degeneration into the vicious forms of any given type.

Given that wisdom in practical affairs, *prudentia*, seems to be very differentially distributed among us, and possessed in exalted degree only by a few, there is something of an argument for aristocracy. Identifying the common good and the means of its pursuit is not an easy task, and only wise and experienced persons are likely to be good guides. The problem is, though, that of choosing or finding the 'best'— hereditary aristocracies have been disappointing to say the least. But in the modern world, bureaucracy gives us another possibility for benign oligarchy, if the officials are chosen competitively, imbued with respect for the law, and supervised properly. Notwithstanding the scandal of the winter of 1999 that led to resignation by the whole Commission, the EC Commission has had some of the qualities for which one might seek. Commission members are drawn from the ranks of very senior political figures no longer with political ambitions of their own to fulfil at national level. Below the level of the Commission itself the Directorates-General are staffed from people of considerable ability, chosen very competitively, with backgrounds in the varied political and administrative cultures of Europe. Moreover, it is ultimately controllable by the democratic element. The Parliament, directly elected by all the citizens of the Union, has some, though still rather too crude and drastic, supervisory powers. For it is able to remove the whole Commission from office, and must approve the budget. In relation to legislation, the Commission takes initiatives, but they must win the approval of the Council of Ministers, who, albeit not directly elected, are in effect indirectly elected through the mechanisms of choosing ministers by means of democratic processes in the member states. In the already extensive and still growing domains of co-decision involving the Parliament, there is a strong directly representative democratic element in the legislative process. So the bureau-cratic–oligarchic element is subject to democratic controls, either through a form of direct representative democracy, or through indirect representative democracy. This is by no means democracy perfect or democracy complete. But it is not a system wholly lacking in democratic elements or democratic spirit. It is in fact a case of a 'mixed constitution'.

In the crisis of March 1999, the whole Commission resigned, led by its president, Jacques Santer, rather than wait for a vote of censure to be carried by Parliament, as would certainly have happened. A commission of inquiry, set up at the instance of Parliament to investigate allegations of irregularity and fraud, found much to criti-cize in the running of the Commission, and particular instances of serious irregular-ity, and neglect or even abuse of powers, by two named commissioners (Cresson and Marin). The President was criticized for failing to ensure adequate diligence on the part of the Commission's own investigative agency. The lack of individual account-ability of Commissioners and of their private offices came in for much unfavourable comment, and with justification. The whole thing was an object lesson on the in-built dangers of oligarchic government where there are inadequate democratic controls on the few who hold power, however well qualified they may be for exer-cising it well.

It is easy to overstate the merits of the idea of a mixed constitution. Even if Aristotle and his successors rightly identified the intrinsic excellence towards which each of the types of government tends in its pure form, this does not guarantee the viability or desirability of some (or any particular) mixture of the three. Sir William Blackstone gave a particularly bland version of the 'mixed constitution' argument in extolling the British constitution's balancing together of monarchical chief executive with (hereditary) aristocratic upper house and democratic lower house in a system of parliamentary government guarded by an independent judiciary that was in turn constitutionally restrained from questioning the final decisions of the sovereign-in-parliament.[12] Jeremy Bentham tartly responded that an argument of the form used by Blackstone might as easily be taken to prove that the British constitution combined together the distinctive vices of each of the pure forms of government, and hence was the worst of all possible constitutions.[13] We may conclude that real systems of government are always analysable into elements of different types (in the Aristotelian or any other typology). But this does not guarantee, even if there are special virtues associated with each type, that any particular mixture will achieve an ideal combination of virtues.

Nevertheless, a reminder about the traditional discussion of the 'mixed constitution'

---

[12] W. Blackstone, *Commentaries on the Laws of England* (New York: Legal Classics Library, 1983), I. 50.

[13] J. Bentham, *A Comment on the Commentaries and a Fragment on Government*, ed. J. H. Burns and H. L. A. Hart (London: Athlone Press, 1977), 461–73, esp. at 471–3 (i.e. *A Fragment on Government*, ch. 3).

is helpful in relation to discussions of the democratic deficit. If we read the critique of the 'democratic deficit' as implying that the current Union is not democratic at all, and that this state of affairs will be intrinsically unsatisfactory until such time as a fully democratic form of government prevails in Europe, we forget the wisdom of the past. Democracy and its particular virtues make a critical contribution to the good ordering of any well-ordered commonwealth, but a satisfactorily democratic form of government does not necessarily submit every single decision to the vote on a basis of one person, one vote. A well-ordered polity may have other elements in its constitution.

The issue about Europe ought not then to be whether it is totally or completely democratic, but whether it is adequately so given the kind of entity we take it to be. From this point of view, it is well to remind ourselves that this is a commonwealth set up through agreements among pre-existing and still coexisting commonwealths, and that each of these, as a constitutional state, enjoys under its constitution the values of democratic answerability of executive and legislature, coupled with independence of its judiciary and some measure of separation of powers. Citizenship of the Union is a citizenship supervening upon citizenship in one or another member state. It carries with it relatively few Union-specific rights as such, though the doctrines of the direct effect and direct applicability of Community Law entail that there are substantial and important rights. These include notably the 'four freedoms' and their corollaries, which Union citizens enjoy under the law of the Economic Community subsumed in the Union.

The executive power of the Union is exercised through the Commission, whose members are appointed on the nomination of Member States' governments, subject to the various checks to which these governments are domestically subject; the whole Commission must be approved by, and can be removed by, the European Parliament. Legislative power is shared between the Commission, which initiates proposed laws, and the Council (of Ministers), and the Parliament, between whom lies the power of final decision. The Council represents the states' interests, and nowadays, on most matters, decides by a system of qualified and partial majority voting among the states. The budget requires approval by the Parliament, and the Parliament (albeit dangerously dependent on in-state party management under prevailing systems of proportional representation) represents citizens directly, though with voting power skewed in favour of citizens of smaller states. This can hardly be dismissed as a wholly undemocratic system of decision-making. But, as we have already noted, the democratic element is to a considerable extent an indirect one, in the sense that the Commission is subject to a double tier of indirect election, while the Ministers who collectively comprise the Council may be indirectly elected only as to a single tier of choice, within their home state, but are there elected or nominated primarily for purposes other than to represent the citizenry on the Council.

In the context of a discussion of the mixed constitution, it is worth remarking that the element yet more obviously lacking than the democratic is in fact the monarchical. I do not, of course, mean that there might be, far less ought to be, a hereditary Queen or King, Empress or Emperor, sovereign lady or lord of the Union.

The absence to which I draw attention is that of a single individual, elected or chosen by some reasonable process, who in a significant sense personifies or bears the overall persona of the Union. There is in fact no identifiable head of the Union or even Chief Executive—some Commission presidents, notably Jacques Delors in the later 1980s and early 1990s, have taken a higher profile and given something of an executive lead to the whole. The dominant tone, however, is one of collective decision-making, of rule by committee, with some evidence that this can erode a sense of individual responsibility on behalf of any particular person. Oligarchy sets the tone both in Commission and Council. The democratic legitimation of the oligarchs (whether or not they constitute in fact an enlightened bureaucracy, an appointed but authentic aristocracy, rather than the petty-tyrannical bureaucracy portrayed in the more nationalistic flourishes of journalism) depends either on the decision-making done collectively in the Council by members of democratically accountable national governments, or on the votes of the European Parliament, still less widely endowed with powers than state parliaments typically are. All in all, what we have is a mixed constitution in which the elements held in rough balance are oligo-bureaucratic and indirectly democratic.

Questions of value: why democracy?

The going question of the paper is whether we have 'enough' democracy in Europe, in the Union and Community themselves, as distinct from in the member states. If there is a constitution of Europe already, but a mixed constitution (mixed both as to constitutional types and as to normative sources), the question is whether the mixture that exists is a reasonable one or a deficient one, and, if deficient, to what measure of 'democratic deficit'. Posing the question by harking back to mixed constitution' theorizing is not mere antiquarian eccentricity. Rather, it provides a salutary reminder that merely to point to some un- or non-democratic element in a given constitutional set-up is not *eo ipso* to damn it. For the issue is one concerning a reasonable balance of elements. And if that is so, we need some basis on which to balance the relevant elements.

   Here, let me cast aside the Blackstonian version of the virtues of the types of constitution, and think of another way to assess what good there is in democracy. Let me suggest a matrix in which to ponder the point. First, let us differentiate individualistic and holistic aspects of social and political value; I mean, let us consider the difference between wondering what good something is for each of us as an individual, and what good something is for all of us as a collectivity of some kind. Let me use an example to highlight the contrast I have in mind. If each of us is musically gifted, for each of us possession of a musical instrument enables us to get the pleasure of using and developing our musical talent, and giving and getting the pleasure of making good music. If we as a group constitute an orchestra, it is good for our orchestra as an entity that the instruments we each have are compatible with the structure of an orchestra of the relevant type (it won't do for everyone to have and be proficient on the French horn). It is also necessary to have a room large enough to practice in and an auditorium to perform in.

Whether in the last resort holistic goods are reducible to individualistic (or, indeed, vice versa), the contrast gives me a horizontal axis for the matrix. The vertical is supplied by the contrast of the instrumentally good versus the intrinsically good. Is music, or the activity of making music collectively and (literally) symphonically, good in itself? Or is it good just for the pleasure it gives? Either answer seems capable of being plausibly supported, but even those who opt for its instrumental goodness (being instrumental to the creation of pleasure) are apt to think of pleasure as being simply good in itself. Anyway, taking the axes as I have suggested them, the matrix they constitute is this:

	Individualistic	Holistic
Instrumental	*Benthamite utilitarian*	*Rousseauian general will*
Intrinsic	*Idealistic self-realization*	*Aristotelian common good*

Could we say something about the value of democracy in this framework?[14] A Benthamite might wish to argue that its value is best located in the top left-hand quadrant. All values are to be understood individualistically, and each individual is to rank equally with every other. Moreover, apart from pleasure or the satisfaction of given interests, which are intrinsically good, all goods are instrumental. This will apply particularly to the goods associated with political or legal institutions. Hence democratic voting arrangements will have value to the extent that (or because it is probable that) they enable individuals to protect or promote their interests. At the same time, considerations of marginal utility will make it likely that there will be trade-offs between individuals such as to guarantee that nobody loses out on the minimal essentials of a decent life.

Followers of Rousseau will perhaps find themselves attending to the top right quadrant. The democratic process working well is essentially holistic, aiming to establish a *volonté générale*, not just an aggregation of individual voices directed at individual self-interest (the will of all). But the process remains instrumental, to the extent that the goods pursued by resolutions of the general will are independent of it, that is, the will is directed at realizing what is in fact good for individuals or for the collective. It is not a will whose very exercise is constitutive of the good. Some defences of representative rather than direct democracy effectively deploy this idea. They suggest that, even if the aim is to produce states of affairs which actually do best serve the aggregate of individual goods, the greater practical wisdom of tried and tested representatives deliberating in a parliamentary assembly will more often achieve this than if each individual has to vote directly on every issue.

---

[14] The idea explored here derives from reflection on a section of Jeremy Waldron's 'Legislators' Intentions and Unintentional Legislation', in A. Marmor (ed.), *Law and Interpretation: Essays in Legal Philosophy* (Oxford: Clarendon Press, 1995), 329–56 at 343–8.

Individualistic argumentation about democracy of a more idealistic than utilitarian stamp might in turn argue that a vital part of individual self-constitution consists in participation in institutions of communal self-government. Taking part in the debate and participating in decision is an intrinsic, not a merely instrumental element in the constitution of the self as an autonomous but fully social self, a moral agent in the full sense. And the constitution of such a self is good intrinsically, not just instrumentally. Yet there is nothing to stop its also being instrumentally good, to the extent that the more such selves there are, the easier it becomes for others to achieve similar development in interaction with them, in ways that involve democratic processes.

Finally, there is a certain Aristotelian line of thought that characterizes the idea of the common good as being something which emerges from and is in effect constituted by a process of collective deliberation and discourse. Deliberation and collective decision are not so much a good way of settling policies that will serve an independently established good, whether the good be conceived individualistically or holistically. Rather, they are themselves a process for disclosing a common good, authenticated by the very process of collectively deliberating and deciding. A position of this kind belongs, obviously enough, to the bottom-right quadrant of the matrix.

It is not important to me to identify with exactness particular thinkers or texts that fit into this picture, though I suspect that obvious enough instances will occur to the reader. My point is rather to draw attention to the fact that each of the arguments for the value of democracy is credible to a considerable degree. The value of having and upholding democratic institutions is not simple, but complex. There are all four of individualistic–instrumental, individualistic–intrinsic, holistic–instrumental, and holistic–intrinsic elements in the value that can be ascribed to democratic institutions. At some very deep level of value-theory ('axiology') or of moral theory, it may be possible or even necessary to show that one perspective is fundamental, the others derivative; but this (even if it be so) would contribute nothing to the present purpose.

Interestingly, if we turn attention to the issue of subsidiarity,[15] we find that reading them against the same matrix may illuminate questions about appropriate levels for decision-making. Supposing we wish to settle the kinds of decision-making process that will best suit some particular subject matter, how might we go about this? First, let us consider the institutions that would be most apt to realizing individualistic goods of a primarily instrumental kind. It can be credibly argued that here the only legitimate role for collective decision-making is to secure legal and institutional conditions for the flourishing of free and fair markets. Within markets, individuals rationally pursuing their self-interest do in fact contribute to the satisfaction

---

[15] The discussion here is schematic and value-theoretical; my own understanding of the historical development of this concept is owed to a brilliant historical essay by Professor Endo of Hokkaido University—see K. Endo, 'The Principle of Subsidiarity: From Johannes Althusius to Jacques Delors', *Hokkaido Law Review*, 43 (1994), 553–652.

of the self-interests of others, and, in the aggregate, individual decisions taken by each for individual ends work to optimize the aggregate outcome in terms of general interest-satisfaction. Contemporary neo-liberals, confusingly styled 'Conservatives' in British party parlance, propound just this view when they argue that the privatization of state enterprises and the empowerment of individuals is the best devolution and the most authentic subsidiarity. Let us characterize this position as that which favours 'market subsidiarity'.

Fairly obviously, of course, market subsidiarity has its limits. It applies only to those goods which are *res intra commercium* in the old civilian conception. Not every good is a market good, and indeed the market itself and the legal–political institutions which constitute and secure markets cannot themselves be market goods. They have in them an element of the necessarily holistic and society-wide, even if we consider their value to be instrumental to the realization of goods that are primarily individualistic in their essence.

So far as concerns the idea of autonomous individuals as self-constituting through processes of collective and interactive deliberation and discourse, aimed at decisions that are necessarily collective, there seems to me to be no doubt that this is a part of human experience and the human condition. But this operates primarily on the small-scale and at local levels. Reflection on our life in a family or similar residential collectivity, in well-ordered workplaces, in clubs and associations, in local branches of political parties, to take but a few particularly salient examples, reveals to us the very real sense in which we can and do come to our full powers as autonomous individuals only by participation. This depends, of course, on the extent to which collective norms enable us to participate in the discourse, deliberation, and decision-making of the collectivity.

Such collectivities are themselves oriented towards goods of various kinds. The more the goods in question are characterized as market goods, the more decision-making processes will have to be geared to efficiency rather than individual or collective self-realization. But market efficiency is, as its very name suggests, always an instrumental concept, and presumably the forms of prosperity that markets generate are enjoyed for other purposes of a kind geared to non-market goods. Let us characterize as 'communal subsidiarity' the need to have a rich and varied range of institutions within which individual self-realization can be fostered and developed. This can be both an end in itself and a condition of satisfactorily pursuing the other goods towards which local and/or private communes and associations may be oriented. Institutions of the kind in view here belong quite as much to civil society as to the state. This reminds us that demands of subsidiarity include demands that the state exercise a self-denying ordinance against seeking to do all good things itself.

So far as concerns the construction of the 'general will' towards projects instrumentally valued either for individual or for common goods, we are clearly in the domain of the political in the strong sense. Here, the conception of democracy in play is some form of representative democracy, rather than direct democracy. The aim is to find forms of collective decision-making which are genuinely open to all, and open to all as equals, but which are effective in forming a rational and durable will expressed in general norms of a lasting kind. Market subsidiarity has an obvious significance in contemporary economic thought, nowhere more than in an 'Economic Community'[16] defined around the 'four freedoms' of the Rome Treaty and its successors. It is therefore one useful test for the adequacy of collective institutions to check how far they are adequate to securing a genuinely collective judgement that settles in a fair way legal conditions for the fair conduct of commercial and industrial activity, without partisan distortion or pork-barrel factionalism. What success by this criterion achieves may be called 'rational legislative subsidiarity'.

Finally, let us consider the possibility of institutions through which discourse and deliberation may come to be constitutive of a common good, or of the common perception of a shared good. This shared good may be itself at the same time an intrinsic good and an instrumental condition of willing mobilization of group and individual effort in fulfilling a common legal order grounded in acts of legislation and in the pursuit of highest-level economic and security policies. The notion of a 'civic *demos*', it will be observed, proves to be conditional on the possibility of this kind of deliberative constitution of a common good, and thus the very idea of a 'commonwealth' deployed in the present paper comes also into question here.

The emphasis must then surely be on deliberation and discourse even more than on will-formation and decision-making. Especially in very large-scale commonwealths, no individual as individual voter has any measurable effect on decisional outcomes. But it does not follow that voting rights are trivial. Any large interest group whose members have voting rights is guaranteed some attention, and the expressive value of standing up for a position may be considerable. But above all, the key right is that to participation in the public debate. It is the ability, both individually and through parties and organized groups of all kinds, to contribute to the public discourse that is vital here.

Moreover, institutions which are least democratic in the form of their decision-making can be decisively contributory to this discursive and rational process and style of identification and constitution of common goods. The judicial process as we witness it in great constitutional courts like the US Supreme Court or the *Bundesverfassungsgericht* or indeed the European Court of Justice or the European Court of Human Rights does not present an image or an actuality of arbitrary decision-making by the will of those in authority. Decisions that bind by virtue of the court's authority are reasoned out and justified publicly in the light of publicly deployed arguments on themes to which all can contribute. People can do this either by way of the general or specialized legal discussion of problems about law and legal policy and principles, or more restrictedly by directly arguing a case before the

---

[16] But consider B. van Roermund, 'Jurisprudential Dilemmas of European Law', *Law and Philosophy*, 16 (1997), 357–76, and MacCormick (ed.), *Constructing Legal Systems: 'European Union' in Legal Theory* (Dordrecht: Kluwer Academic Publishers, 1997), 1–46, 27–46, at pp. 371–4 or 41–4, on the dilemma that 'where there is a market there is virtually no community . . . , while . . . when there is community there is no market'.

Court. That, of course is something which only specially appointed advocates for parties can do (except in so far as *amicus curiae* briefs are admitted at all widely). The institutional arrangements are set up in such a way as to facilitate the careful presentation of every relevant argument on legal points in issue, and to consider them in an atmosphere of cool and rational deliberation. In this way, legal processes better reproduce some of the conditions of an ideal decision procedure than do the deliberations of democratic assemblies. The latter give scope for all opinions to be heard; but the discursive character of deliberation is often all but drowned out in the angry rhetoric of partisan confrontation. In courts, deliberation has a properly discursive character, but rights of audience are tightly restricted and the egalitarian character of a democratic deliberation is simply missing.

The German Constitutional Court in its Maastricht judgment (the *Brunner* case discussed above) doubted the existence of a common public deliberation in Europe, pointing to the absence of common newspapers and cross-referring between different national audiences. At the level of technical discussions of European Community law, European Human Rights law, the Philosophy of Law in Europe, Politics and Government in Europe, and other relevant scholarly disciplines, however, there is a considerable and growing Europe-wide, and indeed World-wide, open forum of deliberation. Newer developments in communications such as the Internet make their own particular contribution here also.

Very much to be regretted, however, is the absence of publicity attaching to deliberations of Council and Commission. The secrecy of discussion at meetings of these bodies and the absence of a full public record of deliberation is entirely inimical to the constitution of an open discourse on the development of policy for Community and Union. Moreover, it contributes to an adverse shifting of the balance between executive and legislature in the domestic politics of the member states. The accountability of the executive to the elected representatives of the people is made less effective to the extent that members of the executive can participate in a secret forum of legislation, participating in the creation of legal norms with direct applicability and effect. Publicity is a necessary condition both of answerability and of a proper public discourse on matters of public concern Europe-wide. However that may be, the demand for effective and open deliberation can be envisaged in the framework of this paper as a demand justified by appeal to subsidiarity at the most comprehensive level of deliberation. This is the level at which the existence of deliberation both is good in itself and contributes to the possibility of a commonwealth, crucial to which is the consciousness of some common good that is genuinely regarded as 'common'. I shall call this 'comprehensive subsidiarity'.

The institutions of a healthily democratic commonwealth would, I suggest give scope to the four aspects of subsidiarity to which I have drawn attention. Due regard to market subsidiarity both enables individuals and corporate groups of individuals to make their own free choices about matters they ought to be free to decide and contributes to enhanced if not always equal prosperity. A due regard to communal subsidiarity underlines the need to have freedom of marriage and freedom of association, and a rich range of voluntary bodies open for participation; also for forms of public self-government at a level local enough to support and reflect senses of civic and cultural identity. Due regard to rational legislative subsidiarity endorses the need for effective representative democracy expressed through legislatures at provincial, federal, and all-Europe levels, while discouraging the construction of all-Europe institutions that would unduly overshadow more local ones. (This is the sense of 'subsidiarity' most strongly written into the Union Treaty.) Respect for comprehensive subsidiarity requires the adoption of practices and fora for deliberation that are as open and accessible as possible, even if direct rights of audience in judicial fora are necessarily regulated and restricted.

Reflecting on the democratic deficit

The argument so far suggests, I think rightly, that the idea of a democratic commonwealth, especially one exhibiting the characteristics of the European Union, being a polyglot, multi-national and trans- or supra-national commonwealth committed both to democracy and to subsidiarity, is a complex, not a simple one. Neither 'rule by the people, for the people' nor 'majority rule', nor 'one person, one vote' nor any other simple concept or slogan will capture it. The different aspects of the value of democracy need to be acknowledged, in their parallelism with different elements or aspects of subsidiarity. An enlightened bureaucracy, provided it is subject to appropriate checks and controls, can also be seen to have an essential utility in a well-constituted order.

Market subsidiarity and communal subsidiarity are as important to a democratic commonwealth as rational legislative and comprehensive subsidiarity. Undue attention to the all-commonwealth institutions rather than the local ones would be unacceptable, and any over-empowerment of the commonwealth at the expense of its parts would impoverish the local levels. Further, reflection on the complexity of the whole suggests the weakness of any 'grand design' approaches to constitution-making for Europe. What is already in place was partly placed there by deliberate contrivance and by iterative agreement in the succession of treaties. It was partly developed by evolution through the discursive and deliberative processes of the European organs and particularly the Court. It does work and has contributed to unprecedented peace and prosperity among the countries included in the Union, whatever storm clouds now hover over the prospects for the common currency established in 1999. It is more probable that further tinkering and marginal adjustment than by an attempt at grand re-design and comprehensive constitution-making (as distinct from a reflective consolidation of the existing *acquis communautaire*) can achieve improvement. Hayek's warnings against the perils of constructivist rationalism are certainly valid for this context.[17] Due regard for comprehensive subsidiarity suggests the evolution of

---

[17] See F. A. Hayek, *Law, Legislation and Liberty*, vol. 1, *Rules and Order* (London: Routledge & Kegan Paul, 1976), 5–9, 14–17, 29–34.

institutions and systems in step with emerging consensus in the public deliberations of the commonwealth.

But certain changes would seem to be desirable in the light of the present discussion. The confidentiality of Council proceedings is indefensible and should be scrapped, and the powers of Parliament, much enhanced in the 1990s, could still admit of enlargement. It must nevertheless be remembered that this is not a state Parliament, nor the legislature of a sovereign federal union. It is the Parliament of a commonwealth of a new kind, a non-sovereign confederal commonwealth constituted by post-sovereign member states. It is a commonwealth with a mixed constitution, and it is necessary to avoid critique of its institutions that expressly or tacitly works from the assumption that the sovereign territorial state is the only legitimate form of human polity. Such an assumption inevitably leads to critique of institutions like the Parliament for failing to be a 'real' Parliament (that is, a state Parliament or a Parliament as closely analogous to that of a state as can be contrived). The burden of my argument has been and is that this is something the European Parliament in its own character is not and has no destiny to become. We must try to take seriously the unique and novel character of this 'mixed commonwealth', and aim for theoretical perspectives that respect its uniqueness and novelty rather than wedging it into old stereotypes.

The discussion of subsidiarity draws attention to the need to reflect on such lower-than-union entities or alleged entities as nations. The concern to avoid constituting the Union as some kind of super-state is a concern that springs, inter alia, from nationalist concerns. These are, however, concerns of a highly suspect kind in today's world. The next two chapters face up to the need for consideration of the question whether there can be any conceivable justification for nationalistic beliefs or principles. I believe that there can, but that the case needs to be stated with critical care.

10

Some Questions of Freedom

Introduction: On two ideas of a free country

We talk often about free human beings, and even today we are all too liable to talk just about 'free men'. In sometimes the same breath, sometimes quite a different one, we talk about 'free countries'. Sometimes we think or speak of a country as being free when it is free from external dominion, meaning that it is self-governing as a sovereign entity, or perhaps a post-sovereign one. Sometimes what we mean by a 'free country' is one with a system of internal governance that leaves people a lot of scope for choice how to live their lives, what to do, and what not to do. Part of the point of 'free countries' in this sense is that people are free to do foolish or undesirable things as well as wise and admirable ones. You might overhear the dialogue 'Mind if I smoke here?'—'It's a free country'. This does not contextually imply that the second party approves of the first party's smoking, but indeed quite the reverse. Yet, however grudgingly and with however censorious an attitude, the non-smoker acknowledges the other's right to make her/his own choice and act on it. When (or to the extent that) a country is 'free' in this sense, the scheme of government, including the law's restraints on wrongdoing, is such as to leave a wide range of choices open to citizens, without seeking excessively to discipline them for their own good. Moreover, there are clearly expressed limits on the situations or ways in which citizens are subject to arbitrary or even broadly discretionary intervention in their lives by agencies of government that can act coercively to enforce their discretionary decisions. The incompatibility of arbitrary rule with the freedom of humans as individual persons has been presented throughout this book as one crucial ground for valuing that respect for the rule of law which clothes the state with the virtue of being a law-state.

There is work still to be done if these two senses of 'freedom' are to be clearly distinguished, but for the moment it may suffice to let these relatively sketchy remarks highlight two distinguishable ideas. Given that they are indeed distinct, the question can be posed whether there are any connections between the two sorts of freedom of free countries I have identified. Can a country be free from external dominion and yet fail to be a free country from the point of view of its citizens' enjoyment of civil liberty? Can individuals have civil liberty even if their country is not a self-governing sovereign state? The answer in both cases appears obviously enough to be 'yes'. It accordingly seems as if civil liberty is not necessary for national sovereignty and national sovereignty not necessary for civil liberty. The two concepts are, it appears, independently variable.

Moreover, it would be among persons of liberal disposition, exactly those most favourable to freedom as civil liberty, that there would be found the gravest suspicions concerning the very notion that true 'freedom' is found in *national* independence rather than individual autonomy. Such persons shun the political rhetoric that promotes the values of 'a nation' as a whole rather than promoting the ability of citizens as individuals and in their freely chosen groupings to choose and pursue what they think valuable, even against actual or supposed national preferences. Liberals, in a word, mistrust nationalism. Nor do they lack instructive examples to exhibit the real grounds for their mistrust. From Hitler to Ceausescu to Milosevic, there has been no shortage of illustrative evils showing how the pursuit of national liberty and national values can lead to denigration, servility, torture, and death for those outside the charmed national circle, and even for many within it.

Liberals, needless to say, are not alone in their mistrusting. For most socialists also, the appeal to national values has been deeply suspect on account of the way it spreads ideological paper over the cracks of class division and exploitation, the real fissures between human beings in capitalistic societies. Jingoism and xenophobia can be whipped up to mask the realities of division, exploitation, and unequal freedom within a country. In 1982, Margaret Thatcher's Government in the United Kingdom sustained a startling recovery in popularity and political fortunes after victory in war with Argentina over the Falkland Islands (or 'Malvinas', as they are called from the other point of view). Socialists saw in this exactly such an instance of the ideological utility of nationalist rhetoric as I have been mentioning. Again, the xenophobia and anti-immigrant stance adopted by parties of the far right in more than a few European (and indeed non-European) countries, and the extent to which they have forced new policies on more moderate parties, could be presented as more glaring examples of this.

Thus from the point of view similarly of liberalism and of democratic socialism, there seems little to be said for nationalism. This holds good even if such a proponent of conservative liberalism as F. A. Hayek can argue that in truth socialism itself always amounts to 'national socialism' in the adversative sense, appealing at the deepest level to tribal instinct rather than respecting individual moral agents as free persons.[1] In Hayek's eyes socialism is as much and in the same way an enemy of freedom as is nationalism, for at bottom they are the same enemy. From the socialist, or social democratic, side of the argument, an available response is that the conservative liberal's conception of freedom is an inadequate and impoverished one. For it gives pride of place to personal freedom only in the sense of 'negative freedom',[2] freedom from excessive legal restriction, and freedom from arbitrary governmental intervention. It thus attends quite insufficiently to positive freedom, ignoring the significance of the freedom, and practical ability, to participate in the social self-constitution of a community, the freedom, and practical ability, to develop and express one's own personality in the collective, but not necessarily uniform, self-expression of all. For

---

[1] See F. A. Hayek, *The Road to Serfdom* (London: G. Routledge and Sons, 1944).
[2] See I. Berlin, *Four Essays on Liberty* (Oxford, Clarendon Press, 1969), ch. 3, 'Two Concepts of Liberty'; J. N. Gray 'On Negative and Positive Liberty', *Political Studies*, 28 (1980), 507–26.

these freedoms to be achieved in reality as practical abilities to act effectively, people have to have the support of the society around them. They must all be given a real chance to do things, and that means securing to everybody a fair, if not mathematically equal, share of commonly available resources. Only then is even equal negative liberty similar in worth for all those to whom the law formally secures it.[3]

In however summary form, with however inadequate elaboration, these few paragraphs may serve as a reminder concerning some questions of freedom that come to the fore the moment one raises the issue of the credibility of nationalism from a political or philosophical point of view. There has been a large majority consensus among philosophers of the later twentieth century concerning nationalism, and that consensus has been broadly hostile and dismissive. Nationalism has been more presented as a phenomenon to be explained in historical or psychological terms, an aberration of romantic idealism, than taken seriously as a topic for normative political philosophy. A brilliant example of this historical-explanatory approach, coupled with what might fairly be considered the standard consensual critique of nationalism, can be found in Kenneth Minogue's *Nationalism*.[4]

Freedom and the end of empires

The whole story of liberal and socialist attitudes has, however, not yet been told. There is another side to the attitudes and policies that found favour among supporters of what one could call 'progressive' beliefs (at least, those who held them considered them progressive) in the second half of the twentieth century. These do not directly contradict, yet do stand in opposing tension against, the ideas reviewed in the last section. We must consider the way in which people of liberal or otherwise progressive opinion responded towards popular self-determination in the context of decolonization. The departure by European imperial states from their colonial possessions overseas, and the nation-state building efforts of the governments of newly independent ex-colonies, were at the time of independence and for a good time afterwards widely welcomed. The sense of rightness persisted even where nation-building in the odd slices of territory left behind by the nineteenth-century imperialists' carve-ups led to authoritarian government, one-party rule, and substantial restrictions in freedom as civil liberty in countries lately come to the freedom of independence from external control. Even where this happened, there is a common opinion, which I certainly share, that the ending of colonial rule was on the whole and in itself good. At the century's end, there remains in the Republic of South Africa, a real hope and a genuine possibility that democracy and civil liberty can thrive now that apartheid is overthrown and majority rule prevailing in a multilingual and multi-ethnic society.

---

[3] See, e.g., B. Crick, *Socialism* (Milton Keynes: Open University Press, 1987).

[4] K. Minogue, *Nationalism* (London: Batsford, 1967). Cf. R. McLaughlan, 'Aspects of Nationalism', in N. MacCormick (ed.), *The Scottish Debate: Essays on Scottish Nationalism* (London: Oxford University Press, 1970), 21–33.

The hope that freedom from external dominion and internal racial tyranny can be matched by sustained constitutional government and civil liberty lends strength to the satisfaction that the colonialist epoch seems finally at an end.

Even more popular in their time among 'Western' intellectuals and progressive thinkers were the movements towards national liberation that came about in Central and Eastern Europe and the former Soviet Union, inheritor of Tsarist empire, through the revolutionary collapse of communism in the years 1989–91. To recall from a yet earlier epoch the emotions awakened by and judgements perpended about the Hungarian rising of 1956, or the Prague Spring of 1968, or the flourishing of the 'Solidarity' movement in Poland around 1980, or to contemplate opinion about the re-emergence of the Baltic republics twice (or three times) conquered during the Second World War, is to remind oneself how equivocal opinions as well as terms can be in this area of discussion. In these cases, there was a widely held supposition that if only oppressed countries could become more free in the sense of enjoying enhanced external independence, they had some chance to become more free in the other sense, with their citizens enjoying greater and more secure civil liberty. Even that may be to overintellectualize the issue. Maybe it is just that, since people so obviously wanted some new deal from the Soviet state, democratic imperatives required applause for every step taken towards their getting it, and most particularly such steps as themselves involved some form of democratic self-expression.

In the case of comparatively recent events, the somewhat impressionistic account given here without elaborate citation of sources will suffice for readers who themselves lived through the years in question and followed the various media of news and opinion.[5] I might perhaps be forgiven for adding a fragment of evidence from my own view of things, formed on an academic visit to Poland in 1988. Everywhere I found an almost palpable sense of a gap between state and the society, a radical mistrust by citizens of 'their' state, and indeed alienation from it. Aspirations of a kind quite ordinary in the perspective of luckier lands to the west went unfulfilled through the inability of the state to respond to views held by what seemed to be the vast majority of citizens. Everywhere also one had a powerful sense of the Polishness of Poland, and yet of a frustration that this was locked into an inefficient and unpopular system of government. So to say, there was here a nation whose state was serving it ill. (If one were to speak of the church, that might have been a different matter. Certainly, the institutional presence of the church made available a focus and locus of alternative opinion and discourse for persons whose attitudes would probably have made them seem the least devout of communicants in different political conditions.) So it was possible to conceive of the conditions for realization of an effective democracy in terms of a hope for re-inclusion of the nation in the state, so that the imperatives of democracy could be

---

[5] Cf. Martin Krygier, *Between Fear and Hope* (Sydney: ABC Publications, 1997), 102–6; to this, and to Martin Krygier's regular contributions about Poland to the Australian current affairs journal *Quadrant*, I am greatly indebted.

considered also to contain an element of nationalism, in the need for a distinctively *Polish* self-determination.

Such an example as this, and the others mentioned, establish a counterpoint, if not quite an antithesis, to the point with which I started. Contemporary moral and political philosophy has on the whole regarded nationalism as a significant but regrettable political phenomenon rather than a political position with a case to make at the level of normative philosophizing.[6] Yet in the face of the general indifference or hostility to the idea of nationalism, there has been a generally cordial response to colonial liberation and national liberation in certain settings, where principles of self-determination of an essentially nationalist sort seem to have been at stake. There appear to be contradictions or at least confusions as to the sorts of free countries it is desirable to have.

In this state of things there is a challenge to which those who are philosophically inclined might essay a response. Can we in any way resolve my questions of freedom by reconciling in any way the two senses of a 'free country', the country that is free because its citizens have liberty, and the country that is free because it has independence itself? Will this lead us to make some sense of nationalism? To pursue this task will call for a certain clarification of confused ideas. So I shall attempt some clarification in the next section, deferring a final conclusion till the following chapter.

On negative liberty

Here, I shall start with a clarification and critique of one civil libertarian conception of a free country. Clearly, there is a great deal to be said for any polity that secures to its citizens the traditional civil and political rights. These are broadly constitutive of what Isaiah Berlin taught us to call 'negative liberty', the liberty that consists in not being required or forced to do or abstain from things one would not freely choose to do or abstain from.[7] The pursuit of happiness requires life and liberty. Mutual respect and self-respect in a moral community require each to have regard to the liberty of others and all ideally to endorse an equal liberty for themselves and everyone else. To this, John Rawls has added the necessary qualification that unequal liberties can be

---

[6] There are, of course, quite a few exceptions, and I am here conscious of indebtedness at least to the late John Plamenatz (see *Consent, Freedom, and Political Obligation* (London: Oxford University Press, 1968)) to Yael Tamir whose *Liberal Nationalism* (Princeton, N.J., Princeton University Press, 1993) I first had the opportunity to see in the form of a doctoral thesis in Oxford University in 1988, to Harry Beran, who has explored issues of self-determination and of secession in a powerful series of articles (see H. Beran, 'Must Secession be Rebellion?', *Politics*, 18 (1983), 49–78; 'A Liberal Theory of Secession', *Political Studies*, 32 (1984), 21–31; and 'A Philosophical Perspective', in A. Macartney (ed), *Self-Determination in the Commonwealth* (Aberdeen: Aberdeen University Press, 1988), 23–35), and to Tim O'Hagan, some of whose ideas on individualism and pluralism I apply or perhaps misapply in this and the succeeding chapter—see T. O'Hagan, 'An Unsolved Dilemma of Liberalism' in H. Jung, H. Müller-Dietz, and U. Neumann, *Recht und Moral* (Baden-Baden, Nomos Verlaggesellschaft, 1991), 53–66.

[7] Berlin, *Four Essays*, ch. 3.

justified where they strengthen the overall scheme of liberty.[8] Perhaps parliamentary or judicial privilege give MPs and judges freedoms of speech that their fellow citizens do not have. Even so, it seems easy to see that the whole scheme of liberty is advanced rather than undermined by according such special privileges of free speech to parliamentarians and members of the judiciary performing the duties of their offices.

In any event, the flourishing of human good in each and every bearer of humanity seems to be furthered by a regime of civil liberty, on one conception of human good. That is to say, for those who regard autonomy as being of the essence of human and moral value, it is only where conditions of liberty admit of each person's autonomous pursuit of the good as they see it that the good life can be truly realized. The appeal to autonomy as a human and moral good is not, however, the only possible way to argue the case for liberal civil liberty. Some may even find it a dangerous mode of argument since it itself depends on a so-called 'perfectionist' ground, namely the idea or ideal of autonomy as a constitutive part of human good.[9] Some wish their theory of liberty to hold a yet more neutral course between visions of the good, and may argue that the special strength and attractiveness of liberalism lies in its refusal to privilege either any philosophical conception or any individual vision or any state-defined imposition of models for the good life.[10]

The natural line for this kind of theoretical approach to take is that of assuming liberty not so much to be conferred on, as to be retained by, the citizen. This suggests that liberty inheres in us in some way anterior to and independently of our social existence, the only question being how far we may lose it or should give it up. Social contract models for legitimating government arise almost inevitably in this setting, whether as historical models or, more credibly, as hypothetical or imaginary contracts like that proposed by John Rawls. Hobbes's question, how much of their natural liberty individuals must transfer to the state, is and remains in some form the basic question from this point of view. The question is not what or how much liberty states should give their citizens; rather, it is how much liberty persons should forego in favour of the needs of government, however these needs are conceived. The continuing theme of one strand of liberal thought is that the needs of government must always fall short of the framing and imposition of any one conception of the good life.

This, however, seems to rest on a deeply implausible vision of human society. For it makes untenably atomistic assumptions about the character of human beings. It is a kind of 'methodological individualism' that imagines there could be individuals anterior to any form of organized society, and that such individuals who could intelligibly come together and agree to constitute one. Nor is it obvious why the fiction of a merely hypothetical contract can get one round the difficulty. It is one thing to

---

[8] See J. Rawls, *A Theory of Justice* (Oxford, Clarendon Press, 1972), 302.

[9] See J. Raz, *The Morality of Freedom* (Oxford: Clarendon Press, 1987); cf. N. MacCormick, 'The Relative Heteronomy of Law', *European Journal of Philosophy*, 3 (1995), 69–85.

[10] So argues Carlos Nino, 'Moral Discourse and liberal Rights' in N. Macormick and Z. Bankowski (eds.), *Enlightenment, Rights, and Revolution* (Aberdeen: Aberdeen University Press, 1989), ch. 7.

make a hypothesis about what could have happened, but did not; another thing altogether to try and work through an imagining of something that could not conceivably happen.

The truth about human individuals is that they are social products, not independent atoms capable of constituting society through a voluntary coming together. We are as much constituted by our society as it is by us. The biological facts of birth and early nourishment and the socio-psychological facts of our education and socialization are essential to constituting us as persons. We are the persons we come to be in the social settings and contexts in which we find ourselves, and whatever sense we have of our identity and character as persons reflects our interaction with significant others in our social setting, and indeed in a more diffuse way is a reflection of our total social milieu. Consider, for example, what a crucial part of anyone's sense of identity is tied up in having a name. Very few people ever choose a name for themselves, and, when they do, it is in substitution for a given one. Yet names are meaningful only within a language and an elaborate coding of what counts as a name. This is significant even for names like 'Malcolm X', which are chosen to make points critical of established naming practices; that is, it is within a web of social practices that we get to be individuals.

Atomistic or methodologically individualistic assumptions seem simply unworkable. All individuals as they really are fall into the class of 'contextual individuals', as Yael Tamir has expressed it,[11] and as will be argued at length in the next chapter. We have a sense of self because of the way we have learned to be ourselves in the contexts in which we have so learned.

This view does not entail any kind of mechanistic social determinism. There is no reason why people cannot come to be autonomous selves within certain kinds of social contexts, and we all have the evidence at least of introspection and also of acquaintance with others to tell us that it is so. Individuals are the very things that people become in social contexts that afford the opportunity of coming to acquire a secure sense of personal identity and a capacity to pursue a life of one's own even within the constraints of given social circumstances. Such individuals are capable of showing the very autonomy in action that the first chapter argued to be of the essence of acting within a normative order. According to the view advocated here, there is value in those forms of social organization that do make possible individuality, individualism, and autonomy, the more so the more these are facilitated. This is achieved by creating protected spheres of legal liberty within which the exercise of individual autonomy is protected. I take it that Hegel's representation of the constitutional state as the concrete embodiment of reason[12] was intended to make just this point.

So far as it was, we ought to accept his point even if not exactly his way of putting it. In any event, we can now see that the absurdity of methodological individualism

---

[11] Yael Tamir, *Liberal Nationalism*, 32–4.
[12] See M. Knox (trans), *Hegel's Philosophy of Right* (Oxford: Clarendon Press, 1952).

in no way entails the rejection of some form of normative individualism.[13] It is impossible to conceive of human individuals as having an existence apart from society, or pre-social or extra-social atoms whose unions come to be constitutive of societies. That in no way precludes one from believing that there are powerful reasons in favour of forms of social organization within which human beings can be constituted as, and can flourish as, autonomous individuals. Autonomy is indeed a fundamental human good, and thus it is a great social value to uphold societies that facilitate it. So when we talk about 'free countries' in the sense of countries enjoying secured civil liberty, we should not think of them as though they just contingently happen to be peopled by free humans; each is partly conditional on the existence of the other.

What then about free countries in the other sense? At least I think it will now be becoming clearer that I have to move towards revising my earlier suggestion that the two senses of 'a free country' are totally independent of each other. The first move is to take up the thesis that some form of democratic self-determination has to be considered both justifiable and valuable on rather the same grounds as the simple negative liberties in the list of civil liberties. Some form of collective self-constitution, some kind of active participation in shaping and sustaining the institutions of social or communal government whose aim is to advance liberty and autonomy, seems to be a necessary part of the whole ensemble of conditions in which the autonomy of the contextual individual could be genuinely constituted and upheld. If autonomous individuals require the context of some sort of freedom-enabling society, then the collective autonomy of the society itself seems a part of the necessary context.

No doubt certain sorts of enlightened despotism and certain sorts of enlightened colonial government can create the possibility of civil liberty and mercantile or professional freedom of trade. No doubt these in themselves are valuable in helping to develop autonomy by creating conditions for its full development. But so long as the state stands apart from and above civil society, there is only a partial autonomy of individuals. This stress on the activist and participatory character of full autonomy, thus of the need for a collective as well as an individualistic component of autonomy, is a point justly taken by democratic and socialistic critics of mere negative liberty. It is a part of the just reply to Hayek's earlier-mentioned critique of socialism. For democratic institutions depend on the ability of each to take part as the equal of every other, and this requires a whole range of basic conditions in the way of freedom from acute need, satisfactory education, and so forth, as well as setting limits, however vague, upon the extremes of economic inequality which are tolerable. Autonomous liberty in a free country requires schemes of redistribution, welfare provision, and educational support which would be absolutely excluded by conservative liberalism of the sort which denies the state any role other than that of the night watchman. Very few people nowadays support that view anyway, and much of our political argumentation seems to me to be more about the how much than the

---

[13] I take his point from Tim O'Hagan, 'An Unsolved Dilemma of Liberalism'; in the next chapter of the present book I re-express it as 'value-individualism'.

whether of redistribution, welfare, and education. In that sense, it remains true that we are still all socialists now, as Sir William Harcourt already remarked a century ago.

So self-determination is after all a vital part of any acceptable conception of liberty as autonomy, self-determination in a dual sense, meaning that there has to be scope both for individual self-determination inside a political community and for the collective self-determination of the community without external domination. This should not be thought a particularly novel finding or conclusion. After all, the International Covenant on Civil and Political Rights and the International Covenant on Economic, Social and Cultural Rights both open with the stipulation that:

All peoples have the right of self-determination. By virtue of that right they freely determine their political status and freely pursue their economic, social and cultural development.

Certainly, in positive international law, this principle has been given a very restricted interpretation,[14] as governing post-colonial liberation but not as implying any right of secession of an internal part from an established unitary or federal state. But, on the face of it, there might be scope for a wider reading as a matter of political or moral theory. That is the question that will occupy the next chapter. The present one having considered the case for some interaction between the two ideas of a 'free country', the next will consider the idea of nationalism against the constraints of fundamental principles derived from the liberal tradition.

---

[14] A certain body of opinion holds self-determination to be more or less restricted in operation to cases of decolonization, and as applying within established states only to the extent of requiring rights of democratic participationm on equal terms by minorities. But see James Crawford, 'Outside the Colonial Context', in A. Macartney (ed.), *Self-Determination in the Commonwealth* (Aberdeen: Aberdeen University Press, 1988), 1– 22, esp. at 21–2.

11

A Kind of Nationalism

Introduction

According to the argument of this book so far, the European Union has brought about a new form of legal and political order in Western Europe. It has created the possibility of politics 'beyond the sovereign state'. Old conceptions of state-sovereignty and of the absolutism of the nation-state are in the process of being transcended, and will perhaps be completely transcended if people realize that this is possible and in certain important ways desirable. The process does not abolish nations as politico-cultural communities. It may create space for the flourishing of nations and, in a significantly qualified sense, of nationalism. This will be a tamed nationalism, a nationalism compatible with the certain essential principles of political morality that deserve to be a permanent legacy of humanistic liberalism to this and successor generations. The key to the idea is that of subsidiarity as discussed in Chapter 9, especially in respect of communal subsidiarity and rational legislative subsidiarity.

The forms of political decision-making that are required in a satisfactorily human existence must be as close to the individuals affected as is reasonably possible. It is in the 'little battalions' that people can really participate in decision-making with a sense that their voice makes a difference, and can through interaction with others become fully responsible beings, participating in communal governance. This is in the first instance a matter of 'communal subsidiarity', to return to the terminology suggested in Chapter 9. Rational legislative subsidiarity does or may require the exercise of law-making powers over a range wider than that of the little battalion, but there is nothing to be said for largeness of scale just for its own sake. Democracy requires a sense of loyalty to the collective decision, which is usually a simple majority decision. The more there is a sense of mutual sympathy between competing opinions in legislative debate, the more it is reasonable to demand (and practicable to obtain) acquiescence in majority votes. Where there is a sense of local or national community, this is of value to the end of sustaining the kind of mutual solidarity that trust in democratic institutions presupposes. Moreover, where there are distinctive civic institutions connected with a territory, and especially if these include substantial elements of law and legal tradition, the convergence of the imperatives of communal and rational legislative subsidiarity is obvious. This comes into alliance with the democratic idea that those who are subject to a special legal system should have the ultimate say about its contents, hence the residents of such a territory should also possess democratic legislative institutions. The case of Scotland is a material illustration here, but this is not a result of special pleading, simply an illustration of principles independently derived.

The case that has to be made is a difficult and delicate one. No cause, perhaps not even that of class warfare or that of religious extremism, seems more readily exploited to the ends of inhumanity than that of a 'nation'. The twentieth century began in a clash of great empires. These were all in some degree characterized by tension between a dominant imperial culture and the aspirations of subject peoples and nations, but all were multi-ethnic. One by one, the empires imploded. The Versailles Treaty attempted to implement a principle of national self-determination, but with very imperfect success. The Second World War grew out of some of the failures of Versailles, exhibiting in the Holocaust and in other ways the intolerable brutality of racist species of nationalism. In the succeeding years, the principle of self-determination, though asserted as a universal human right belonging to 'peoples', was applied only in relation to decolonization, and international lawyers hold that it has either no, or only restricted, application in the case of minority nations within union states.

The last empire to collapse was that of Russia, transformed into the USSR, and dissolved with the economic, intellectual, and political collapse of soviet Marxism. The same events led or contributed to the dissolution of federal Yugoslavia, among and within whose former republics savage ethnic-nationalist conflicts broke out. Finally, in March 1999, the North Atlantic Treaty Organization (NATO) conceived itself forced to intervene in Kosovo to prevent a humanitarian disaster, the extirpation of Kosovo Albanians by forces of, or irregulars loyal to, the Republic of Yugoslavia, by this time little more than alter ego of the Serbian state. In Russia, the first reaction was of nationalist resentment against the militarism of the West, intervening in the internal affairs of a sovereign Slav state.

Nationalism through all this has been reviled by enlightened thinkers, and has often deserved no better. In the last chapter, some of the reasons for this attitude were considered. Why not then forget completely about nationalism?

There is a difficulty to be faced: multi-nationality and multi-ethnicity have always been features of empires, and empires at their best have treated ethnic plurality in a reasonable and tolerant way, though usually with at very least a tacit assumption of the superiority of the metropolitan culture. Democracy, however, has never been successfully combined with empire, and the rise of democratic ideals and movements has accompanied, and even played a part in causing, the downfall of empires. In some form, nationalism is then implicated in the nation-building of a post-imperial period, often at a high cost to ethnic, national, or religious minorities within emergent and putatively democratic nations. Where democracy has failed and one-party dictatorship or military rule has supervened, nationalist rhetoric has played a considerable (though not exclusive) part in ideologically sustaining dictatorship, often through victimization or demonization of minorities.

Nobody who is minded to make out a case for nationalism of any species, however qualified, dare ignore these evidences of history. But there is another side, as the preceding paragraph suggests, namely that concerning democracy. If one does believe in democratic forms of government, perhaps for the reasons suggested in

Chapter 9, perhaps for egalitarian ones considered in Chapter 10, the question arises concerning the political entities within which democracy should have place. Within what group of people does a majority vote constitute a genuine mandate for legislation or executive policy-making, such that the minority can be called upon to acquiesce in it for the sake of democracy? Is there any right of secession from an established state or empire? If considerations of subsidiarity are added to the agenda in the manner suggested above, one may conclude that nations are among the groups that merit some consideration in the context of democratic constitution-making.

Nations, however, have been considered highly suspect entities. Perhaps they are 'entities' that can find a sort of 'being' only within an ideological form of false consciousness. Perhaps their only reality is that embodied in the deeds, often evil deeds, that men and women do under appeals to nation or national rights. Unless this can be shown to be false, the discussion comes to an abrupt end. The next section argues on behalf of a basis for continuing the discussion.

Identifying nations

What is it that makes a 'nation' or a 'country', in the sense of a place to which a person might belong, not just a territory arbitrarily marked on a map? Three ways of thinking about this have gained prominence in contemporary discussions. One way stresses civic institutions, public offices, public agencies and officials, churches in their secular activities, common and authoritative rules with a territorial scope. These define a country and the nation that inhabits it. Another stresses culture and language, a heritage of literature, music, and dancing, a way of life associated with a geographical home, a landscape celebrated in song and story. A history of the common doings and sufferings of those who share in the culture that itself enshrines popular memories of historical triumphs and disasters. A nation, as such, has a culture. The third way stresses common ethnicity, common ancestry, and common ancestral struggles. The nation is the community of fate, the community of ethnic bonds.

The models need not be interpreted as exclusive. Civic institutions can generate and become a focus of common culture; cultural identity can lead to a demand for common civic institutions, or adaptation of non-civic institutions to civic purposes (consider the Catholic Church in Polish history). A sense of shared ethnicity can lead to common institutions and cultural folk-ways, or, more probably can be inferred from the existence of these. Culture, indeed, seems a kind of middle ground between the civic and the ethnic. The civic and the ethnic conceptions of the nation are opposite poles, or contrasting ideal types. Real countries and nations may fall nearer one pole or the other, and this will show up in the ideas about the common culture that prevail.

Given these models of a 'nation', it seems reasonable to suppose that we may need at least two models of nationalism, where the latter is understood as a principle advocating the right of persons who constitute a nation to national self-determination and continuing national self-government in some form. Under a civic conception of the nation, the nation which exercises the right of self-determination is constituted by a sense of common belonging among those who share civic institutions, with no exclusiveness towards any person or group willing to participate in them. The issue is that of acceptance of the jurisdiction of the civic institutions. Ethnic nationalism focuses on the self-determination of the historically given—perhaps even genetically given—community of culture and of ancestral belonging.

Subsequently, we shall consider the possibility of a kind of 'liberal nationalism'. To this, the idea of civic nationalism is strongly material. 'Civic nationalism' identifies the nation in terms of its members' shared allegiance to certain civic institutions. These are understood in broad terms to include, for example, legal norms and institutions, political representative organs, branches of public and local administration, the organization of education, churches and religious communities in their secular aspect, and other like institutions having an understood territorial location to which they refer. Institutions of civil society as much as of the state are relevant here. Territorially located civic institutions can be objects of allegiance, understood as 'ours' by the people among whom they perform their functions. As civic institutions, they are necessarily of great political significance to the community which, to an extent, they define.

Naturally, it is possible, and perhaps desirable, for such civic institutions to go the length of including a constitution and the full panoply of statehood. Perhaps without that the civic quality of civic institutions is too precarious. But it would be a mistake to require this by definition, for to do so is simply to endorse the in-principle challenged assumption that the states that currently exist comprise also the totality of nations, at any rate, the totality of nations that can be understood in the civic sense. Whether or not the civic nation is or has a state, or *a fortiori* an independent sovereign state, the point of the idea of a civic nation is that it is in principle open to voluntary membership. The community defined by allegiance to institutions is open to anyone who chooses to dwell in the territory and give allegiance to the institutions. Departure to a different place and different allegiances is also possible, and not traitorous. One is guilty of treachery only if one remains in place and surreptitiously undermines the institutions of that place while ostensibly giving them respect and allegiance. (There is all the difference in the world between such surreptitious subversion and open criticism, however robust, of civic institutions considered stultifying, obsolete, or the like.)

To contrast with this is the conception of nation as a racial or ethnic community. This may be defined as the possessor of a distinctive culture, including perhaps a language thought of as the special possession of those and only those belonging to the original ethnic community, grounded ultimately in some kind of shared ancestry or genetic bond. Nationality so defined is necessarily and unavoidably given. It has no voluntary element nor any opening thereto. Nations are communities of fate, with compulsory membership and no right of exit. You either are a member of this nation or not; if you are, it has a claim on your loyalty whether you like its institutional arrangements and cultural manifestations or not. Ethnic nationalism thus focuses on a shared ethno-historico-cultural identity as defining the community whose self-determination is in issue. This entails some exclusiveness of attitude towards those deemed not to possess the relevant ethnic identity.

We should avoid seeing or defining the civic and the ethnic in straightforward either/or terms. As was said above they are more ideal types than exclusive alternatives. For of course communities identified by common loyalty to common civic institutions develop cultural practices and institutions around them. Further, people in one country or another tend to have more or less long-standing familial and historical associations with given places and the institutions that exist there. Thus the community of allegiance will easily and naturally perceive itself as also a community of culture and of historical belonging, and places with their ancient place-names and characteristic, partly man-made, landscape can exercise a powerful grip on human imagination and emotions. On the other hand, the community that conceives itself primarily in terms of blood and belonging, ancestral culture and history will also develop its own institutions, and may tacitly acknowledge a kind of adoption of incomers who over time come to accept the institutions. As was noted above, 'culture' is the middle ground between civic and ethnic poles.

There remain all-important differences of emphasis and degree. It is plainly enough evident that a political commitment to rights of personal individuality and autonomy is one that restricts its endorsement to the claims of civic nationalism, with only such associated elements of the cultural or ethnic as are compatible with personal freedom and autonomy.

The idea of a culture in its historical and geographical setting does have a genuine part to play in the argument here. In Iceland, for example, or in Wales, or in Tuscany, one has a sense of an ancient way of life, a language rooted in its historic place, with place-names of ancient origin expressing the continuity of settlement and of cultural and social identity in that place. None of this is incompatible with free movement of people and gradual change over time. But there is surely a sense of loss, loss not only for the minority, but also for human cultural diversity, if the weight of migration is sufficient simply to eliminate or obliterate all that went before. Cultures have value in terms of identity to their possessors. To everybody, they are a manifestation of the variety of human experience and the multiplicity of human identities, also of the continuity of past and present, and the challenge of continuity into the future.

None of this would justify preservation of cultures in culture-dishes, so to say. Universal theme-parks would be just as depressing as universal and identical hamburger joints can be. (Anyway, the two are frequently found in juxtaposition.) The insensitive onward march of majority cultures propagated through the media of mass communication and information technology almost inevitably triggers a reaction of defensiveness towards threatened species of language and potentially despoiled cultural habitats. Many of the bearers of majority cultures are highly and laudably sensitive to this, and surely the growth in awareness of diversity and in appreciation of the manifold contemporary politics of identity (though not the violent or terrorist forms it takes in some places) is indicative of this.

In recent papers, the social anthropologist Anthony Cohen has advanced the notion of what he calls 'personal nationalism'.[1] His idea is material to the present discussion. It is that nations are not real entities at all, but elements ultimately of individual consciousness. For any country or nation, each of us has her or his own conception of it, and our sense of identification is not with some objective 'out-there' entity, but rather with our own idea of the nation. To use an example of mine rather than his own one, there must be as many Englands as there are English people, and these are not all the same thing. Rather, there is at best a partially overlapping consensus of England-ideas from the point of view of those who self-identify as English, and then also, perhaps, from the point of view of self-defined outsiders. England as a nation is not something that justifies the overlapping consensus, but an idea that emerges from it, to the extent that any consensus does in fact emerge.

This is in many ways an attractive idea given its tendency to liberate national consciousness from anti-individualism. The problem is in the use of the term 'nationalism' here. The 'ism' is an intrinsically political idea, one that argues for the political relevance of the shared national consciousness, however many share it. Some of the difficulties of democracy, for example, notably the difficulty concerning who counts as a potential voter, are soluble by reference to nations as legitimate units of self-determination. It may, indeed it must, be the case that social entities like 'nations' depend on human consciousness and human use and wont, and human interpretations of usages customs and ways of life. But the step from overlapping but not in-principle identical or even closely similar states of individual consciousness to a seriously arguable political principle seems an inordinately long one—and indeed that may be the true upshot of Cohen's 'personal nationalism'.

On the other hand, it might point toward, or warn of the risk of, a somewhat manipulative political style. Persons with necessarily different and possibly competing personal conceptions of a nation could be expected to struggle for possession of the public institutions and symbols through which to privilege 'their' nation over other conceptions or pictures of it. This would be the 'nation' of persuasive definitions,[2] not of existing reality. There may well be very much more than a grain of truth in the idea that rival entrepreneurs of identity work at seeking to capture the nation-idea for their personal vision of a country and culture. No doubt, nationalist politicians do deploy nation-conceptions in an essentially ideological spirit in the always-ongoing power struggles that characterize political parties within themselves and in competition with rivals.

---

[1] See A. P. Cohen, 'Personal Nationalism: a Scottish View of some Rites, Rights, and Wrongs', *American Ethnologist*, 23 (1996), 1–14, 'Peripheral Vision: Nationalism, National Identity and the Objective Correlative in Scotland', in Anthony P. Cohen (ed.), *Discriminating Relations: Anthropological Essays on Boundary, Identity and Authenticity* (London: Routledge 1999), 186–218.

[2] See C. L. Stevenson's discussion of 'persuasive definitions' in his *Ethics and Language* (New Haven, CT: Yale University Press, 1963), ch. 9.

But there is another side to this as well. For personal conceptions of nations do also have some objective correlative.[3] In the case of the civic nation, there are civic institutions and durable forms of normative order. From the opening chapter of this book, it has been assumed that normative order can have objective existence, not unconnected to states of momentary consciousness of individuals, but not simply constituted by these. Normative orders of certain kinds are explicitly connected to jurisdictional space, that is, to some demarcated place or places. These places are also the sites for associated material and non-material cultural objects and practices. The cultural objects and practices flourish through their being made, being interpreted, being developed, and being appreciated by humans. In these states of consciousness do indeed reside the personal and subjective nations of those individuals who have national consciousness at all. If there were no such states of consciousness, it is unimaginable that there could be anything at all in the way of a politics of identity connecting to national belonging as one strand of the personal identity of human beings.

Cultural activities and objects, like legal ones (law being, indeed, a part of culture in its broader sense) are, as noted, subject both to interpretation and to innovation. To both, each interpreter or innovator brings a personal and individual style and understanding. This is both a condition and a consequence of the kind of social formation that makes possible the flourishing of personal autonomy. Of course this means that a 'nation', not only in the personal but also in the civic sense, is, through the self-conceptions of members an always evolving, always diversifying, always contestable, cultural community. It is so because of the overlapping but also diverging ideas of those who identify with the civic nation. In due course, we shall return to the idea mentioned already in Chapter 10, that individuals are not independent atoms, but 'contextual individuals'. It is already possible to see and reasonable to claim that the 'context' that makes each of us a contextual individual is no straitjacket of deterministic and fatal identity, but itself something always evolving and in some degree negotiable. Evolution and negotiation occur in the interactions of persons and their mutual exchange of interpretations of their context, country, and culture.

Accordingly, Cohen's idea of 'personal' nationalism is, perhaps already in his own version of it, but certainly in an available and attractive adaptation of it, an important corollary of the civic ideal type of nationalism. In this guise, it is a useful or even a necessary step in the argument for a liberal interpretation of nationalism. The liberal interpretation for which I shall argue can be stated in terms of this principle:

the members of a nation are as such in principle entitled to effective organs of political self-government within the world order of sovereign or post-sovereign states.

Given the civic nationalist conception of membership in a nation, this has promise of being a principle compatible with certain basic liberal ideas that merit support,

---

[3] I borrow the idea of the 'objective correlative' from T. S. Eliot, *The Sacred Wood: Essays on Poetry and Criticism* (London: Methuen, 7th edn. 1950, repr. 1960), 100–2, though in this context its application is somewhat different from that stipulated in the literary context by Eliot.

even if some liberals' ideas of the constitution of individuals and of society cannot be accepted without qualification. It is, I shall claim, a principle, not an absolute rule. This means that in any real-life situation there may be competing principles, such that it is a question of weighing and balancing to decide how far and in what ways our principle is susceptible of implementation without injury to equally important, or more important, values and principles.

It is often said, and rightly, that on any reasonable definition of 'nation', human beings have too many of them, too badly distributed, to allocate a territory and a sovereign state to each of them.[4] Sometimes this is taken to justify a do-nothing policy, accepting the states that we have, with all their pretensions to sovereignty and to nation-statehood. If the only alternative were bloodshed and war, I would agree. But if it is injudicious to increase excessively the number of states, it may in the alternative be possible to diminish their pretensions, and thus to adjust the position between those nationalities who have and those who have not a fully sovereign state of their own. The principle of subsidiarity again springs to mind as a useful principle for liberal reflection in this context. The argument for the principle must now be made.

Liberal nationalism?

The question for review here is whether there can be such a thing as liberal nationalism. The answer, of course, depends on what you mean by 'liberal', for liberalism has been a quite vigorously contested concept, as much among its supporters as among its opponents. The strategy here will not be to offer an addition to the plethora of definitions there have been of 'liberalism', but rather to argue for certain basic principles that have in one form or another had a prominent place in liberal thought. I shall argue for what I call 'liberal nationalism', under a considerable debt to Yael Tamir's book of the same name,[5] but nothing turns on the felicity of the name, for what matters is the soundness of the principles. There is, I firmly believe, an important place in the contemporary world for a liberal nationalism. This 'liberal' version of nationalism is one for which it is vital to argue most vigorously just now. Otherwise, we leave the field wide open for intolerant, illiberal, racist or even fascist forms of nationalism. This case has to be upheld against arguments that say liberal ideals are wholly incompatible with nationalism in any form, and so-called liberal nationalism is a mixture of contradiction in terms and dangerous illusion.

Liberalism in the version I favour shades over into social democracy,[6] rather than embracing a purely market-economical view of the good society; it also rejects atomistic

---

[4] See E. Gellner, *Nations and Nationalism* (Oxford: Basil Blackwell, 1983), G. Gottlieb, *Nation Against State* (New York, Council on Foreign Relations, 1993), ch. 3.

[5] See Y. Tamir, *Liberal Nationalism* (Princeton NJ, Princeton University Press, 1993).

[6] See N. MacCormick, *Legal Right and Social Democracy* (Oxford, Clarendon Press 1982), ch. 1.

and contractarian assumptions about the constitution of society, as will appear shortly. This social-democratic liberalism is both universalistic and individualistic.

It is universalistic because it holds that whatever rights or duties attach to any particular human being in given circumstances must be considered as universalizable in a simply logical sense. The same rights and duties must attach to any human being in like circumstances. It also upholds universalism in an inclusivist sense. There is a presumption in favour of more inclusive over less inclusive characterizations of relevant human circumstances. Universality is a necessary feature of moral justification. Hence morally justifiable political principles have to be universalizable, and principles that have a narrowly discriminatory application to narrowly specified characteristics or external circumstances of individuals are to be considered suspect despite being logically universal in form. The less inclusive the categories they stipulate, the stronger the justification they require.

For example, 'all white male adult citizens may vote in Parliamentary elections' is narrower than 'all male adult citizens may vote in Parliamentary elections'. It in turn is narrower than 'all adult citizens may vote in Parliamentary elections', and it than 'all citizens may vote in Parliamentary elections', and it than 'all human beings resident in the state may vote in Parliamentary elections', and it than 'all human beings may vote in Parliamentary elections'. Assuming that we are referring to a particular state's Parliament, we may be inclined to think a voting qualification based on citizenship justified. If not that, we may favour at least a residence qualification, since a Parliament's chief task is to legislate for and supervise the government of the territory of the given state and those who live there and are committed to its long-term wellbeing. Many might go further and argue that some degree of political maturity is relevant to voting, and hence that a restriction of voting rights to adults (judged by a relatively arbitrary age-qualification) is justified. But all attempts to provide satisfactory justifications for voting qualifications on such other bases as gender or skin-colour have been totally discredited, in an instructive way. The grounds of exclusion, unlike immaturity, have no relevance to a person's capability for participation in public decision-making. One can justify some narrowing of principle from 'all human beings may vote' down to a more restricted formula; but some further narrowings fail to find relevant justification, hence the presumption in favour of inclusiveness is undisturbed.

The individualistic element to be argued for has two internal principles. The first makes an assumption about value, namely, the assumption that nothing can be deemed a fundamental human good unless it is capable of being enjoyed as an enhancement of life by a human being as a distinct individual. The second makes an assumption of value, namely the assumption that a social situation where human individuals have scope for self-development and self-realization through autonomous decisions and choices, taken either individually or in free collaboration with others, is of value both to the self-realizing individuals and to others. Of these principles, the former rejects claims on behalf of superhuman or collectively human entities to be repositories of ultimate human values—there cannot, for example, be 'national values' enjoyed by nations as such but incapable of being enjoyed or experienced as values by human individuals as individuals. The second asserts a particular claim on behalf of individuals: there is special political value in securing a social situation where self-aware individuality and self-fulfilment are possible for individuals.

Neither of these individualistic principles adds up to or gives any support or backing to such absurd, or anyway wrong, theoretical positions about the character and existence of human beings as social atomism or what is sometimes called 'methodological individualism'.[7] It is clearly not possible to understand humans as intrinsically extra-social atoms who come together voluntarily or otherwise to form human societies or communities, in the manner envisaged by contractarian thought. Nor can human individuals be conceived as existing with the very nature they have independently from or in abstraction from social relationships and connections. Nor can social organizations, activities, or phenomena be described or conceived in terms of simple aggregations of individual human actions. Without the participation of individuals, it would be logically impossible for there to be families, football matches, and symphony concerts, but there is no individual activity or aggregation of individual activities that amounts to constituting a family, playing a football match, or playing a symphony. Moreover, the individuals who take part in these activities have acquired an individuality, and a sense of their own being and character, through participation in a multiplicity of also irreducibly social relationships and activities. We have all known since Aristotle said it that humans are irreducibly social animals; Yael Tamir adds, in a happy turn of phrase, that human individuals are necessarily 'contextual individuals',[8] familial and social interrelatedness with other persons being for each individual elements of the context essential for individuality. More will be said of this later.

Accordingly, the value of individual self-realization, though it depends on extensive political and economic liberty for individuals, also depends on a substantial degree of support for individuals so that each may have the social and economic backing with which coming to maturity as a potentially self-realizing individual is possible. It also gives reason to oppose acceptance of legally conferred economic liberties so extensive that differences of wealth between different persons can reach an extent that makes impossible any serious adherence to an ideal of equality of self-respect among different persons. Equality of this sort is essential to their participation as equals in the same political community. The upshot is that when one adds

---

[7] I here ascribe a strong sense to 'methodological individualism'. I treat it as postulating that there are individual human beings whose character as such is independent of any social location or setting, and, further, that anything which can be predicated of society or community or about human beings collectively is reducible either to predicates about individuals severally or to some averaging statement about individuals in the aggregate. This leads to the conclusion that 'there is no such thing as society', for there is only a multiplicity of individual actions and interactions. For a softer, and more defensible version of 'methodological individualism', see A. P. Hamlin and P. Pettit, 'The Normative Analysis of the State', in A. P. Hamlin and P. Pettit (eds.), *The Good Polity* (Oxford: Basil Blackwell, 1989), and G. Brennan and A. P. Hamlin, 'Economical Constitutions', *Political Studies*, 44 (1996), 605–19 at 606–7.

[8] See Tamir, *Liberal Nationalism*, 32–4.

together universalistic and individualistic principles in the senses here proposed, one establishes relatively clear criteria for preference of certain political programmes, situations, and systems.

One ought always to prefer social situations in which there is more rather than less autonomy for individuals, and situations in which more individuals are able to pursue self-realization over those in which fewer can. One ought to rule out forms of self-realization involving the exercise of autonomy by some individuals in ways that exploit others through denial of or severe constraint upon their chances for achieving real autonomy as individuals. (Slavery is an extreme example, but others can be envisaged, including the condition of women in many types of society.)

The commonly recognized human rights of the present epoch, those for example contained in the European Convention for the Protection of Human Rights and Fundamental Freedoms, or in the UN Covenants on Civil and Political Rights and on Economic and Social Rights, correspondingly express basic requirements for human autonomy. This is because of the way they are linked with a set of reasonable assumptions about the human condition and about human goods in contemporary human circumstances. The need for some recognition of economic and social rights is tied up with the bar on improperly exploitative exercises of autonomy. This entails a need accordingly to supplement substantially, though not to supplant, the market as the mechanism for distribution of social products. Due observance of human rights by governmental officials, with some form of judicial scrutiny, is a reasonable contemporary requirement for anything that aspires to be a socially just state. Constitutional entrenchment of human rights is highly desirable. Where it is missing, the kind of external guarantee of human rights achieved in countries such as the United Kingdom through the European Convention, coupled now with non-entrenched domestic enforcement of the convention rights, is a requirement for any serious pretension to a just foundation of social order in the state.

In summary, the liberal principles advocated here are universalistic and individualistic. They do give a large place to the working of markets but at the same time they require also state intervention of a redistributive kind, and require states to be subjected to a guarantee of human rights. This is not very original, and nowadays not even particularly controversial. Relative unoriginality is, however, a virtue in this present context. For the task of the moment is not to reconcile nationalism with any highly eccentric conception of the good society. Rather it is to establish whether any kind of nationalism can be found that is fully compatible with a reasonable, acceptable, and quite commonly accepted vision of the fundamentals of a just and free society. The tenets I have set out exhibit, I think, just such a commonplace quality. The time has therefore come to move towards an investigation of such a nationalism.

Movement in that direction is best achieved through reflection on possible objections to the supposedly liberal principles I have sketched here.

Objections to abstract individualism

The ideas of universality and of individualism that I have supported here sometimes attract criticism for ignoring the true substance, the flesh-and-blood actuality, the idiosyncratic and personal character, of real live beings. Immanuel Kant is usually picked out for especially unfavourable mention in such a setting, and not without reason. For the idea of universality or indeed universalizability found its classical expression in Kant's 'categorical imperative', whose simplest form requires the moral agent to act only upon such maxims of action as can at the same time be willed as universal laws applying to every moral agent.[9] Notoriously, this categorical imperative of Kant's addresses humans as purely rational moral agents, as 'noumenal' or 'intelligible' or rational selves, not as the sensual-cum-rational creatures that humans actually are. Notoriously, it fails to make contact with the merely phenomenal world of desires, friendships, pleasures or pains. It poses moral demands of an abstract kind, apart from earthy reality. Between abstract universal principles and concrete decisions affecting real people there is often considered to be an unbridgeable gap.

Liberal individualism comes often under similar attack. The 'individual' of liberal individualism can be so conceptualized as to lack the true individuality that makes real people real to us—and to themselves. Likewise, the abstract equality of all rational agents or legal persons before moral or economic principles or before the law ignores or obscures the huge inequalities that divide and differentiate different members of class- and gender-divided societies, to say nothing of differences of skin colour or ethnicity. The promise of equal and identical human rights for all is hollow mockery in real societies whose institutions, including those articulated around legal rights, constitutional rights, and human rights, have evolved and been designed under the guidance of the dominant groups of the societies whose institutions they are.

The proper response to these by no means unreasonable lines of criticism is to revise the position in such a way as to ensure that real flesh-and-blood individuals are built into it in the first place. Kant may (though the point is disputable) have held that rational agency is extraneous to the phenomenal world of desire, feeling, and fellow-feeling. But we need not. The rationality we ought to contemplate is the rationality of at-the-same-time flesh and blood humans, each belonging in a particular familial, social, and historical context. The principles we set up are principles that have to take account of human sense and sentiment. The acceptability or unacceptability of a universal principle depends on our view of its impact on flesh-and-blood humans.

It is indeed necessarily true that general principles have an abstract quality, and address individuals in terms of some of their qualities. They address us as persons

---

[9] See, e.g., H. J. Paton, *The Moral Law* (London: Hutchinson University Library, 1948, repr. 1961), 84, Paton's book being a translation of and commentary on Kant's *Groundwork of the Metaphysic of Morals*.

wishing to vote in an election, or parents, or promisers, or scholars, or citizens of a state, or members of a nation, for example, and they necessarily do so in abstraction from the totality of our personal qualities. This, however, is not an abstraction that ignores concrete human realities. It is simply a logical feature of having principles that are the same principles for everybody, or for every participant in some actual or ideal dialogue or discourse. It does not require us to ignore the fact that people have a multiplicity of other characteristics seen from a multiplicity of possible points of view and schemes of classification.[10]

What happens if we examine our principles in the light of the fact that humans have a multiplicity of features potentially relevant for moral deliberation either at large or (even more) in relation to particular situations engaging particular individuals? The answer seems clear: it has to be the case that there can be a plurality or even a multiplicity of acceptable and relevant principles bearing on any particular situation of moral significance. So it must be acknowledged that any final judgement in any concrete case will involve taking into account a plurality of potentially applicable principles. To reach a satisfactory final judgement calls for a capacity to enter sympathetically into the position of all parties involved, and to weigh the subjective importance for them of the interests and values at stake.

On this view, it is always possible that the final judgement about what is right for one person at her junction-point of relevant and applicable principles differs from the equally sound judgement about another person at his junction-point. For differences of individual character and situation may entail different relative weight in the given context even of the same abstract principles. Here is a trivially easy, and indeed rather abstract, example: Two people have promised to attend an important meeting, but a third party is dangerously ill. One of the two is a close and valued relative of the ill person, while the other is merely a colleague and friendly acquaintance. Then the former ought to visit the hospital at the cost of missing the meeting, while the other ought to attend the meeting rather than visit the hospital. Another example: somebody who is a native speaker of a minority language might have to weigh different factors about whether to rear her children as speakers of her language than one who speaks a widely used language like English, yet surely everyone has in principle the right to rear her child in her own native language.

We should reject any approach which says or suggests (as, for example both Kant and his contemporary follower John Rawls[11] at least seem to suggest) that ideas about individuals as moral agents have to be formed in abstraction from their flesh-and-blood actuality. Every individual, to take up again Yael Tamir's vivid phrase, is a 'contextual individual'. Each of us occupies a physically distinct human

---

[10] Cf. Onora O'Neill, *Towards Justice and Virtue* (Cambridge, Cambridge University Press, 1996), 73–89, for a robust denial that abstraction and universality in principles mandates uniformity of treatment of individuals. The original version of this section of the present chapter was written and published before O'Neill's book was available. It states with magisterial and wonderful clarity the point that I have been trying to put.

[11] *Theory of Justice*, 50–62 (on 'veil of ignorance' that deprives all parties of any individuality).

body from every other. Each has a unique (identical twins aside) genetic inheritance, and each a unique (identical twins included) social situation, in the form of
a set of relationships to other individuals, and to communities and cultures, and
social organizations, associations, and institutions. To become a full human individual involves things like acquiring a name, learning to speak a language and
becoming acculturated into some culture, or into some subculture in some idiosyncratic mix with some wider and more inclusive culture or cultures. Schooling
and further education, work and the workplace, marriage and family, friendship,
engagement in sport or voluntary activity or politics, and all suchlike engagements
and relationships with other persons, make us the persons we come to be. Such
things account for the continual evolution of character and individuality in our
lives as human persons.

The Scottish Enlightenment must here be added to the German. Francis
Hutcheson and even more his intellectual successors David Hume in Edinburgh and
Adam Smith in Glasgow, observed and argued with great force that humans as moral
and practical beings have ties and links of sympathy and fellow-feeling with other
individuals. They have like ties in a more diffuse way with larger groups and communities of people. These particular links of sentiment are not just accidental features
of phenomenal human beings aside from their rationally intelligible moral character.
They are a part of what makes it possible for people to have moral character at all.[12]
It is in one's becoming capable of seeing the world as it must seem from someone
else's point of view that one can grasp the validity of a universal principle applicable
to both of us, and be motivated to act on it. Without the gift to see ourselves as
others see us—and to feel their potential engagement in situations in which we are
engaged—we would lack the psychic equipment essential to entering into any moral
discourse whatsoever with others.

This is all a matter of what it is subjectively like to be a human being. Our feel-
ings and attachments and bonds with and commitments to other people participate
at least as fully in what makes us human and makes us individual as our faculty for
rational calculation, universalization, and abstraction. Again, it must be insisted that
contextual individualism, although it treats 'individuality' as a morally significant
abstract category, is properly envisaged as applying that abstraction to each human
being as she or he is. And each human being finds her- or himself at a unique junction-point of genetic and social influences. Each has also, and inevitably, a distinctive self-awareness, which may quite likely be grounded in conscious reflection on
these influences and on abstract principles. The abstraction involved in universalistic individualism need not and should not amount to a bland indifference to the
concrete and contextual individuality of the human individuals it envisages. It would
be self-contradictory if it were. For it would treat everybody as uniformly the same,

---

[12] For a profound and thorough discussion of this theme, see K. Haakonssen, *The Science of a
Legislator: the Natural Jurisprudence of David Hume and Adam Smith* (Cambridge: Cambridge University
Press, 1981).

whereas individualism asserts difference, but difference within universalistic (not uniform) equality.[13]

Universality and abstraction express our commitment to impartiality in interpersonal dealings; but the impartiality proper to abstract moral thought sometimes reveals the legitimacy of a strictly qualified kind of partiality in practical conduct. I should be impartial among qualified applicants in allocating municipally owned council houses as a local authority councillor. But I should not be equally impartial in the face of need when it comes to allocating beds in my own house. Family members there have rights to prior consideration even over others whose needs, objectively considered, may be greater. Moreover, even in the case of a public housing authority, impartiality seems to have its limits. Residence in the local authority area, and certainly permanent residence in the state in question, if not indeed citizenship of that state as well as residence, are quite properly taken into account alongside of need. The criterion for access to municipal housing is not pure neediness, nor is the whole homeless population of the world admitted to the housing list.

The right to reside in a country is not impartially allocated either. Amidst all the controversy about immigration and rights of asylum, it is widely taken for granted that governments do and should treat existing citizens and established residents differently from those who seek to change their domicile by moving from one country to another. In discussions of asylum, mere economic motivation—which includes attempting to escape from starvation—is treated as different from political persecution. That someone only wants to escape abject poverty is not an accepted ground for automatically permitting international migration. Yet if the only principles at stake were ones concerning human need, this could not be so. As Tamir observes, most current liberal theories take for granted the legitimacy of states (and frequently denominate them 'nation-states').[14] They then work out elaborate theories of justice in the political sphere that simply take states as the given and obvious units of political discourse and practice, and discuss the special obligations of governments to citizens and of citizens to each other. Nationalism is not a widely favoured doctrine, but unargued nationalist or statist ('nation-statist') assumptions in fact lie unexamined behind such theorizing. The hidden assumptions should be taken out of their closet and either brought up to scratch as an acceptable part of liberal political philosophy, or the whole project should be abandoned.

However that may be, the following seems to be a reasonable interim conclusion to the argument. To make sense of the idea of an individual, we have to acknowledge that no individual is without some social location and context. To be credible, individualism must have as its theme contextual individuals. The ostensibly paradoxical opinion of Alasdair MacIntyre that the individual is as much an abstraction as society loses its puzzling quality in this light.[15] Individuals, not least

---

[13] Cf. again O'Neill, as cited above in note 21.

[14] Cf. Tamir, *Liberal Nationalism*, 99–102.

[15] A. MacIntyre, *A Short History of Ethics* (London: Routledge & Kegan Paul, 1967).

autonomous, self-determining individuals, come to maturity in social contexts that are essential to their development and formation. Societies are conceptual communities supervening on the sets of relations among people who can come to be what they are only by virtue of the relationships in which they participate, and whose sense of themselves would be radically different if they were to have emerged from some different set of relationships, even if their biochemical and genetic make-up were otherwise unchanged.

One of the corollaries of the categorical imperative considered earlier is the duty of respect for persons. In Kant, this no doubt refers to purely abstract rational agents. Robin Downie and Elizabeth Telfer have, however, given much the same idea a more satisfactorily substantial quality in their book of several years ago.[16] With them, if with necessary adaptation to the ideas now in play, we should insist on respect for persons as implying respect for persons-as-contextual-individuals.

Nations in the 'civic' sense are communities of a certain kind, explained above. They are cultural, but not necessarily ethnic, communities of persons conscious of their attachment to a country (a geographical space) and its civic institutions and culture as historically evolved parts of human social reality. Culture and institutions are attached to a given place, a country, and are of special significance to those who live there, because they belong to (or in) it as much as it belongs to them. This is a critical part of the context of the contextual individual in many parts of the contemporary world. For communities of this kind seem to be among the most affectively dominant contexts in terms of which human beings acquire a sense of identity, individuality, and belonging. Probably nobody identifies solely with the national community—it would be a poor and thin kind of identity for someone who did. Everyone has some other focal points of their sense of identity, be these family, city, parish, workplace, professional community, religious tradition, trade union, school, college, or whatever. Quite probably some have a sense of identity that wholly lacks any national component. Certainly, nations as relevant communities are a comparatively modern cultural form. They may prove to have belonged merely to a passing phase in human history—but, even if this turns out to be so, the phase has not yet passed. If many humans, as humans are today, include in their subjective sense of individuality and identity the idea of belonging to a certain nation or national culture, then respect for persons as contextual individuals must include respect for that aspect of their individuality. Moreover, it is likely that individual self-fulfilment will require a political context involving some opportunity for collective self-government. This implies a right, which is eminently universalizable, whether or not all who possess it would wish to exercise the right, or to exercise it in a determinate political way. It seems fully compatible with the two liberal principles of universality and individuality, in the sense put forward in the earlier argument.

[16] R. Downie and E. Telfer, *Respect for Persons as a Moral Principle* (London: Allen and Unwin, 1969).

Nationalism as political

There is at least a prima facie case for some kind of right to respect for national identities as a part of respect for persons, for implicit in respecting human individuals is respect for whatever goes into their individuality. Morally justifiable political principles have to take account of a sense of nationality that is intrinsic to the fabric of individuality, to whatever extent such a sense is vital for many individuals to their sense of themselves, and to their self-respect in being acknowledged members of some recognized and respected community of people. But how do such principles lead towards defining nationalism as some kind of political idea?

As for a definition of nationalism, Kenneth Minogue in his classical *Nationalism*[17] gave this characterization of the idea:

Nationalism is a political movement which seeks to attain and defend an objective which we may call national integrity.

No great stress has up till now been laid on politics in the sense of programmes for political action, yet it is obviously right to accept Minogue's stress upon this in a definition of nationalism. Nationalism is indeed a political movement or programme, or a family of overlapping movements or programmes. The character of members of the family may, however, differ quite largely, depending on the other elements or principles built into such a movement or programme. Here, the aim is the construction (if possible) of a liberal nationalism. This will take national integrity seriously, but advance claims for it only in a way that is compatible with the basic liberal principles already enunciated.

The issue is not only about the sense of identity or belonging that individuals have, nor only about the moral rights we may found upon that. The issue is also about individuals acting collectively to attain and defend identity through distinctively national political institutions. Culture is conceptually essential to the being of a national as distinct from some other kind of human community, yet purely cultural, or related religious organizations or the like, cannot usually guarantee a nation's integrity, however significant a role they may play alongside of more strictly political institutions. Even so, the question may arise as to which institutions of state, or which political arrangements, meet the need described.

To take the case of Scotland, the absence of the full panoply of statehood is not incompatible with maintaining certain institutions of state. Even before 1999, there was a complete system of courts and of civil and criminal justice, and there was an administratively devolved executive branch of government under the Secretary of State for Scotland. There was, and is, an established national church (and the nonestablished churches have a Scottish national mode of internal government), and there are all manner of state and public bodies such as National Library, National

---

[17]   London: Batsford, 1967.

Museums and Galleries, national orchestras and opera companies, national sporting associations active in international sport, national newspapers, broadcasting stations and so on. There is no doubt that such institutions and agencies have over many years played a powerful role in sustaining and even in part defining our contemporary sense of Scotland and of 'Scottishness'. One form of nationalism in Scotland for long argued that the defence and nurturing of such institutions was the most desirable way of upholding Scotland's position as a contemporary nation embedded in a larger state (and some would say more comprehensive nation). The Conservative Government of John Major, in rejecting proposals for any move towards a devolved or independent Scottish Parliament, argued that Scotland flourished better as an integral part of a British state that actively fostered Scottish civic institutions within that state.[18]

Others argued that further political and constitutional change was required for the securing of Scottish identity and enabling Scotland as a politico-cultural community to thrive fully in contemporary circumstances, and this argument has now prevailed to the extent of setting up a Parliament with powers of limited home rule. One reason in favour of this was essentially that in favour of democratic institutions. Processes of autonomous self-realization are of fundamental value to humans, as argued earlier. Sometimes this requires no more than negative liberty and private opportunity to get on with one's own life. But a life that is a human one can only be lived in society, and the legal framework within which one's liberty and privacy are shaped is necessarily a common framework for the collectivity in which one lives. How shall the laws that define the framework then be made and upheld? By external fiat, or by some process of participatory decision-making?

The latter engages individual autonomy in a collective process of law-making. The self-determining individual participates in determining the collective conditions of the common life which form the essential context of individualistic self-realization. So by liberal premises, democratic and thus partially autonomous processes of decision-making about common rules are preferable to purely heteronomous processes. It has been said that good government is preferable to self-government; despite the fact that some experiments in self-government have ended in catastrophic failure, this is unacceptable. Good government in a real sense has to be self-government, even though not all self-government is good, and sometimes effective externally imposed rule may be better than home-grown chaos.

But democracy as majority rule always poses the questions: What majority? A majority of whom? The current state of debate in Ireland, and the question whether relevant majorities must always be all-Ireland majorities or must for some purposes be majorities in Northern Ireland only, provide a vivid example of how problematic this can be. Any answer to the question anywhere has to include some perception of common and mutual loyalty such that a momentary minority can reasonably accept to go along with a majority choice. In some communities there is the possi-

---

[18] See the White Paper *Scotland in the Union: A Partnership for Good* (1993: Cm. 2225).

bility of a reasonable understanding that all political majorities are in principle temporary, and all political minorities likewise. This suggests that there must be some ground of belonging other than the mere existence of a legally constituted constitution that confers power to vote and rules about the establishment and working of a legislative assembly. Thus viable political societies have an existence conceptually apart from any particular constitution giving them a determinate legal character.

This both explains and justifies the ideas of nation or people that are enshrined in legal attempts to grasp at the right of self-determination as a collective right. The International Covenant on Civil and Political Rights and the International Covenant on Economic, Social and Cultural Rights both open with the stipulation noted at the end of Chapter 10:

All peoples have the right of self-determination. By virtue of that right they freely determine their political status and freely pursue their economic, social and cultural development.

Notwithstanding the assertion of this right in such solemn and authoritative documents, a common response among intellectuals is one of extreme scepticism alike towards nationalism and towards claims for national self-determination outside of such very special contexts as decolonization. This scepticism has commonly challenged the whole idea of the 'nation' and has denied the principle of 'self-determination' as a moral principle. Kenneth Minogue's *Nationalism* is (as already noted) itself a highly sceptical account. He describes nationalism as a political phenomenon, but in terms of the holding of ideas that in his view are mainly false and mischievous. He considers, and largely deplores, the effects of nationalism. But he does not entertain it as a justifiable political ideal in any form.

Among persons of liberal disposition, exactly those most favourable to universalistic and individualistic ideas, there has been a long-standing suspicion of the notion of national independence or integrity. There has been a similar distaste for politics that promote the values of a nation as a whole as against those that promote the ability of citizens as individuals and in their freely chosen groupings to choose and pursue what they think valuable, even against actual or supposed national preferences. Liberals on the whole mistrust nationalism. Yet I have tried to show how self-determination as a collective right of appropriate groups may be derivable from principles that are fundamental to liberalism, together with assumptions about 'contextual individuals' that seem to square with experience. If that is so, there must surely be forms of nationalism that are fully compatible with forms of liberalism. It may even be that forms of liberalism incapable of giving place to liberal-nationalist values or of properly allowing for the 'contextual' character of the contextual individual, that is, the real human being, have to be rejected on that account.

Perhaps even yet we have not sufficiently pursued one key point. Why in this setting are people apt to insist on such ideas as self-determination for such puzzling entities as 'peoples' or 'nations'? The doctrine that 'peoples' have the right to self-determination was once taken for granted as an element in liberal internationalism.

In such a classical work as his *Representative Government*[19] of 1861, John Stuart Mill considered it obvious that the members of smaller cultural or ethno-cultural group-ings ('peoples', perhaps?) like the Welsh or the Basques, or the Scots Highlanders ought to seek their good in some larger and more politically advanced 'nation' respec-tively England (then the common name for the United Kngdom) or France. Anyway, the doctrine itself has been found problematic because of the difficulties of applying it in concrete cases. Woodrow Wilson's famous attempts to apply the doctrine after 1918 through the Versailles settlement were far from successful. All the problems of sorting out people from people, and minorities within minorities within minorities, have led many to the same position as Hugh Seton-Watson,[20] who rejects the basic idea as not merely impracticable but essentially chimerical, postulating the existence of metaphysical objects such as 'nations' or 'peoples' where no identifiable such enti-ties really exist.

This is a challenge that has been answered already. People are 'contextual individ-uals'. Our sense of identity arises from our experience of belonging within significant communities such as families, schools, workplace communities, religious groups, political associations, sports clubs—and also nations, conceived as cultural communi-ties endowed with political relevance. A nation is constituted by a sense in its members of important (even if internally diverse) cultural community with each other based in a shared past, a 'heritage' of common ways and traditions, including at least some of a family of items such as language, literature, legend and mythology, music, educational usages, legal tradition, and religious tradition. In connection either with a shared set of civic institutions or with a claim (perhaps more based on myth than reality) to some common ethnicity, all of the things just mentioned cumulatively are regarded as bearing on the legitimacy of government. At least, governmental practices and decisions that denigrate or belittle any of the focal elements in a given national consciousness are abuses of power. Nations exist wherever there are substantial numbers of individuals who share in some degree a common consciousness of this kind. This gives them a possibility of mutual loyalty and a common patriotism of the kind that seems essential to any form of long-run viable democracy.

Accordingly, such national identities do carry political aspirations. The relation between the existence of a nation and the conditions of governmental legitimacy was noted a moment ago. So respect for nationality does require some acknowledgement of political demands grounded in the needs of national communities for political conditions hospitable to their continuance and free development. Further, the whole idea of the desirability of creating the conditions for autonomous self-determination both of individuals—contextual individuals—and of the groups and associations in which they find themselves leads back to the claim of self-determination as quite properly a claim on behalf of each nation on similar terms to any and every other.

---

[19] J. S. Mill, *Utilitarianism, Liberty, and Representative Government* (with intro. by A. D. Lindsay) (London: Everyman's Library, J. M. Dent and Son, 1948), 363-4 (and see chapter 16 throughout).
[20] H. Seton-Watson, *Nationalism and Communism* (New York: Praeger, 1964).

This is fully capable—and only capable—of being stated thus as a universal principle. It couples up naturally with the earlier noted and equally universal imperative of equal allowance for equal respect among national identities, just like other identities.[21] But, of course, this depends on adhering to what was earlier characterized as the civic conception of a nation, and to principles of government that tend strongly towards the pole of civic and away from that of ethnic nationalism. A part of the odium attaching to nationalism (and richly earned by not a few nationalists in political arenas from Bosnia-Herzegovina to Kurdistan, Kosovo, and elsewhere) lies precisely in its failure to universalize and treat essentially like claims in like manner. But this in itself can no more discredit the legitimate claims of a liberal nationalism than the rampant selfishness and non-universalism of some individualistic persons discredits of itself universalistic liberal doctrines of political individualism. The unacceptable face of ethnic nationalism is no part of civic nationalism.

Related to this last point is a hitherto unexplored implication of the whole argument up to this point. It concerns the non-exclusiveness and non-absoluteness of national claims. Since the French Revolution, there has been until a few years ago an insistence both on the exclusiveness and on the absoluteness of national rights. Nation states were sovereign states, and sovereignty had to be absolute. There was a parallel doctrine of unity. For every state, there was but one nation, whatever violence this might do to the facts of history or the consciousness and self-respect of minorities. Ernest Gellner[22] has pointed out how the politics of large-scale modern political societies has required an assertion of a 'flat' common nationality through educational and communications systems, has required, that is to say, an assertion of a 'nation' for the state. Historians have tended to treat these theses as paradigmatic for nationalism, and thus to treat nations and nationalism as features exclusively of the post-revolutionary world. I have elsewhere argued that this is an unduly restrictive model for a descriptive theory of nationalism that could fit credibly with the history of, for example, the British Isles.[23] Rather, the virulent doctrine of the sovereign and absolute nation-state which arose after the revolution, important though it may have been in the rise of modernity, is but one conception of a concept with a longer past and, I hope, still a future.

---

[21] A. Vincent, 'Liberal Nationalism: An Irresponsible Compound', *Political Sudies*, 45 (1997), 275–95 argues *inter alia* that there is no reason for a liberal to privilege a sense of national belonging above other forms of association that give individuals a sense of belonging, and that there is a contradiction between any form of liberalism and any allowance of political claims based on nationality as such. I hope the present argument has shown both that there is a real connection between the 'national' component in a person's identity and political claims to collective self-government in some form. Given a civic conception of nation and nationalism, such claims are fully universalizable, though they do not yield uniform results in different concrete cases. This avoids the contradiction that Vincent asserts, and is not, in my respectful submission 'irresponsible'.

[22] E. Gellner, *Nations and Nationalism* (Oxford: Basil Blackwell, 1983).

[23] See MacCormick, *Legal Right and Social Democracy* (Oxford: Clarendon Press, 1982), 256–61.

Nationalisms differentiated

So it is indeed proper to distinguish various strands within nationalism. It is a phenomenon with more than one face, and the contrasts extend beyond the simple polarity of civic and ethnic, important as that is. There is the imperialistic nationalism of successful nation-states. This is a nationalism of which I have already spoken slightingly. It has often both attacked internal minorities and imposed itself on external victims or rivals, defining enmity so as to justify territorial aggrandisement and enhanced state power.

At the same time, it defines a tendency towards exaltation within the state of a single dominant national tradition and culture, and a disregard for minorities or deviant traditions. It is easy to read this in the reported speeches of Vladimir Zhirinovsky in Russia, or of Slobodan Milosevic in Yugoslavia, now completely dominated by Serbia. Nationalism in this sense always shades over towards fascism, and is the enemy of human liberty. Nationalism of this kind, and appeals to nationality and identity, are often used ideologically (in the adversative sense) to stamp out liberal democratic parties and socializing institutions like free trade unions and social democratic parties, exalting national unity against any mere partisanship or any politics of class rather than country. Nationalism in this mode tends toward the ethnic polarity, and in that aspect becomes the embodiment of exclusivism, intolerance, and racial hatred. In this model, nationalists cannot see the universal of humanity in the many versions of human identity, but only the particularity of the favoured or asserted nation exalted over all its internal or external rivals. It is because this has become such a prevalent image of nationalism that it can be difficult even to get a hearing for the possibility that nationalism could have a different and acceptable face.

There is a different face, though, and one that starts from a universally statable principle, not from pure particularism. The principle is that of the right of self-determination of those politico-cultural communities that have evolved as 'nations' in the history of Europe and, no doubt partly under European influence, elsewhere. This principle is not only compatible with, but has as its necessary corollary, the duty of mutual respect among those who claim the right. The assertion of national aspirations does not have to be, and rationally ought not to be, a ground for the denial of other aspirations similar in kind. This is a principle which can and should be recognized among the principles of right (or justice) that set the terms of shared democracy in a large-scale confederal commonwealth like the European Community.

Further, if one asks about the values represented by the principle of self-determination, these unquestionably include a certain appreciation of cultural individuality and diversity. If I ask why there should be a Catalonia after years of a unified Spain, why there should be a Lithuania or an Estonia after two generations of incorporation in the USSR, the answer must presumably include the proposition that the existence of these cultural diversities and the possibility of their political recognition adds to the wealth of human experience and enhances human possibilities. No less important, of course, is the proposition that there are many people who want this to be, and to be recognized as Catalan, or as Lithuanian, or as Estonian, and to enjoy the same opportunities of individual and collective cultural self-expression in that identity as can easily and uncontroversially be enjoyed by those who identify with the state culture of Castilian or Russian or the like. But for such wishes to be rational, they must be for a state of affairs which is itself of some value. That is satisfied if we ascribe positive value to variety in the human experience; the existence of a plurality of expressions of human culture adds to the richness of life. This seems to me a value with much positive appeal. It is a value each can appreciate for herself or himself as an individual, even though that which is appreciated has an irreducibly collective rather than purely individualistic character.

But what is then required is some form of universally statable acceptance of diversity in human groupings with mutual respect and like rights to respect. So conceived, nationalism is absolutely incompatible with fascism, racism, or majority discrimination against national (or other) minorities. The critique of nationalism in its virulent forms simply would not apply to nationalism defined as implying a right and duty of mutual respect among diverse national traditions, with appropriate political expression of national identities.

The question seems to me not to be whether this argument is rationally acceptable, but whether the state of affairs that it envisages is a serious practical possibility given the real political, sociological, and psychological circumstances of human beings now. It might be argued that any political approach which allows of, let alone contemplates celebrating, the collectivity as such, the cultural group, the nation, is bound to lead on into the kind of mass hysteria, the mindless self-exaltation and other-denigration, the exacerbation of suspicions and hatreds, the intercommunal violence, the massacres, the death camps, that history has so often associated with actual movements of national self-determination, and that political science predominantly deems to be inevitable concomitants of anything meriting the name 'nationalism'.

The years of disappointment in the 1990s which followed the year of triumphs and liberations in Eastern and Central Europe in 1989–90 seem almost to prove the point. Certainly, newspapers throughout democratic Europe are full of foreboding about the outbreaks of destructive and intolerant nationalism that have blown up in many parts of Central and Eastern Europe, and the new fascisms that creep up on the countries of the West. Movements that started with the joy of the liberation of individuals and their societies have continued into more questionable and exclusivist reassertions of the nation and of national authoritarianism. Or so it is said. But the truth by no means seems to bear this out everywhere. So far, at least, conditions in the Baltic republics, for example, do seem to be a good deal closer to those required by a tolerant and liberal democracy than those in many other parts of the former USSR, though these countries have had difficulty in coming to terms with the equal entitlements of ethnic Russians now settled there.

Anyway, to carry on with arguments stated elsewhere in the present work, I should like to suggest that the problems associated with nationalism lie more with the state and with statism than with the nation. The doctrine of the self-sufficiency of sovereign states led in some nineteenth-century thinkers to a doctrine of their right to dominate to whatever extent they had power to dominate.[24] Such an approach legitimated imperialism and the nationalistic wars of the nineteenth and earlier twentieth centuries. Here may be found in large part the source of the odium attaching to nationalism. For the idea that the 'nation-state' must have absolute and uncontrollable control of a territory and all (everyone) that is found within it necessarily creates incurable tension between those who are defined as belonging and those who are defined as not belonging, or who so define themselves. The contemporary fate of the Kurds, who lack a state, but who define themselves (and are for some purposes defined) as not Iraqi, makes a dismal contrast with that of the Kuwaitis. The latter have, on however shaky historical foundations, a state of their own, and thus have had their national independence rigorously vindicated under full authority of the United Nations. The Kurds have the further problem that they are distributed among four states, none of which is hospitable to their maintaining a distinct identity.

The principle of national self-determination becomes morally and practically problematic because (or when) it is coupled to the concept or doctrine of the absolutely sovereign state. For in this form it stipulates that whoever constitute a nation have the right (unless they freely renounce it) to constitute themselves into a sovereign state. But the distribution of people and territory makes all the familiar problems almost inevitable once you try to implement this principle. Both Ernest Gellner[25] and Gidon Gottlieb[26] have persuasively argued that there are too many possible nations for the capacity of our planet and its geopolitical systems to embrace as many states. In the world as we find it, there can be no practical universalizability of the right to respect for national identity and the duty of mutual respect if one insists on strong self-determination coupled with the doctrines associated with state sovereignty.

On the other hand, the world being one in which there are sovereign states, which clothe themselves also in the trappings of nationality, the sense of, and the reality of, injustice to national minorities who are denied a full place in this scheme of things is obvious. It is one consequence of the non-universalizability of the maxims governing the international order of sovereign states under the current arrangements approved by dominant majorities (or, just as likely, minorities). Thus it appears that problems of national minorities are practically by definition injustices, but injustices of that special kind whose rectification cannot but involve the infliction of like injustices on different persons or groups.

---

[24] See, for example, James Lorimer, *Institutes of the Law of Nations* (Edinburgh: Blackwood 2 vols. 1884), vol. 2, pp. 201–6.   [25] Gellner, *Nations.*
[26] G. Gottlieb, *Nation Against State* (New York, Council on Foreign Relations Press, 1993).

European opportunities?

Hence arise some among the grounds for optimism about the new order represented by the European Union according to the analysis offered in this book. For this is a new form of political order, a new kind of 'commonwealth', which offers the hope of transcending the sovereign state rather than simply replicating it in some new super-state, some new repository of absolute sovereignty. It creates new possibilities of imagining, and thus of subsequently realizing, political order on the basis of a plural-istic rather than a monolithic conception of the exercise of political power and legal authority. By creating a framework of political and economic order across many states and national cultures, and by guaranteeing free movement of people, goods and services throughout the whole, Europe necessarily weakens somewhat the idea of the exclusive territoriality of its parts. This does not, however, derogate unaccept-ably from internal jurisdictions and democratic institutional authorities within the parts.

In such a setting, it is possible to escape from the apparent conceptual necessity for some single repository of absolute institutional sovereignty (as distinct from underlying popular sovereignties). This in turn makes possible a solution of the problem considered above. Choices between claims of different nations can cease to be choices between rival claims to sovereign statehood over disputed territories and populations. They can become choices about allocation of levels of political author-ity within a transnational commonwealth embracing many nationalities and cultural traditions or groupings. The principles that guide such choices will have to be worked out as more determinate norms developed out of the broad idea of subsidiar-ity. In this way, difficulties of choice will be somewhat eased. The recognition of one identity ceases to be necessarily at the price of denying another.

These are, at any rate, possibilities. Dire events in Kosovo in the Spring of 1999 make them seem perhaps almost naïvely hopeful, as war yet again flares up in Europe. On the other hand, the war itself is predicated on the absence of any absolute sovereign right in Serbia-dominated Yugoslavia to resolve in its own geno-cidal way its own problem of an ethnic (Albanian) minority in Kosovo. There are emerging doctrines of international law[27] that authorize intervention on behalf of the international community where a humanitarian disaster, by way, for example, of murderous ethnic cleansing, is reasonably apprehended. The intervention was a collective one by the NATO alliance, not by individual states as such. Certainly, the

---

[27] A highly important parallel development in international law, that lies somewhat outside the self-imposed limitations of the present book is revealed in the *Pinochet* case, in which the House of Lords has ruled that sovereign immunity can no longer be claimed on behalf of a former head of state in respect of crimes against humanity such as torture, genocide, or mass murder committed while he or she was acting as head of state. In general international law, the absolute frontiers of the state set up by the non-intervention principle have been breached by the priority now accorded to fundamental human rights. See *R. v Bow Street Magistrates, ex p. Pinochet Ugarte* [1999] 2 All E.R. 97.

justification of the intervention in the form it took is highly controversial as a matter of law, and depends on a quite strained interpretation of materials that could well be read in a different light. But the different light in question is one that would insist on the role of the United Nations rather than NATO, and would deny the authority of a regional alliance to take on the role of international police force by its own say-so. In fact, even in this scene of horrifying events and grave crimes, the thesis of post-sovereignty is, if anything, strengthened. Whether nationalism can have a liberal and universalizable variant is not a question that would cut much ice in the Belgrade of 1999. But the mutual recognition of rights of Serbs and of ethnic Albanians within Kosovo is what the principles here stated would prescribe. The application of such principles through a practical and durable constitutional settlement is a matter greatly dependent on local variables. The deepest tragedy is that one practical attempt to achieve something of this kind was blown away with President Milosevic's refusal to accept the Rambouillet agreement, followed by a resort to scorched earth tactics in Kosovo itself.

In truth, even (or especially) in the face of dire events, it seems that there are important reasons to consider the issue of nationalism in the light of broader and deeper principles, and to work out in what way and under what constraints national aspirations can and should be recognized as legitimate in the conditions of the contemporary world. The world and the Europe that are to come will not, I think, find it possible to abandon every sort of nationalist principle. The realistic, but profoundly difficult, aim ought to be that of securing acceptance only of liberal nationalist principles, and of trying to devise institutional frameworks in which, whatever nationalisms remain in being or come into being, they confine themselves within the constraints of liberal principles in their practice.

In the final chapter, I shall reconsider the contemporary situation in the United Kingdom in the light of the ideas elaborated here, and in earlier chapters of the book.

12

New Unions for Old?

Introduction

Throughout the European Union, there is a growing tendency to a kind of two-tier confederalism. Germany and Austria are already federations. Spain has developed a pattern of 'autonomous regions' led by Catalonia (Catalunya) and the Basque Country (Euskadi), which both have more extensive devolved powers than the other regions, and which have substantial pro-independence national movements and parties. The federation of the three Belgian regions, Flanders, Wallonia, and Brussels grows steadily looser. In Italy, Sicily and the Val d'Aosta have extensive powers of regional self-government within the state, and other regions are beginning to raise the argument for a 'new federalism'. France has established a typically well-ordered form of regional government, and has granted substantial internal home rule to Corsica. The developments in the United Kingdom noted in Chapters 4 and 5 above, involving the establishment of a Scottish Parliament and Executive, a Welsh Assembly, and an Assembly and power-sharing executive in Northern Ireland, take their place in that context. There is a new diffusion of power that answers to the growth, all over the world, of what can justly be called the politics of identity. Communal and national identities, so far from dwindling in significance in a world of globalized information systems and increasingly globalized commerce and capitalism, play a significant and indeed a growing part in politics within states and among them, and in the strange commonwealth that is the European Union.

This is a phenomenon that has benign forms, though also some ugly manifestations. The argument stated in Chapter 11 for a 'liberal nationalism' perhaps indicates why it can be benign, and suggests the principles whereby to secure its being so. Inside Great Britain, the national movements in Scotland and Wales that have won the establishment of limited domestic home rule have done so in an entirely peaceful, constitutional, and democratic way. There is here a stark contrast with the embittered history that has steeped Ireland's independence from Britain, and the contests over the status of Northern Ireland, in so much blood of all communities involved.

Federating the United Kingdom?

Looking at insular developments in the light of the European mainland, it is tempting to see the new pattern of devolved governments in the UK as yet a further instance of quasi-federalism inside a state which itself is confederated with the other member states of the Union. The emergent picture is of Europe as a confederation of federations together with smaller unitary member states of a more homogeneous kind. This squares well with the value of subsidiarity as that was discussed in Chapter 9. The UK, especially under the sway of the 'diffusionist tendency' discussed in Chapter 5, seems to fit the broader picture.

There remains, however, an acute problem—how to deal with England? If the UK is becoming a kind of federation, is England to be within it one federal state, or a patchwork of federal regions? Each solution has its own problems, and both are bedevilled by the absence of any widespread popular wish to create new units of government and new assemblies, though this may be changing in some parts of the country. There are now to be Regional Development Agencies and 'Regional Chambers' in the regions of England. In particular, there seems to have been some growth of opinion in Yorkshire, and in Tyneside and the North East of England in favour of emulating the Scots and Welsh in seeking directly elected assemblies or parliaments, and of securing a similar budgetary settlement. Yet if developments along these lines do take off, and subsequently spread to other regions of England, there will remain important differences with Scotland. Scotland has a distinct legal system, with now a legislature to attend to its reform, and a similar situation obtains in Northern Ireland. No one, however, is seriously suggesting a regional sub-division of the English common law; so a provincial devolution of general legislative powers is unlikely to extend further than to Scotland and Northern Ireland. In that case, the UK Parliament will remain the sole legislature in respect of the general law in force in England. Meanwhile the Welsh Assembly's legislative powers are limited and depend on the delegation of particular statutory powers of regulation, so the greater part of Welsh private and commercial law, and much of Welsh public law, will go on being reserved to the powers of the UK Parliament at Westminster, though the leading opposition party, Plaid Cymru, challenges the finality of this settlement.

This means that there is inevitably a strangely uneven and unequal quality built into the kind of quasi-federalism the UK can have, and it is difficult to conceive of a fully federal constitution that could elide these problems. At all points, it appears that members of the UK Parliament representing Scottish constituencies will have a disproportional voice in relation to laws in England and Wales. Yet they will effectively cease to have any substantial say in the extensive issues of Scots law that lie within the stewardship of the Scottish Parliament.

In any event, there is a considerable body of opinion in Scotland that would deplore any development that apparently reduced Scotland in status to equivalence with a region of England, rather than recognizing its status as one of the two kingdoms that were founder nations of the first United Kingdom. We saw earlier (Chapter 4) that Scotland has always been something of an anomaly inside a theoretically unitary 'nation-state', and it is not clear that she would be glad to yield up this status as an anomaly. So perhaps the best idea would be to aim for a constitutional settlement recognizing England as one state of a federal UK, establishing a separate Parliament and executive branch to handle the matters devolved to the English state.

This solution, looking to make England one state of a redesigned and fully federal

United Kingdom, is in fact the least workable of all. The problem is one of relative economic weight and population size among the units to be federated. England has more than nine elevenths of the population of the UK, Scotland one eleventh, and Wales and Northern Ireland the balance. Yet federal government presumes some equilibrium among the federated units, and a reasonable balance that can be struck between central government and state governments. It is easy to see why this should be so. In a federation like the USA or Australia or Switzerland or Germany, there are of course differences of size and economic weight between different states or cantons. But the whole federation is considerably greater than even the biggest states or cantons, and the large ones are not single mammoths among pygmies, but are in some kind of a balance with other large ones, while, for small ones, there is safety in numbers. Hence the federal government outstrips in scale any of the federated parts, and the whole economy of the federation is clearly differentiated from that of even its largest component.

This shows why any full-dress federation that would constitute England, Scotland, Northern Ireland, and Wales as the states of a federated United Kingdom is not seriously imaginable. Whatever line England was minded to take in economic policy, the United Kingdom could follow no other. In legislative questions, either England would be able to override the smaller states, or there would be a severe democratic deficit in any blocking arrangement that enabled the two-elevenths to protect their position against the nine. The typically federal balancing act between a population-based lower house and a state-based upper house is unachievable between the four 'home countries'. The only way out is to regionalize England, as noted. But to reinvent the kingdoms of the Anglo-Saxon Heptarchy as federal states would only solve one problem by generating others, according to the argument already stated. For the moment, there is no democratic will in that direction, anyway.

The United Kingdom is thus in the process of switching from inconspicuous anomaly to highly visible anomaly in the constitutional position of the elements in the union. The admirable and seemingly inexhaustible pragmatism of English public life may swallow this anomaly, as it has many others in the past. It is not inconceivable that the curious troika of English Constitution, British State, and Scottish anomaly will rattle along in a new form, with the sledge ever under repair as it crosses and re-crosses the frozen wastes. It is not inconceivable that the right way to resolve the difficulties inherent in the emerging constitutional settlement is to put up with imbalance. The idea of 'variable geometry' in a constitution has been put in circulation around various European compromises. For example, some states are in and some out of the Schengen scheme for abolition of internal frontiers, and some are in and some out of Economic and Monetary Union and therewith the Euro-zone. It perhaps smacks of 'constructivist rationalism'[1] to demand abstract symmetry in constitutions. It may be that 'variable geometry' in constitutions is simply a sensible

---

[1] See F. A. Hayek, *Law, Legislation and Liberty*, vol. 1, *Rules and Order* (London: Routledge & Kegan Paul, 1976), 5–9, 14–17, 29–34.

and pragmatic way of accommodating to real differences between the parts that make up a whole. Variable geometry may be the very thing for the United Kingdom in the long run. The answer to the problem that an English state cannot be effectively separated out from a workable United Kingdom may simply be the present one, namely, declining to separate it.

That is the effect of using the United Kingdom Parliament as the legislature both for England and for Britain, and United Kingdom Ministers as (in most cases) both English and British, while Scotland, Northern Ireland, and Wales have each a separated executive and (Scotland more extensively than the others) a separate legislative Parliament. These have, of course, exclusively Scottish, Northern Irish, and Welsh functions, and remaining British functions in the countries remain with the UK Government answerable to the Westminster Parliament. This on the one hand sets up the possibility of the government of England being disproportionately affected by representatives of the other countries, depending on electoral arithmetic, yet on the other entails that in most instances the policies and politics of the UK are firmly in the hands of the English majority. These are the points of strain in the system, where anomaly may some day precipitate crisis.

Union in Europe with a Council of the Isles?

A different solution is available, however, one favoured by a substantial body of opinion in Scotland. If we look to the European Union, we find there a mix of large states and small, with the whole always substantially more than even the largest part. In a curious inversion of normal federal government, the assembly that represents states as such, the Council of Ministers, has the primary legislative role (with ultimate policy direction of the Union in the hands of the the European Council, comprising heads of government or of state of the Union). The directly elected European Parliament plays in legislation and supervision of government a role more akin to that of a traditional senate or upper house. Here again we note that the European Union remains a confederal commonwealth, not an embryonic federal union enjoying sovereignty as a comprehensive entity.

In these circumstances, the better solution to the constitutional relations between the component nations of the UK may be that of seeking separate membership within the European Union. This is exactly the meaning of the Scottish National Party's proposal for 'independence in Europe'. The kind of (old sense) 'federal' relationship[2] with England that Scots hoped for in 1705 and 1706 is available, and probably only available, in this larger framework. By contrast, devolution within the existing union, on the variable geometry principle, is really just incorporating union with parliamentary pendicles in Scotland, Wales, and Northern Ireland.

A further straw in the wind that blows in this direction is the creation of the

---

[2]   This idea was discussed in Ch. 4 above, at pp. 56–8.

'British/Irish Council', or 'Council of the Isles' following on the Belfast Agreement of Good Friday 1998. This is to be an intergovernmental consultative body that will comprise heads of government or ministers from the governments of the UK and of Ireland, and from the devolved administrations in Scotland, Wales, and Northern Ireland, and from the constitutionally independent islands within the domain of the British Crown, the Isle of Man and the various Channel Islands. Conspicuously missing, at present, is England as such. But that omission is not incurable. The Council of the Isles could be the embryo of a body akin to the Nordic Council that links together the constitutionally independent countries of the Nordic group. A council so conceived would maintain community in policy and in usefully harmonious aspects of law among the various parts of this archipelago once (or if) they became mutually independent member states of the European Union, as indeed Ireland, formerly also an incorporated member of the UK union, already is. The proposal for such a Council of independent but closely associated countries had been put forward already in 1996 by a Committee reporting to the Scottish National Party,[3] though at that time it seemed something of a remote aspiration. The Belfast Agreement of Good Friday 1998 gave an essentially similar idea the early prospect of concrete realization.

The argument here can be linked back to the discussion of 'liberal nationalism' in Chapter 11. There, it was suggested that 'Liberal nationalism is a morally permissible and indeed morally imperative position, but its point is that nationalism must not be interpreted as a moral absolute.' Further, a principle of liberal nationalism was stated in these terms: 'the members of a nation are as such in principle entitled to effective organs of political self-government within the world order of sovereign or post-sovereign states.' Clearly, in the light of other possibly relevant principles, this self-government need not in every case take the form of wholly independent sovereign state. One occasionally hears it argued that 'independence in Europe' is no real independence, and that the Scottish National Party has given up nationalism to the extent that its ambitions are addressed to that goal.[4] On the contrary, the policy position adopted is fully compatible with asserting the rights of the nation as such to a frame of government suited to it and chosen by its people. But it also implicitly acknowledges the reality of a world in which a principle of liberal or civic nationalism, albeit morally mandatory, is at the same time not morally absolute, and must be balanced against other values in seeking a practical, political solution in any case.

Other relevant values include solidarity[5] of people across national boundaries, and reasonable openness of boundaries in contemporary circumstances. As an

---

[3] *Scotland's Government: The Transition to Independence* (Peterhead: Scottish Centre for Economic and Social Research, 17 Maiden Street, Peterhead AB42 6EE, 1996).

[4] See G. Brown and D. Alexander, *New Scotland, New Britain*, cited below n. 4, at pp. 25–6.

[5] There is an intended response here to the claim about 'solidarity' contained in the 1999 Smith Institute Pamphlet by Gordon Brown and Douglas Alexander (G. Brown and D. Alexander, *New Scotland, New Britain*, London, Smith Institute, 1999), arguing in favour of solidarity against 'separatism' (pp. 42–3). It is a poor view of solidarity that confines it within national boundaries, whether or not these are state boundaries.

offshoot of the principle of self-determination (in a more extensive interpretation of self-determination than currently prevails in international law), the liberal national-ist principle is limited in favour of other human rights. The principle that nations are entitled to their own organs of self-government cannot justify arrangements that would override or endanger the fundamental human rights either of nationals or of strangers, nor would it justify resort to violence or unconstitutional action. It is better to suffer evil than to inflict it. Patient resort to all constitutional avenues of improvement, even within imperfectly fair and democratic constitutional arrange-ments, are more likely to yield satisfactory results in the long run than apparently quicker and more ruthless measures. Such measures almost inevitably rupture the fabric of the society they seek to advance. The history of the progress the Scots and the Welsh have made to self-determination, with an almost total absence of inter-personal violence, indicates what is possible, as does the rather striking example of the 'velvet divorce' achieved by Czechs and Slovaks some few years ago.

Taking all that into account, it seems to me that there is a framework, or a set of frameworks, within which it is possible to achieve ends that many people would find desirable, and which the present argument justifies deeming desirable. The ends are ends of national self-government, together with an acknowledgement of special historical bonds of solidarity among the countries of Britain and Ireland, and indeed with a sense of British nationhood held by some, though by no means all, and not a majority in Scotland at least. The others are ends of partnership toward peace and prosperity, these being ends that certainly do not stop at the shores of British or Irish Isles. Europe within the Union, after its century of civil war, is seriously in the business of making resumption of internal hostilities all but impossible, and must seek at all costs to extend this zone of peace eastward and southward. It is in the process of dismantling or redefining the state sovereignties that expressed themselves in destructive and inhuman wars. It is also, though too feebly, extending hands of help to less fortunate regions, and collaborating in the wider scheme of free trade enshrined in the World Trade Organization and its constituent treaty.

Other desirable ends are a full acknowledgement of equality of national dignities notwithstanding great differences of size or of economic weight. This whole ensem-ble points unequivocally, in my view, to seeking the evolution of the Council of the Isles into a league of nations equal in the mutual regard of countries that are fully self-governing, but that are also post-sovereign states in the way characteristic of the members of the European Union. The Union, and within it the European Community, constitute the strong framework that keeps open markets among all participating states, and that seeks to fix fair competitive conditions while attending on the same or similar terms to promote protection of employees and consumers from exploitation and the common environment from degradation. This is done under a common rule of law, upheld by the European Court of Justice. Fellowship within such a confederal commonwealth seems to me better and more readily achiev-able and intelligible than any vain attempt to transform the UK into a federal state.

If that were not so, the argument would be a more balanced one between these two possibilities from the point of view of liberal nationalism.

The question remaining is that of how one might seek to get there from here. On that question, the Scottish National Party commissioned in 1995–6 a report from a Working Group chaired by the late Dr Allan Macartney, with myself as his deputy, the remainder of the committee being experts independent of party allegiance.[6] The Committee's remit was to examine the steps that would have to be taken and the issues that would have to be resolved to ensure the most speedy and satisfactory attainment of independence for Scotland, in the event of an adequate electoral mandate being achieved to set that process in train. This report *Scotland's Government: The transition to independence*[7] was published in the summer of 1996. It still seems pretty well right to me, and the present essay is much informed by it.

The key point is that 'independence' has to be transformed from an abstract ideal to a concrete proposal. How is this done? There are two aspects: the internal—internal to Scotland, that is—and the external.

Internal questions

Internally, people can no more be asked to vote for independence in the abstract than they could be asked to vote for a devolved parliament in the abstract. Devolution became a concrete proposal through the work of the Constitutional Convention and successor groups, and finally in the White Paper that provided the effective framework for the subsequent Scotland Bill (now the Scotland Act 1998). The Scottish electorate voted on 11 September 1997 for (or against) what had become a quite specific proposal. Not everybody was interested or expert enough to study the detail and the fine print. But everybody knew, or ought to have known, that the fine print existed, and had been studied closely by competent people both for and against. The choice that the Scots electors made on 11 September 1997 was by a huge majority, and but few voices remain to say that the choice was an unwise one that the voters will come to reject. Even if it were so, what they could by no means be said is that the vote was on an obscure question, ill understood by the voters. A quite concrete proposal for constitutional change was before the people. They understood it, and they voted for it.

Independence in one aspect is readily understandable, and will become more so as the Scottish Parliament elected in May 1999 settles to its many tasks. For it is a Parliament with wide legislative powers which are nevertheless limited powers. They

---

[6] The other members were Malcolm Anderson, Professor Emeritus of Politics in Edinburgh University, Professor Michael Lynch, most distinguished Scottish historian of his generation, and Neal Ascherson, outstanding journalist, subsequently Liberal Democrat candidate for West Renfrew in the 1999 Scottish parliamentary election, Mungo Deans, then senior lecturer in Public Law in the University of Dundee, and David Murray, Professor of Government in the Open University

[7] Cited above, n. 3.

are limited because of the powers reserved to Westminster and because of the continuing legislative authority retained by the UK Parliament to legislate for Scotland as for every part of the UK regardless of the devolution settlement. Independence would have the effect of de-reserving all the reserved powers, and terminating the sovereignty (or asserted sovereignty) of the present United Kingdom Parliament in respect of Scotland. Positively, this would mean acquiring power over all the natural resources and revenue sources existing within Scotland, acquiring power to discontinue (or to continue on stipulated terms) the use of Scottish soil and territorial waters for the Trident missile system and the submarines that bear it, or for other weapons of mass destruction, and all such other matters as are currently reserved ones.

This shows what happens when one removes reservations and restrictions. But it is necessary also to think about the positive provisions that have to be made to set up a fully independent state. This has so far been the subject of remarkably little calm and disinterested public discussion. Yet an independent Scottish state is not just the dependent one with the conditions of dependency discarded. It has to become a duly constituted state with a properly framed constitution. The constitution of a people should be something broader than the programme of any single political party. For a constitution is the charter whereby a whole free people together resolves to regulate, discipline, and exercise its freedom.

The Scottish Constitutional Convention of 1989–96 very regrettably declined to give the same attention to the drafting of a possible independence settlement as its members did to the devolution proposals eventually enacted into law. The task therefore remains before the people to determine the kind of constitution they desire if they choose to become independent. In concrete terms, the choice of independence has to be the choice of a constitution. A constitution is the required framework for an independent Scotland.

Thus the idea of an independence referendum is, effectively, the idea of a referendum whether to adopt or to reject a constitution. The constitution proposed should have been devised with the participation of all those citizens interested enough to take part in preliminary deliberation. So far as concerns such deliberation, the Scottish National Party has indeed prepared a draft constitution at the centre of its constitutional policy. In the character of a draft constitution, it answers such key questions as:

- Who shall be citizens?—All persons principally resident in Scotland and all those who were born in Scotland, with no restriction on dual citizenship; a free right to renounce citizenship, with no loss of residential rights in the case of renounced citizenship; absolute prohibition on any loss of citizenship otherwise than by fully voluntary renunciation.

- Who shall be head of state—The Queen and her successors, represented as Head of State when not in Scotland by the Chancellor of Scotland, speaker of the Parliament; with provision also for an early referendum on the specific question whether to retain the constitutional monarchy or change to a republic with elected President.

- What form of legislature?—A single-chamber Parliament elected by a fair system of proportional representation; with provision for delaying legislation by exercise of powers of a two-fifths minority in Parliament, the delay being open to override by referendum

- Where shall lie executive power?—It shall be vested in Prime Minister and Cabinet elected from and answerable to Parliament, with fixed term Parliaments and diminution in powers of Prime Ministerial patronage; any continuing prerogative powers should be subject to repeal and replacement by provisions in Acts of Parliament.

- What judges?—Independence of the Judiciary guaranteed, with continuity of Court of Session and High Court of Justiciary as supreme and final courts for Scotland.

- What recognition of human rights?—An entrenched Charter of Rights based upon the European convention, but with some strengthening in light of Scottish legal tradition (e.g. '110 day rule', public right of access to open countryside).

- How secure a constitution?—Entrenchment of the constitution, with requirement of three-fifths parliamentary majority and confirmation by referendum in case of any amendment.

When this was first put forward in 1977 (there have been certain revisions since then), much of it seemed radical and controversial. Curiously, its elements seem to have become the subject of what is in effect a radical consensus. The Scottish Parliament that now exists is a single chamber Parliament, elections to it are by proportional representation, and the European Convention has been adopted into the domestic law, thereby entrenching human rights in the Scottish context. Subsequently, in a slightly weaker form, the Human Rights Act 1998 will put the same rights in force in the whole United Kingdom.

In that light, it might well be comparatively easy to establish a quite broad consensus very quickly on a hypothetical proposition. 'IF Scotland were to become independent, THEN this should be the constitution.' No one has to be pro-independence to have a right to consultation on that hypothetical. Those who oppose as well as those who favour independence have an equal right to be heard on this, for if the proposal carries, it will be the constitution of the whole body politic, dissenters as well as assenters.

In contesting any Scottish parliamentary election, the Scottish National Party asserts its claim to place the issue of independence before the people, and the other parties, with equal legitimacy, oppose both the claim that a referendum on this issue is either timely or desirable, and *a fortiori* the asserted desirability of independence. Whenever sufficient Scottish National Party members are returned, it will be fully legitimate in democratic terms for them to raise the independence issue. But, as we have seen, this requires some anterior consensus on the kind of constitution that should lie at the heart of that proposal. It would be possible, for example, for Scottish National Party members to convene an extra-statutory meeting of all Members of the Scottish Parliament willing to take part in discussing the draft constitution. These could delegate inquiries to a committee or commission to consult as widely as possible within a fixed time-span, and on that basis to produce a definitive draft of a Scottish constitution for agreement by the full consultative assembly.

Under devolution, the constitution is a reserved matter. So amending it lies outside the power of the Scottish Parliament. The Scottish Executive, however, has power to raise issues of good governance for discussion with United Kingdom Ministers. There would accordingly be no constitutional obstacle to the Scottish Parliament legislating to provide for an advisory referendum. In substance, the question would be whether or not the draft constitution should be adopted. In form, it would be whether or not the Scottish Executive should be advised to propose to United Kingdom Ministers that they enter into negotiations for and in due course make legislative provision for recognition of Scottish independence on the basis of the draft constitution.

External questions

At this point, the discussion turns necessarily from the internal to the external aspect. Issues that it is essential to decide arise not only within Scotland, but also between Scotland and the present partners both in the United Kingdom and in the European Union. Although the Departments that formerly made up the Scottish Office have now become ministerial departments under the Scottish Executive created by the Scotland Act 1998, vital ministries of state such as the Treasury, Trade and Industry, Social Security, Defence, and Foreign Affairs do not exist in any separate form in Scotland. For independence to be achieved, they would have to come into being, and with them the full competence to run a comprehensive independent government. Common assets and liabilities of the present United Kingdom would have to be reviewed and partitioned equitably, and public utilities reorganized on an appropriate basis. Individual rights like pension rights would require to be continued in new forms under new authorities.

Therefore there would have to be negotiations. The United Kingdom Government could represent the other countries, the devolved Scottish Executive Scotland, and each could then appoint commissioners to carry out negotiations to establish terms of a consensual separation, as commissioners once decided those of a consensual union. In some respects, privatization has, paradoxically, greatly simplified the issue of division of public utilities, for neither state owns or will own them. The development of 'next steps agencies' in non-privatized areas has separated the policy and supervisory function of government from the actual administration of services. The administration of services is quite substantially decentralized in a way that would facilitate the setting up of distinct service agencies in the two (or more) successor countries.

With good will, there is no reason to suppose that the process of settling the basis of a division need be an excessively protracted one. The setting up of adequate public mechanisms to run an independent Scottish state need not take more than two years, even though (as parallel instances like that of Slovakia and the Czech Republic show) there would be a further period after achievement of mutual independence when the successor states would still have work to do in running some matters of common concern while agreeing a basis for final division, or setting up permanent collaborative arrangements. The key, of course, is 'good will'. Why should England treat Scotland well if Scotland is in the process of departing from a union of three hundred years? If there were no other answer, such as English decency and a sense of fair play, the answer 'common self-interest' is a very obvious one. Any suggestion of a turbulent or resisted move to independence, or indeed any prolonged period of uncertainty about the stability and permanency of governments, is likely to cause severe loss of confidence internally to these islands and also overseas. That would be deeply damaging to everyone, as damaging in the City of London as in Glasgow or Edinburgh.

If it became clear that the Scots wished to achieve independence, it has long been generally conceded, as readily by those who hope they will not as by those who hope they will, that they have a legitimate right to do so. It would therefore be in everybody's interest for both governments involved to cooperate in a constructive spirit so as to bring the constitutional change about with minimal detriment to the people of either or any of the countries. If there are to be allegations about people behaving as 'wreckers', they should be reserved in the hope that no one will earn that epithet, either in the circumstances of a staying-in-union, or in circumstances of its being dissolved.

Finally, there is the European Union issue. In so far as the Union is constituted by international treaties, the law of state succession clearly applies. The Convention on State Succession has not yet received sufficient accessions to be in force of its own right, but it may be taken as indicating what are the present norms of customary international law. If so, both (or all) successor states to the United Kingdom continue subject to all obligations and rights of Union membership as a matter of international law. In so far as the Treaties have been recognized as the constitution of a 'new legal order', the 'European Commonwealth' discussed above, issues beyond those of state succession arise. But the Greenland precedent shows that there is no automatic departure from the Union when a part of a state achieves internal self-government even if it does so with the express desire to leave the Union. For Greenland's negotiation of partial independence from Denmark was pursued on purpose to take Greenland outside the European Union (that is, its predecessor Communities) and yet it was assumed that there must be subsequent negotiation leading to treaty amendments before Greenland could be acknowledged as having ceased to be within the union. By parallel reasoning, if Scotland, or indeed England, wanted to leave the Union, this would call for protracted negotiation and finally treaty amendment to make possible a departure from the Union that would be lawful in the perspective of European law.

It would seem, therefore, that in the event of the United Kingdom dividing into two or more successor states, there would be a need for hard negotiation concerning representation and voting rights in the various organs of Union and Community, with Treaty amendments to bring these into effect. But it does not seem that the constitution of Europe, as discussed in the present book,[8] could be interpreted in terms other than such as would make it obligatory on the Union to secure representation according to prevailing norms for member states that emerged from the division of an existing member state.

Conclusion

It is a matter of satisfaction, that ought to be more commented on than it has been, that England and Scotland achieved a union in peace and by negotiation, and they have now revised it by introduction of wide-ranging devolution in total peace and good will. The question of independence has been brought to the centre of the public agenda without the scratching of a finger or the shedding of even one drop of blood. Whatever comes next, it can be achieved and surely will be achieved in the same way. It can be done well with mutual good will, and there is no sign that mutual good will is lacking.

It is very clear, notwithstanding opinions of another tenor occasionally heard, that Scottish independence could not possibly occur by inadvertence. It would come at the end of a process that would take some time, but that need not amount to an inordinately protracted period. At the time of final choice, the voters would vote in as well-informed and thoughtful a way as can be contrived in a mature democracy. Whether they will do so in the early or the remote future remains to be seen. The argument of this book shows that the prospect is a quite reasonable one. The principles discussed indicate that it is one among a range of reasonable choices, not that it is a required or obligatory outcome. This is appropriate to a work of philosophy that seeks to enhance understanding and to advance practical principles that are relevant to the real world in its contemporary condition. General principles do not settle concrete cases, and the settlement of this kind of case is a matter for the political process, in which the philosopher has no larger a voice or vote than anyone else.

---

[8] But for a radically opposed view, see R. Lane, ' "Scotland in Europe": An Independent Scotland in the European Community', in W. Finnie, C. M. G. Himsworth, and N. Walker (eds.), *Edinburgh Essays in Public Law* (Edinburgh: Edinburgh University Press, 1991), esp. at pp. 151–3. I acknowledge the force of Lane's argument, and the learning in which it is grounded, but I respectfully think that he does not sufficiently attend to the character of the situation when a union state that originally united by agreement subsequently dissolves the union by agreement, in the context of membership of a larger entity of the kind in question.

General Index

Index of Names